LIVES OF THE GREAT ROMANTICS

GENERAL EDITOR: JOHN MULLAN
VOLUME EDITORS: JOHN MULLAN
CHRIS HART
PETER SWAAB

From H. Meyer's 1812 engraving of a portrait by George Sanders which appears in 'Famous in My Time', vol. 2 of *Byron's Letters and Journals*, edited by L. Marchand (John Murray, 1973)
By courtesy of John Murray (Publishers) Ltd.

LIVES OF THE GREAT ROMANTICS
BY THEIR CONTEMPORARIES

VOLUME
2

BYRON

EDITED BY
CHRIS HART

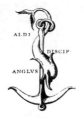

LONDON
WILLIAM PICKERING
1996

Published by Pickering & Chatto (Publishers) Limited

21 Bloomsbury Way, London, WC1A 2TH

Old Post Road, Brookfield, Vermont 05036, USA

© Pickering & Chatto (Publishers) Limited 1996

BRITISH LIBRARY CATALOGUING IN PUBLICATION DATA
Lives of the great romantics: Shelley, Byron and Wordsworth
by their contemporaries
1. Shelley, Percy Bysshe, 1792–1822 – Criticism and interpretation
2. Byron, George Gordon Byron, Baron, 1788–1824 – Criticism and
interpretation 3. Wordsworth, William, 1770–1850 – Criticism and
interpretation 4. Poets, English – 19th century 5. English poetry –
19th century – History and criticism 6. Romantics – 19th century –
History and criticism
I. Mullan, John II. Hart, Chris III. Swaab, Peter
821.7'09'145

Set ISBN 1–85196–270–0.
This volume ISBN 1–85196–272–7

LIBRARY OF CONGRESS CATALOGING-IN-PUBLICATION DATA
Lives of the great romantics : Shelley, Byron and Wordsworth / by
contemporaries ; edited with introduction and notes by John Mullan,
Christopher Hart, Peter Swaab.
    p. cm.
Includes bibliographical references.
Contents: v. 1. Shelley –– v. 2. Byron –– v. 3. Wordsworth.
ISBN 1–85196–270–0 (set)
1. Poets, English––19th century––Biography. 2. Shelley, Percy
Bysshe, 1792–1822––Biography. 3. Byron, George Gordon Byron, Baron.
1788–1824––Biography. 4. Wordsworth, William, 1770–1850––Biography.
5. Romanticism––Great Britain. I. Mullan, John. II. Hart,
Christopher. III. Swaab, Peter.
PR105.L58   1996
821'.709––dc20
[b]   95–21350
                                                              CIP

This publication is printed on acid-free paper that conforms to the American
National Standard for the Permanence of Paper for Printed Library Materials

Printed and bound in Great Britain by
Biddles Ltd
Guildford

To Karen

CONTENTS

ACKNOWLEDGEMENTS

I would like to thank the staff of the University Library of Cambridge for their unfailing helpfulness while helping me collect the materials for this volume. I would also like to thank Dr Nigel Leask for the encouragement and advice he has given over the past four years, and also the Master and Fellows of Queens' College Cambridge for their friendship and financial support during the time of this project. Most of all I would like to thank my family, and in particular my wife Karen. I need hardly say why.

INTRODUCTION

In November 1812, when Byron was struggling to disentangle himself from his affair with Lady Caroline Lamb, he wrote to Lady Melbourne one of a series of letters which have revealed to posterity perhaps the most open, and yet most curious epistolary friendship of the poet's life. The young poet and the older society dame (though she was only just old enough, Byron said teasingly, for him not to have designs on her) continued for more than two years to exchange intimate secrets, often concerning people to whom one or the other was related. They had like minds, shared the same politics, and were similarly irreverent about the foolishness of the Whig high society in which they both moved. This particular letter contains the usual mix of flirty half-confidences – Byron claims the greatest attraction of marriage to Annabella Milbanke was that it would give him a relation to Lady Melbourne – and also a good deal of social gossip which is today entirely lost to us because of the mixture of half-references and abbreviations Byron and Lady Melbourne used in correspondence with each other. In this particular case, however, Byron interrupts his flow with an aside which must have sent a shiver down the spine of his biographers.

> At M[iddleton] – & before – my memory really fails me – I never laughed at P – (by the bye this is an initial which might puzzle posterity when our correspondence bursts forth in the 20th century) nor can I possibly pronounce where all was '*proper*' who was the 'properest' but I am sure no one can regret the general *propriety* half so much as I do. (Marchand, II, p. 240)

Byron was right – the initial *has* puzzled twentieth-century literary historians – but this is hardly the most important feature of this aside. In his recognition that his correspondence with Lady Melbourne was likely to be publicized at some point in the future Byron was signalling an aspect of his life which was to inform almost the entirety of his behaviour. He showed his awareness of the inescapably public nature of every thing he did. He had come to recognize already at this relatively early stage in his career that the combination of his social standing and his unprecedented literary stardom would deprive him for ever of a private life – in one sense in which we understand the term today. He was the Regency English equivalent of a media celebrity; and, trapped inescapably in the glare of publicity, he would have to consider every word and every action in the light of its effect on his public image.

This was not a challenge that Byron attempted to meet by conformity to the most obvious behavioural norms of his class in his day. At its most basic level his process of image formation involved a habitually dramatic – perhaps even melodramatic – approach to documenting the events of his life. More than this, it entailed a compulsive literary twitch which made him recount and embellish his life story, as fascinatingly and as irritatingly as Coleridge's Ancient Mariner, often when prudence would have suggested keeping quiet about it. In *Some Observations Upon an Article in* Blackwood's Edinburgh Magazine (1820) Byron struck back against John Gibson Lockhart's critique of *Don Juan* with an only tangentially appropriate *apologia pro vita sua* that would have reminded his intended readers of just those personal faults that had drawn such condemnation onto his head in the previous years. In this passage he relates the consequences of the breakdown of his marriage to Annabella Milbanke at the end of 1815:

> The Man who is exiled by a faction has the consolation of thinking that he is a Martyr, he is upheld by hope and by the dignity of his cause real or imaginary, – he who withdraws from the pressure of debt may indulge in the thought that time and prudence will retrieve his circumstances – he who is condemned by the law has a term to his banishment – or a dream of its abbreviation – or it may be the knowledge or the belief of some injustice of the law or of its administration in his own particular; – but he who is outlawed by general opinion without the intervention of hostile politics, – illegal judgement, – or embarrassed circumstances, – whether he be innocent or guilty must undergo all the bitterness of Exile without hope – without pride – without alleviation...
>
> The fashionable world was divided into parties, mine consisting of a very small minority – the reasonable world was naturally on the stronger side – which happened to be the lady's as was most proper and polite – the press was active and scurrilous – & such was the rage of the day that the unfortunate publication of two copies of verses rather complimentary than otherwise to the subjects of both – were tortured into a species of crime or constructive petty treason. --- I was accused of every monstrous vice by public rumour, – and private rancour; my name which had been a knightly or a noble one since My fathers helped to conquer the kingdom for William the Norman, was tainted. – I felt that, If what was whispered and muttered and murmured was true – I was unfit for England, if false – England was unfit for me. ----I withdrew – But this was not enough. – In other countries – in Switzerland – in the shadow of the Alps – and by the blue depths of the Lakes I was pursued and breathed upon by the same blight.--- I crossed the Mountains – but it was the same – so I went little farther, and settled myself by the waves of the Adriatic, – like the Stag at bay who betakes him to the waters. (Nicholson, pp. 94–5)

Byron's prose, written in the heat of his fury at what was in fact a surprisingly mild and perceptive review, threatens to run away with him. His story becomes incredible: he is Frankenstein, pursued by a nameless monster across Europe; or he is Caleb Williams stalked by the opprobrium of Godwin's oppressive conservative society across England. Of course the reference to either of these heroes brings to mind the radicalization of Byron's politics by the late eighteen-tens – in the passage he figures himself as a radical persecuted hero – but much more than politics is at stake here. For the Byron of these lines would have brought to mind the Byronic hero of the earlier poetry, only here having finally convinced his readership that he is as evil as Byron had always claimed he was, and shrinking from the outraged recriminations he earns as a result. This of course had never been Byron's intention in inventing the Byronic hero, who was attractive because the show of mysterious evil that surrounded him was just that – a pose – and bore little relation to the charming aristocrat the poet himself was known to be. Byron's audience, in other words, imagined an uncrossable chasm between the heroes and their author, so that even if they called him 'the Giaour' or 'Childe Harold' (as they had called Matthew Lewis 'the Monk') they never seriously believed that the villainy and repulsiveness Byron always claimed for his heroes was a realistic description of himself. And this was a step that modern critics have repeated. Byron's heroes, it is now thought, should not be regard as embodying Byron's guilt at some crime that he committed during the largely undocumented latter phase of his tour around south eastern Europe. Instead they can be seen as a multivalent expression of Byron's feelings of alienation from aristocratic Whig society – one couched in an appealingly fashionable literary language which was designed to lodge him in the very heart of the society from which he proclaimed his own distance. The Byronic hero thus took up an uneasy double stance with regard to the *ton* of Whig London. However, by the end of the eighteen-tens, history – as it was seen by some – had intervened to undermine this position. Byron's bluff had been called; his literary enemies had helped London reread the Byronic hero so as to make him not a charming senti-mental Wertherish outcast but a moral (and, it was whispered, sexual) deviant with a heart every bit as black as the expression Byron had always given him. Even the most carefully-planned literary creations can be upset by the passage of time; the delicate fabric of Byron's purely 'literary' self-fashioning was torn down and trampled into the mud of reality by the outrage in the Tory press following his exile from England. His hero, like Frankenstein's monster, had returned to haunt him; the aporia between Byron's life and that of his fictional heroes had finally been crossed. The literary had come crashing into the factual.

That this should have infuriated Byron was understandable; he had lost control of his own creation – the Byronic hero – and found it turned against him by a hostile English social world. The enigma Byron had always left at the heart of his hero – why *was* he so mysterious, so melancholy, and so guilty? – was rapidly filled during 1816 by London society. The answer seemed easy; the mystery behind the creation of Childe Harold, and the Giaour, and Conrad, and Selim, and Lara – and now most tellingly of Manfred – was that of Byron's guilt at his own sexuality. Was he not after all rumoured to have attempted the most unorthodox sexual conduct with his wife – and, even worse, with his half-sister Augusta? What Byron was discovering was a lesson modern historians and literary theorists have since formalized – that reality (in this case that of his personality) is, except through their own experience, rarely directly available to an audience, but is mediated by its transmission through spoken report, newspaper columns, literary texts, and any other medium available. A barrier a writer attempts to erect between himself and his work is unlikely to survive absolutely, and Byron in particular was always going to be confused with his heroes, however much he protested (in *Some Observations*)

> it is at once ludicrous and vexatious to be compelled so frequently to repeat the same thing – that my case as an Author is peculiarly hard in being everlastingly taken or mistaken for my own Protagonist. --It is unjust and particular.--- I never heard that my friend Moore was set down for a fire-worshipper on account of his Guebre -- that Scott was identified with Roderick Dhu or with Balfour of Burleigh; – or that notwithstanding all the Magicians in Thalaba – any body has ever taken Mr. Southey for a Conjuror. (Nicholson, p. 90)

As so often the tone of the argument is whining and slightly embarrassing; the point, of course, is that neither Moore nor Scott nor Southey had returned obsessively in their work to depict one particular kind of hero – one who physically resembled his creator, and shared with him (in *Childe Harold's Pilgrimage*) a common curriculum vitae. The point about calling the heroes 'Byronic' is not that they were created *by* Byron, or resembled him in some vague undefined way, but that to an unimaginable extent for Byron's audiences from the Regency period to the present day these heroes *were* Byron, and *are* Byron. They are in a certain way no less reliable as sources for what the 'real' Byron was like than the self-proclaimed truth and reliability of the memoirs written by those who knew him.

This clearly takes us straight to the question of the purpose of studying memoirs of Byron's life. But before pursuing this question it is worth seeking some idea of what the memoirists represented in this volume had to encounter when they committed their likenesses of Byron to paper; taking a look, in other words, at the actual process through which Byron presented himself to his memoirists. There are at least two good reasons for doing this.

Firstly, because Byron had an especially complex way of projecting his personality even on the level of quotidian encounters with the people he knew; he was consistently reluctant to 'let his guard down' and appear 'as he really was'. Like many aristocrats accustomed from early age to being the centre of attention Byron was invariably aware of an audience of onlookers, and adjusted his behaviour accordingly. For him even the most mundane encounters of everyday life involved putting on an act, and it should never be lost sight of when reading memoirs written of him that very few people indeed ever saw him behaving in a relaxed and 'unaffected' way – however anachronistic this concept may be in this context. Secondly, and more tendentiously, because the process by which Byron put on his act of personality – this masquerade which his onlookers were invited to interpret as the expression of 'the real man' – may in turn be regarded as no more than an exaggerated and therefore more clearly visible version of the process of the production of personality which characterizes the existence of everyone – and not just of great poets like Byron.

A particularly interesting place to start is by reading a brief account of a young woman's first glimpse of Byron, recorded in her diary on 25 March 1812. Byron was at this time nearing the height of his popularity with the English upper and middle classes. He had achieved dramatic success with the first two cantos of *Childe Harold's Pilgrimage*, and his extreme good looks, social connections, aristocracy and celebrity had drawn him into the most select circles of London life. He was lionized by all, and his enormous attractions were not lost on his onlooker:

> Saw Lord Byron for the first time. His mouth continually betrays the acrimony of his spirit. I should judge him sincere and independent – sincere at least in society as far as he can be, whilst dissimulating the violence of his scorn. He very often hides his mouth with his hand when speaking. He professed himself very partial to music, and said he could not understand how any one could be indifferent to it. It appeared to me that he tried to control his natural sarcasm and vehemence as much as he could in order not to offend; but at times his lips thickened with disdain, and his eyes rolled impatiently. Indeed the scene was calculated to shew human absurdities. There was the listless gaiety which so surely bespeaks the absence of enjoyment. Waltzing was in vain attempted to give animation; Music was listened to *as a duty; Thought* was engrossed by *self;* What a picture of the first-rate society of London! (Lovell, pp. 50–1)

The writer, who was Byron's future wife, went on to tell her mother Byron 'talks much, and I heard some of his conversation, and sounds like the *true* sentiments of the Speaker'. The minuteness of Annabella Milbanke's observations helps compensate for her lack of perception. Clearly visible through her description is a picture of a young fashionable Byron putting on a show of being *ennuié* – of suffering from the accidie which was so much the fashionable ailment of Regency High Society London (though equally visible is Byron's irritation at the waltzing, a practice from which his deformed foot excluded him). Of course Byron knew he was being observed by young ladies like Miss Milbanke, just as he knew that already there were Dallases recording his every gesture. And he knew how to speak so as to sound as sincere as Milbanke thought he was (when in fact the one sentiment he does express – his fondness of music – is only weakly supported by the evidence we do have of his tastes). The case should not need overstating. Gesture and expression were considerably more formal and more evolved in Regency England than many modern critics usually allow – this was after all the time of Lady Hamilton and her 'mimeoplastic art' (see Holmstrom) – and the postures Byron is described as adopting were largely derived from the unwritten rules for the comportment of a fashionable young unmarried man. To be bored and contemptuous, in other words, was hardly to assume a novel attitude. Yet what is visible in this passage is rather more than this. Byron can be seen pushing the fashion for *nil admirari* to the limit; he does more than merely conform to the expected attitudes of Regency London: he embodies them, magnifies them, and adds the ingredient of what has come to be known as 'Byronism'.

We might turn to Samuel Rogers' description of the first meeting of Byron and Tom Moore, in November 1811, for a more explicit look behind the scenes at the functioning of this process. The friendship between Byron and Moore was one of the most intimate either man enjoyed, though it had had an inauspicious start. Following a savage review of his poetry by the critic Francis Jeffrey, Moore and he had fought a duel which was interrupted by the police. They discovered that Jeffrey's gun had not actually been loaded – an omission which instantly made both men the laughing stock of London, and which led Byron to parody Moore in *English Bards and Scotch Reviewers* with his reference to the Irishman's 'leadless pistol'. Moore almost succeeded this time in firing off a challenge to Byron, but in one of the strokes of luck that characterized his charmed existence his challenge was suppressed by a friend of Byron's, and he never received it. The two men exchanged increasingly friendly letters, and Moore arranged for them both to meet at the house of Samuel Rogers, the famous banker and poet. The speaker is Rogers himself:

> When we sat down to dinner, I asked Byron if he would take soup? 'No; he never took soup.' – Would he take some fish? 'No; he never took fish.' – Presently I asked if he would eat some mutton? 'No; he never ate mutton.' – I then asked if he would take a glass of wine? 'No; he never tasted wine.' – It was now necessary to ask him what he *did* eat and drink; and the answer was, 'Nothing but hard biscuits and soda water.' Unfortunately, neither hard biscuits nor soda water were at hand; and he dined upon potatoes bruised

down on his plate and drenched with vinegar. – My guests stayed very late, discussing the merits of Walter Scott and Joanna Baillie. Some days after, meeting Hobhouse, I said to him, 'How long will Lord Byron persevere in his present diet?' He replied , 'Just as long as you continue to notice it.' – I did not then know, what I now know to be a fact, that Byron, after leaving my house, had gone to a Club in St. James's Street and eaten a hearty meat supper. (Lovell, pp. 41–2)

This sort of anecdote is by no means rare in accounts of Byron's life in London between 1811 and the time of his departure for the Continent. Although at times Byron's bouts of fasting were provoked by the need to keep his weight down in order to lessen the pain from his club foot, this is not the issue here – he is quite ready to eat once he is out of the glare of the spotlight of fashionable society. Byron is out to preserve his good looks – he had a tendency to gain weight rapidly – but he is even more concerned to play the part of the mysterious ascetic, thereby remaining the centre of attention. It was not always an act he was able to maintain for long; other accounts describe Byron beginning similar evenings silent and uncommunicative and ending them the soul of the party. And once anyone was admitted into the inner circle of Byron's friends he seems rapidly to have let his posture slip. But to the majority of London society in these early years Byron was unaccountably mysterious; he conformed only enough to keep himself within the pale of select society, and after that he was concerned to maintain his difference from the norms of the young aristocratic men of his circle.

This process visibly repeats itself in the accounts of those who knew Byron throughout the first half of his career as a literary celebrity (once he reached Venice things began to change). In May 1817 the famous sculptor Albert Thorwaldsen was commissioned to produce a bust of Byron. His description of his sittings is illuminating:

In Rome, when I was about to make Byron's statue, he placed himself just opposite to me and began immediately to assume quite another countenance to what was customary to him. 'Will you not sit still?' said I; 'but you must not make these faces.' – 'It is my expression,' said Byron. 'Indeed?' said I, and then I made him as I wished, and everybody said, when it was finished, that I had hit the likeness. When Byron, however, saw it, he said, 'It does not resemble me at all; I look more unhappy.' (Lovell, p. 212)

The anecdote is a relatively straightforward description of Byron's attempt to control the dissemination of his image, and of course this was nothing unusual for patrons of artists like Thorwaldsen. What is significant about the passage, however, is not the appearance that Byron wanted Thorwaldsen to convey (which after all sounds like only an extreme version of the conventional portrait faces of the rather serious poets of the Romantic generation): it is the fact that the passage displays the mechanics of a praxis that Byron refused to confine to the sphere of artistic representation. This can be seen by comparing it to two other accounts, this time descriptions of Byron far from the artist's studio. The first is that of an anonymous correspondent of Thomas Moore's, describing Byron aboard the Salsette en route from Constantinople to Zea in July 1810:

> Perceiving, as he walked the deck, a small yataghan, or Turkish dagger, on one of the benches, he took it up, unsheathed it, and, having stood for a few moments contemplating the blade, was heard to say, in an under voice, 'I should like to know how a person feels after committing a murder.' (Lovell, p. 34)

The second was written by William Harness, and records an incident which took place during his stay with Byron at Newstead Abbey during Christmas 1811:

> He told me more than once that his father was insane and killed himself. I shall never forget the manner in which he first told me this. While washing his hands, and singing a gay Neapolitan air, he stopped, looked round at me, and said, 'There always was a madness in the family.' Then after continuing his washing and his song, as if speaking of a matter of the slightest indifference, 'My father cut his throat.' The contrast between the tenor of the subject and the levity of the expression, was fearfully painful: it was like a stanza of *Don Juan*. (Lovell, p. 45)

The writers seem half aware of the clumsiness of Byron's amateur melodramatics (one can easily imagine how un-*sotto* was the *voce* in which Byron expressed his wish in the first passage) yet their effect is hardly diminished. Byron visibly acts the creation of the character who was to populate his Tales – and has slightly more success than he enjoyed while trying to suggest to an experienced professional like Thorwaldsen that a ferocious scowl was his most characteristic attitude.

This of course lies very near the heart of the reason why London was so ready to believe the most scurrilous rumours about him in 1816. To some extent Byron himself had laid the foundations of his downfall in the eyes of the public, and he had done it by acting himself into a corner. If we pause to examine the picture Byron's London would have gained of him had they invariably taken him at his word, the events of 1816 become less surprising. Byron was a man from a tainted family – his father was a mad suicide, he claimed, and a previous Baron Byron had certainly been involved in a fatal duel in dishonourable circumstances with William Chaworth, the head of a neighbouring family, in a Pall Mall tavern in 1765. Byron himself had had a string of affairs with a number of mysterious women. One of them, he may have told others besides Claire Clairmont, 'was a young girl whom he had seduced and had two children by; she wanted him to marry her, but he would not and went to the East and she committed suicide and was buried in a cross row which was the reason he could not erect a stone to her memory' (Lovell, p. 188). It is unlikely that rumours of Byron's bisexual tendencies had reached London society before he went into exile, but exaggerated and embellished accounts of his affairs in the East (he attempted ineffectually to scotch the story that he was implicated in the plot of *The Giaour*) more than made up for this. Besides this he was supposed to have partaken in infernal nocturnal orgies at his ancestral Newstead Abbey; possessed a wine goblet made out of the skull of a dead monk he had found buried in his grounds; held unorthodox religious views and espoused the pro-Napoleonic Whiggism of the mildly disreputable Holland House society; and frequented the company of several characters from the seamy side of London society. He trod the tightrope of fashionable disreputability which had been occupied by characters such as the Hollands, Fox, and Sheridan – and had as a result only a precarious balance when the winds of rumour began to blow at the start of 1816. It is worth noting, however, that the scandal surrounding his marital breakup is no more responsible for Byron's reputation as a 'satanic' poet (in Robert Southey's phrase) than were the rumours Byron himself had spread about his earlier life. Satanism for Southey was associated inexplicably with Byron's politics – all the members of the so-called 'Satanic school of poetry' were left-leaning Whigs or radicals – and the reason they were satanic were that they had fallen from the heaven of political favour and righteousness by supporting such fallen causes as those of Napoleon Buonaparte and the rioting members of the working classes in Nottingham and Manchester.

The obvious question to address at this point is that of why Byron *chose* to adopt a series of postures with so little relation to what we do know of his life – why, in other words, he persisted in staging in the practice of his everyday life the personality of the Byronic hero of his poetry. The obvious way to begin is by examining his life. Byron was chronically self-conscious. We shall never know how much this was owing to a deformed foot which made him limp painfully, and on occasion made him the laughing stock of beggars in the street; but in a fashionable society given to dancing, tight shoes and the minute inspection of appearance that the dandies had posited as the *sine qua non* of respectability, the attention a limp and a platform shoe would draw cannot be underestimated. And there may have been other reasons for Byron's feelings of 'diffidence', as he himself described his sensations on appearing for the first time in his nobleman's robes at Cambridge University. Although by no means impecunious, Byron was burdened throughout most of his life by enormous debts which led him finally to sell his family home Newstead Abbey. He stood, until the publication of *Childe Harold's Pilgrimage*, a little outside the pale of fashionable society, and had suffered cruelly when Jeffrey (understandably) excoriated him for the rather miserable collection of poetry he published in 1807, *Hours of Idleness*. He was petrified at the thought of anyone detecting what may have been a faint Scottish accent, and had a morbid dread of becoming fat. Yet, of course, none of this satisfactorily explains the scale of the poesis of Byron's social persona – the extreme 'mobility' (to use his own word) which saw him habitually represent his own personality through the filter of the villains of Radcliffe, Shakespeare, Milton and Schiller.

We may get a little closer to the truth if we take account of Byron's sense of humour. However trivial it may sound, there is ample evidence that Byron took lasting pleasure from convincing people that he was guilty of the most terrible crimes; and that the more gullible the person, the more delight Byron took in convincing them of his guilt. To the plodding and humourless John Galt this was the worst of sins:

> It cannot be controverted, that there was an innate predilection in the mind of Lord Byron to mystify every thing about himself: he was accentuated by a passion to excite attention, and, like every other passion, it was often indulged at the expense of propriety. He had the infirmity of speaking, though vaguely, and in obscure hints and allusions, more of his personal concerns than is commonly deemed consistent with a correct estimate of the interest which mankind take in the cares of one another. It was a blemish as incurable as the deformity of his foot. (Lovell, p. 74)

While to Walter Scott, who had a little more sympathy with his fellow-poet's taste for this sort of practical joke, Byron's 'love of mystifying' (as he called it) was a little more excusable:

> I believe that he embellished his own amours considerably, and that he was, in many respects, *Le fanfaron des vices qu'il n'avoit pas*. He loved to be thought awful mysterious and gloomy and sometimes hinted at strange causes. I believe the whole to have been the creation and sport of a wild and powerful fancy. In the same manner he *cramd* people as it is termd about duels, and what [not], which never existed or were much exaggerated. (Lovell, p. 116)

There are numerous other testimonials to the same effect. What tends to drop out of sight in the two descriptions, however, is that this habit of 'mystifying' was not the invention of Byron's unique poetic imagination, but a fashion of Regency society, who usually called it 'bamming' rather than Scott's 'cram[ming]'. Although Byron's predilection for this extremely common form of practical joke appears to have been unusually strong, and to have been infused with a tendency towards black humour, there was little in the way he went about spreading his tall tales (such as the one retold by

William Harness above) which would have seemed unusual to his social circle. And at least – unlike figures like Trelawney – Byron never took his own bams to the point of actually believing them himself.

It is likely that this habit of bamming was responsible for a large part of the mythology – perhaps demonology would be a better word – which surrounded Byron during his years of fame. And when it was combined with an undeniably romantic personal history and a knack for publicizing his work by suggesting that it contained personal revelations, the combination would be more than enough to account for the extreme difficulty Byron's memoirists have encountered in matching their recollections to the story told by his more accurate biographers. And yet we may still wonder *why* Byron should have taken such a compulsive liking towards this particular form of fiction-making – why he should have taken the art of the 'bam' to such an extremity that the task of extricating him from the web of his literary and social fictionalizing now seems almost impossible.

Perhaps we can get a little closer to the truth if we remind ourselves that Byron was not just a young aristocrat, but one who was known above all as the first poet of England. Poetry in Regency society was on the verge of becoming fully professionalized. It was already a full-time career for many, and the number of those who enjoyed any commercial success by publishing what they had written in their spare time was quickly diminishing. As Raymond Williams and Pierre Bourdieu have pointed out, artists in the latter half of the eighteenth century had been liberated from the bondage of having to produce for a particular patron or a given occasion, but were instead exposed to the pressures of the marketplace – to the 'dull compulsion of the economic'.[1] There they were obliged to sell their wares just like any other trader – a descent that was particularly degrading for this most immaterial of professions. In reaction to the threat of being plunged into the banausic world of commerce, Romantic poets like Coleridge and Wordsworth, the story goes, develop a so-called Romantic Ideology which figured the artist as a unique category of being whose thought and work was independent of mundane or material influences. The artist, like Toussaint l'Ouverture in Wordsworth's sonnet, possesses an unconquerable mind that is as impregnable to commercial pressures as it is to the oppression of tyrants. He may not therefore be regarded as a member of the British middle classes: instead he falls outside the class system altogether. He is a special class of person, and is therefore rescued from an embarrassing confusion with the bourgeoisie.

Whatever may be the demerits of this rather simplistic account of the

[1] R. Williams, 'The Romantic Artist' in *Culture and Society* (London, 1958) and P. Bourdieu, 'The Market of Symbolic Goods', in *The Field of Cultural Production*, edited and introduced by R. Johnson (Oxford, 1993), p. 114.

formation of the famous 'romantic ideology' – and there are several – it is of some use to us here. As an aristocrat Byron was of course not subject to quite the same pressures as were his middle-class poetic rivals, but this is not to say that the practice of publishing poetry was without its problems for him. Ever since Locke's description of a career of writing and selling poetry as 'incompatible with the calling of a gentleman' there had been a pervasive suspicion in aristocratic English life of any nobleman who exposed himself to commercial judgements by venturing to publish his work. This was as strongly felt in the Regency period as in any of its predecessors, and aristocratic poets like Lord John Russell found themselves looked down on for degrading themselves by selling verse. For Byron the perils of going into print were obvious, and he attempted to counter future criticism by ostentatiously handing over whatever profits he gained to parasites like Dallas. However, this could not allow him to escape altogether the charge of writing for commercial gain; it must have been as clear to Byron as it was to his friends that donating to them the profits of the sale of the copyrights of his poems was just another way of paying them – just another way of turning his talent to account.

The habit of 'bamming' his way through life may have been one way of countering this. Instead of being just another nobleman open to accusations of having demeaned himself for the sake of lucre, Byron became a mysterious personality more interested in and more interesting for his cult of self than the marketing of his poetry. People at the parties Byron went to were not principally interested in his wonderful poetry – although of course this was a huge attraction. They were interested in Byron himself. His cult of personality could thus become an aristocratic equivalent to the heroic status accorded to the poet by Shelley and Coleridge and the others. However, there would clearly be substantial differences between this and the aims of Byron's particular method. For most of Byron's fellow poets the imperative was to distinguish themselves *as poets* from the rest of commercial society; the emphasis of their arguments therefore lay on emphasizing the qualities that set poets apart from the rest of mankind. For Byron, on the contrary, the ostensible intention was to draw the attention of society away from the poetry itself, and towards the man and his attractions. The medium and the profession were far less important than the message – and this no doubt explains why so much of Byron's poetry written between the success of *Childe Harold's Pilgrimage* and his move to Italy can often seem careless and slipshod. Poetry was not for him a carefully-crafted medium for the transmission of vatic utterances; it was a hobby of a bewitching young aristocrat which could be dashed off as he changed for dinner. The poet, it was to be hoped, would slip from sight entirely: the onlooker would be left instead with the fascinating image of the man. This is why so few of the heroes of

Byron's work are poets or artists – a feature that sets him apart from most of his Romantic colleagues – and why he is extremely reluctant (in verse at least) to debate the nature of poetry and the role of the poet. It is also why Byron was so determined never to have his portrait painted with the usual poetic accompaniments of a pen and a manuscript.

To accept this interpretation, however, would risk being wholly taken in by what had been by a long way the most instinctively brilliant marketing campaign to date in English literature. Byron was interested in selling poetry. Even as far back as the publication of the first two cantos of *Childe Harold's Pilgrimage* he had been keenly aware of the implications of John Murray's decision to publish the poem in the expensive quarto format ('a cursed unsaleable size', he had complained). Although he was a deeply self-conscious young man, he was also aware of his physical attractions, and he worked hard at deepening the mystery surrounding his personal history and love life. And he made it blatantly clear in the huge majority of long poems that he wrote that it would take no very sophisticated analysis to see in them a wealth of insights into his character, and into the awful events people had been led to believe clouded his past life. The result, of course, was that Byron became a walking advertisement for his poetry. In return for buying John Murray's expensively turned-out editions, people could hope for insights into the scandalous liaisons that had been previously hidden behind the doors of the aristocracy; they would feast in a world of oriental fantasy, painted with a personal touch and interest that only an aristocratic Grand Tour could have brought; and of course they could thrill in the knowledge – or the belief – that they personally were privy to the mind of the famous Lord Byron. The pose of not being interested in poetry or the role of the poet, in other words, can be seen as a way of expanding the market for Byron's works. And besides, as Byron never had a problem selling gargantuan quantities of his work there was little reason to agonize over the nature of the poet and the role of his work. Byron was, for the book-buying British public, the spirit of the age.

This reading of what looks like the thorough-going commercialization of Byron's status as an aristocratic poet is clearly incompatible with his hope of maintaining distance from the materialistic motivation of the marketplace. In fact the process was even more threatening to Byron's feelings of noble purity than might first appear, for two reasons. The first comes from a reading of his poetry that recognizes the ubiquity of the aristocratic hero in almost every major work from *Childe Harold's Pilgrimage* through the Tales to *Manfred* and beyond. The rank of these heroes of course matches that of their creator: and this was one of the key attractions of Byronism for the British and European audiences. But the implication of this is that aristocracy in itself is used in Byron's poetical career as a commercial tool – it is an incentive to buy into Byronism and the Byronic hero – and this is clearly radically incompatible with the anti-commercial imperative of aristocracy. It may in fact be seen as a betrayal, or an exploitation, of a rank that should in theory have kept Byron out of the marketplace. The second threat posed by Byron's decision to pursue a career as an author comes when we consider the audience he addressed in his poetry – and above all in the oriental tales and the later cantos of *Don Juan*. Byron was not a writer whose appeal was confined to the upper classes. Relative to the standards of literacy of his day, and to Regency poetry publishers' production runs and pricing strategies, Byron was a writer of mass appeal. His tales of oriental 'gothicism' – to stretch a term – were read and enjoyed by the customers of circulating libraries, by women, and by the middle classes. And the cheap cantos of *Don Juan* that John Hunt brought out in an effort to counter pirates like Onwhyn were read by many more. As John Klancher has recently shown in *The Making of English Reading Audiences*, Byron (and to a lesser extent Scott) was able to address an audience that could only have been dreamt about by his predecessors. And by writing in an accessible, sentimentalized style, avoiding too heavy a larding of classical references, he not only encouraged this audience, but defined it, or 'interpellated' it. In other words – to simplify the argument – he made himself as popular as possible: and this was not a practice with which the most blue-blooded of England's aristocrats would have felt comfortable. But nor was it something that Byron himself accepted unequivocally as the price of success, and the image-formation of his own particular version of romantic ideology may be read as a struggle to symbolize – and thus create – the desired distance and alterity from the grubby grasp of commercial publishing.

If the motivation for this act of self-fashioning was fundamentally different from that of Stephen Greenblatt's new men of Elizabethan and Jacobean England, it was no less artificial (see his *Renaissance Self-Fashioning*). But what Byron probably didn't reckon with was the incredible success of the 'Byron' he had created in the years between his death and the present day. Of course to a large extent this has not been a phenomenon unique to Byron – it is common to all of the major English Romantic poets – though in the years following Byron's death the public's fascination with his life, and the mythologies surrounding it, easily outstripped the interest in other literary celebrities. The memoirs from which this volume is extracted form only a tiny part of the hundreds of documents published on the subject of the recently deceased, and writers in the 1820s and 1830s soon opened up a number of other literary markets besides the obvious areas of the biography and memoir. Soon the Byron fan was able to choose from his bookseller's shelves a number of inquiries into the poet's morals, and defences of them; personal testimonies to the poet's character, and judgements of his place in literature; illustrated editions of his poems, and of recently discovered (or more likely forged) poems by him. It was an industry that Byron had attempted to influence before his death by controlling the rights to his Memoirs, but an industry that of course eventually took its own way. In more modern times, of course, the rise of the professional English Literature academic has ensured the continuation of the Byron industry, and it is a testimony to the power the Byronic hero and the Byronic story are still able to exert that a surprising number of critics have been unable to extricate themselves from what is felt to be a continuing need to defend Byron's character. Although G. Wilson Knight's quixotic defence of Byron's Christian virtues may have been an extreme point in the struggle, even today the flame of the Byron shrine is kept burning by many devotees to whom mentions of his affair with his half-sister, and of the numerous relationships he enjoyed, remain decidedly *infra dig*. If Byron himself is no longer available to work quite as hard at the process of image formation, many of his modern fans are quite prepared to take a hand in assisting him. It is as if the self-fashioning of his lifetime has become contagious; the Frankenstein's monster of his poetry has found a mate, and born progeny. For many modern critics, to be a 'Byronist' implies far more than merely studying his work: it entails an obsessive quest to find nuggets of value in even the most slapdash of his poetry. Byronic critics suffer from almost as much of an identity crisis as Byronic heroes, and it is not uncommon to read in their work or hear in their conversation the vocabulary and cadences – and even the favourite quotations – of their favourite author. Byron's obsession with the self he created in his work has cast a long shadow, and his critics have often struggled to escape it.

As the most famous memoirs concerning Byron were those written by the poet himself, which Hobhouse and Kinnaird persuaded Moore to burn in the flames of John Murray's parlour fire, any book titled the 'memoirs' of the poet will clearly have to define its aims very carefully. It is worth saying first what this book is not. It is not intended to endorse any established notion of Byron's character. Nor does it provide a thorough exploration of the Byronic myth, or a précis of the myriad techniques Byron used to impress the personality he wanted to convey onto the highly impressionable substance of his acquaintances. For this the reader is better directed to the work of Peter Thorslev or Philip Martin. Instead this book is a hybrid, deliberately offering fewer, but much lengthier extracts than its two valuable predecessors, Ernest Lovell's *His Very Self and Voice* and Norman Page's *Byron: Interviews and Recollections* (1985). First and most simply, its intention is to transmit a sense of the character of Byron as it was described in the accounts of the most widely-read work of those who knew him. Second, and equally important, it aims to shed light on the characters of these witnesses

themselves. Byron counted amongst his acquaintance many of the most
interesting characters of his day, and the accounts of their relationship with
him are of intrinsic value for the insights they give into their own personalities. Besides this, however, is the importance of contextualizing the many
anecdotes that are told about Byron within these memoirs. Byron's age was
one given to the *bon mot* and anecdote, many of which were learned by rote
and treasured before being produced over dinner at just the right moment.
The anecdote, it was believed, was a privileged source of information which,
like a *haiku*, would reveal a disproportionately large amount of information
about the subject of the tale. In presenting these anecdotes within their
parent narratives it is hoped that some sense of where they fit into the overall
aims of the writer may be realised. Thus we may be able to gain some sense
of the accuracy and trustworthiness of this particularly complex form of
synecdoche.

More important than any of this, however, is an aim which may just be
glimpsed in the background. It is an undeniably Quixotic aim, but one
which nevertheless bears at least initial scrutiny. This is that by reading the
memoirs of those who knew Byron, and consequently attaining some idea of
the intentions of these writers, it may be possible to glean some insights into
the character of the poet. This is to say that the larger scope of these extracts
may enable the reader to begin filtering out the personalities and agendas of
the memoirists, leaving behind the personality of Byron himself. Clearly the
residue can not be taken to be the 'real Byron'; this would be to push
optimism too far – to endow such constructs as 'personality' and 'character'
with the aura lent to them by twentieth-century psychology. It should, after
all, be born in mind that reading these Memoirs may be like attending an
identity parade in which it is highly unlikely that the wanted man is present
at all. But it may offer a close approximation of the real Byron as he
appeared to the audience of his day – an audience not only for his poetry,
but for the bamming and posturing that so often characterized his everyday
behaviour.

BIBLIOGRAPHY

References to works are by author's or editor's names, and volume and page number. If a person is author or editor of more than one work, an abbreviated form of the work's title is used (e.g. Hunt, *Recollections*, p. 30).

Primary texts

Dallas, R. C., *Recollections of the Life of Lord Byron from the Year 1808 to the end of 1814* (London: Charles Knight, 1824)

Galt, John, *The Life of Lord Byron* (London: Colburn and Bentley, 1830)

Gamba, Pietro Count, *A Narrative of Lord Byron's Last Journey to Greece* (London: John Murray, 1825)

Guiccioli, Teresa Countess, *My Recollections of Lord Byron* (London: Richard Bentley, 1869)

Hobhouse, John Cam, Lord Broughton, *Recollections of a Long Life* (London, 1909)

Hunt, Leigh, *Lord Byron and Some of his Contemporaries: with Recollections of Friends and Contemporaries* (London: Henry Colburn, 1828)

Hunt, Leigh, *The Autobiography of Leigh Hunt: with Reminiscences of Friends and Contemporaries* (London, 1850)

Kennedy, James, *Conversations on Religion with Lord Byron and Others* (London: John Murray, 1830)

Medwin, Thomas, *Journal of the Conversations of Lord Byron: Noted During a Residence with his Lordship at Pisa, in the Years 1821 and 1822* (London: Henry Colburn, 1824)

Moore, Thomas, *The Works of Lord Byron* (London: John Murray, 1832)

Scott, Sir Walter, 'Character of Lord Byron', in *Pamphleteer* 47 (London, 1824)

Trelawny, Edward, *Recollections of the Last Days of Shelley and Byron* (London: John Murray, 1858)

Secondary texts

Bourdieu, P., 'The Market of Symbolic Goods', in *The Field of Cultural Production*, edited and introduced by R. Johnson (Oxford, 1993)

Greenblatt, Stephen, *Renaissance Self-Fashioning from More to Shakespeare* (Chicago: Chicago University Press, 1980)

Holmstrom, K. G., *Monodrama Attitudes Tableaux Vivants* (Stockholm: Acta. Univ. Stockholmiensis, 1967)

Klancher, Jon, *The Making of English Reading Audiences 1790–1832* (Madison: University of Wisconsin, 1987)

Knight, G. Wilson, *Lord Byron: Christian Virtues* (London, 1952)

Lovell, Ernest (ed.), *His Very Self and Voice* (New York: Macmillan, 1954)

Marchand, L. (ed.), *Byron's Letters and Journals* (London: John Murray, 1973)

Martin, Philip, *Byron: a Poet before his Public* (Cambridge: Cambridge University Press, 1982)

Nicholson, Andrew (ed.), *Byron: the Complete Miscellaneous Prose* (Oxford: Clarendon, 1991)

Thorslev, Peter, *The Byronic Hero: Types and Prototypes* (Minneapolis: University of Minneapolis Press, 1962)

Williams, R., 'The Romantic Artist' in *Culture and Society* (London, 1958)

CHRONOLOGY

1788   Born on 22 January to Captain John Byron and Catherine his second wife.

1789   Catherine Byron moves to Aberdeen, taking the young George with her.

1794–8   Attends Aberdeen Grammar School.

1798   Becomes Sixth Baron Byron of Rochdale. He and his mother travel to the family seat, Newstead Abbey in Nottinghamshire.

1799   Begins school at Dr Glennie's in Dulwich. Suffers excruciating and ineffectual medical treatment for his clubbed foot.

1801   Enters Harrow, where he remains until 1805.

1803   His meeting with Mary Chaworth provokes a lifelong passion – which at this time is unreturned.

1805   Goes up to Trinity College Cambridge, where he is to meet Matthews, Davies and Hobhouse. He later describes his 'diffidence' on first arriving at Cambridge, but soon begins making friends, and eventually joins the University Whig Club.

1806   *Fugitive Pieces* privately printed.

1807   *Poems on Various Occasions* privately printed. Also publishes *Hours of Idleness*, which enjoys a modest success.

1808   *Poems Original and Translated* is published. Leaves Cambridge for Newstead Abbey.

1809   Takes his seat in the House of Lords. He is incensed at Lord Carlisle's insistence that he undergo the formal procedure to prove his title. *English Bards and Scotch Reviewers* is published in response to the stinging attacks of some critics – notably Francis Jeffrey – on *Hours of Idleness*. Leaves for Spain at the start of a modified Grand Tour.

1810   Completes the first two cantos of *Childe Harold's Pilgrimage*. Spends most of his time in Greece, and parts company with Hobhouse. Swims the Hellespont and indulges in a lifestyle of extreme sexual irregularity.

1811   Returns to England via Malta and a brief affair. Three deaths mar the year: those of his mother, of Charles Matthews, and of John Edleston, the Cambridge choirboy for whom Byron had felt the most intense of attractions. Meets Thomas Moore and Samuel Rogers, who share his political views, and to whom he takes an instant liking.

1812   Awakes to find himself famous following the publication of *Childe Harold's Pilgrimage*. Affairs with Caroline Lamb and Lady Oxford, both members of the Holland House high society into which Byron is received.

1813   *The Giaour* and *The Bride of Abydos* published, and Byron's spectacular success continues. Meets de Staël and Leigh Hunt, and probably begins his affair with his half-sister Augusta.

1814   *The Corsair* is published, with a claim from John Murray to have sold over 1000 copies on the day of publication. *Lara* also published to slightly less acclaim. Byron becomes engaged to Annabella Milbanke. The 'Ode to Napoleon Bonaparte' marks his bitterness at what he feels is a personal betrayal by Napoleon of the values which left-wing Whigs like he had seen in him. His fame in England continues unabated.

1815   Marries Miss Milbanke on 2 January. His first daughter, Ada Byron, is born. The Byrons settle in London, and are troubled by bailiffs. Byron's liaison with Augusta continues, and relations with Annabella become troubled.

1816   Publishes *The Siege of Corinth*. The Byrons separate; by April a deed of separation has been signed and he has left London for the Continent. To this day the causes of the separation remain a mystery. *Childe Harold III* written and published, following Byron's tour around the ruins of central Europe recently vacated by Napoleon. By the end of the year Byron is in Venice, and publishes *The Prisoner of Chillon and Other Poems*.

1817   Natural daughter by Claire Clairmont, whom he calls Allegra, is born. Byron revels in the hedonistic atmosphere of the Venetian carnival, and publishes *Manfred*. Writes *Beppo* and the fourth and final canto of *Childe Harold's Pilgrimage*. At the end of the year finally succeeds in selling Newstead Abbey, the home of the Byrons for hundreds of years. He is utterly *déraciné*.

1818   Meets and falls in love with Teresa Guiccioli. Publishes *Beppo* and *Childe Harold's Pilgrimage IV*, and begins *Don Juan*, in its day the most monumental document of English Romanticism.

1819   Follows Count Guiccioli and his young wife to Ravenna and then Bologna. The first two cantos of *Don Juan* are published, to equal measures of acclaim and disgust (in England at least). Enjoys the Venetian carnival once again, and entrusts his memoirs to Thomas Moore for posthumous publication.

1820   Byron's friendship with Count Pietro Gamba involves him increasingly in anti-Austrian revolutionary politics. Teresa is formally separated from her husband. Teresa forbids Byron from continuing *Don Juan*.

1821   Enters the Bowles controversy on the side of Pope, and publishes *Marino Faliero, The Prophecy of Dante, Sardanapalus, Cain*, and *The Two Foscari*. Meets Edward Williams and Trelawney and the so-called 'Pisan Circle' is formed when they join fellow-expatriates Medwin and Shelley in Pisa. The Englishmen are also joined by Teresa Guiccioli, who has followed her brother and father, banished by the Austrians for their revolutionary pastimes.

1822   Byron resumes *Don Juan*, but John Murray's increasing scruples about the politics of the poem leads Byron to entrust the remainder to John Hunt for publication. Allegra Byron dies in her convent. Leigh Hunt and family join the Pisan circle. Shelley drowns, and the planned radical newspaper *The Liberal* is strangled at birth. Byron publishes *A Vision of Judgment* and *Werner*, and travels to Genoa.

1823   Byron is elected a member of the London Greek Committee, and sails for Greece on the *Hercules* to join the Greek nationalists in their struggle against the occupying Turks. He publishes *Heaven and Earth, The Age of Bronze, The Island* and *Don Juan VI–XIV*.

1824   Arrives in Missolonghi. *The Deformed Transformed* and *Don Juan XV–XVI* are published. Byron suffers fits and fever, and dies on 19 April. His body is conveyed to England, and he is buried at Hucknall Torkard church in Nottinghamshire.

COPY TEXTS

The following extracts are reproduced in facsimile except in one or two cases (indicated in the headnote) where texts have been reset due to the poor quality of originals. Breaks between excerpts (which may cover paragraphs or whole volumes) are indicated by three asterisks:

☆ ★ ☆

In order to fit texts comfortably to the pages of this edition certain liberties have been taken with the format of the original: occasionally right-hand pages have become left-hand pages (and vice versa) and text from consecutive pages has been fitted onto a single page. Endnotes in this edition refer to Pickering & Chatto page and line numbers. Readers wishing to consult the passages in the original are referred to the table below.

TEXT NO.	PROVENANCE	ORIGINAL PAGE NUMBERS	P&C page no. ff
1.	reset	170–73	1
2.	CUL	14–21, 60–62, 151–6, 172–7, 278–91, 322–7	9
3.	CUL	124–37, 160–67, 270–75	54
4.	CUL	48–54, 64–7, 188–204, 292–7, 324–41	83
5.	CUL	191–7, 33–44	139
6.	CUL	34–92	163
7.	CUL	9–23, 228–59, 268–77	227
8.	CUL	55–95, 133–40, 220–26, 321–32	275
9.	CUL	277–320, 321–42	344
10.	CUL	24–49, 126–35, 222–8	412

CUL – the texts are reproduced by kind permission of the Syndics of Cambridge University Library.

Sir Walter Scott, 'Character of Lord Byron' (London, 1824)

The voice of Sir Walter Scott represents, more than that of any other of Byron's memoirists, the judgement of the literary, intelligent and Tory part of the nascent English middle class. Not that Scott himself would have considered himself a member of such, even in retrospect: but the measured, reasonable and above all moralistic tone of his memoir are characteristic of the central discourse through which this class was to create itself – a discourse which defined itself above all in contrast with the 'decadent' and 'immoral' upper classes. To this extent it is important to realise that Scott's memoir is the only one in this collection written as journalism. His censorious but above all moderate assessment of Byron represents, to a limited but useful extent, the conclusion many of the most important figures (Francis Jeffrey and John Lockhart are only two examples) in this most seminal of media in the formation of the British middle class had reached in their estimate of Byron.

Born in 1771 in the College Wynd, Edinburgh, Sir Walter Scott was the ninth child of Walter Scott, Writer to the Signet. He was lamed in childhood by polio, the first in a series of debilitating illnesses by which he was plagued throughout his life. Byron, who was himself club-footed, later claimed that this lameness was one of the things that had endeared Scott to him. After a training in his father's legal firm Scott read law at Edinburgh University, and in 1792 was called to the Bar. He became a practising barrister in Edinburgh, and it was not until the early eighteen hundreds that the first signs of his future literary celebrity became apparent. The publication of *The Minstrelsy of the Scottish Border* (1802) and *The Lay of the Last Minstrel* (1805) marked the start of a career writing poetry which was to see the publisher John Murray advance the spectacular sum of one thousand guineas for *Marmion* (1808) – a poem which was to repay his investment handsomely when it sold twenty-eight thousand copies by 1811. In terms of sales Scott was already by some way the leading poet of his day, and in 1813 he was offered the Laureateship vacated by Sotheby. He turned the offer down on the grounds that he felt unable to produce poetry with the regularity demanded of a laureate, though by this time he was well aware that he was in any case no longer the darling of the poetry buying public. Byron had arrived.

Resigning his claim to the throne of British poetry with the stoicism characteristic of many of his public pronouncements ('Byron beat me') Scott turned his energies instead to prose, and resumed a novel he had started several years previously. This was *Waverley*, published anonymously in 1814 to phenomenal acclaim. It was in its day the most successful novel ever published in the English language, and earned Scott well over two thousand pounds by the end of the year. Over the next decade and a half Scott churned out successors to his novel with phenomenal assiduousness, earning himself a fortune and a baronetcy, though not officially admitting authorship of the Waverley novels until 1827. His fiercely Tory politics (he vigorously defended the action of the Manchester Magistrates at the Peterloo riots) gained him the favour of the Tory establishment, and in 1822 he helped stage manage the visit of George IV to Edinburgh, the first visit to Scotland by a Hanoverian monarch. At the end of 1825, however, the crash of the London Stock Market brought financial ruin, when Scott's involvement with the Ballantyne brothers' printing company, and his investment in his publisher Constable, left him with debts of nearly £135,000 – a gargantuan sum by the standards of the day. However despite continuing ill health (including partial paralysis) and the loss of his wife he succeeded in writing himself out of debt by the time of his death in 1832. It was an achievement which he thought would be as celebrated by posterity as anything he had done during his lifetime.

Had Sir Walter Scott been a man to take offence easily his relationship with Byron would have been quite different to the warm esteem in which the two men came to hold each other. Following the *Edinburgh Review's* lambasting of *Hours of Idleness*, his first widely-available collection of poetry, Byron had visciously but rather predictably lashed out at the literary establishment of his day in *English Bards and Scotch Reviewers*. Despite the fact that Scott himself had earlier suffered in the pages of the same journal (Jeffrey had derided the antiquaitedness of *Marmion*) Byron evidently regarded him as fair game, branding him 'Apollo's venal son' and damning Scott for racking his 'brains for lucre not for fame'. It was just one of the attacks that Byron was to regret bitterly, when bathing only a couple of years later in the acclaim that greeted *Childe Harold's Pilgrimage*. Before long Scott became for him the 'Monarch of Parnassus' and the two men were to meet and take an instant liking to each other in London. The acquaintance was to be short-lived: but their mutual regard and respect were to stay with them until the end of their careers. When news of Byron's death reached Scott in Edinburgh he wrote 'we feel almost as if the great luminary of Heaven had suddenly disappeared from the sky'. And Byron was no less generous about Scott, the 'Ariosto of the North'. 'I like no reading so well,' he told one correspondent, and 'I have read all Walter Scott's novels at least fifty times' (see Marchand, V, p. 255; VII, p. 48 and VIII, p. 13).

This in itself is no reason to suppose Scott had an especially privileged understanding of Byron's character. But there was probably no man of the age who was able half so well as Scott to sympathize with the peculiar pressures of Byron's career. Scott knew what it was like to be feted as the leading poet of the day; he was familiar with the financial rewards this could bring; he had similar literary tastes to Byron; and he is frequently accused of having the same aristocratic (for which read snobbish) temperament. He was in some respects a John the Baptist figure for Byron, blazing a trail for him and casting a sympathetic paternal eye on the younger poet as he struggled to cope with the pressures of his celebrity. Yet there were at the same time real differences between the characters and thought of the two men. Diametrically opposed in their political sympathies, they were also sharply differentiated by their approach to the increasingly heated question in the 1810s of personal morality. The two men had radically different perspectives on history, and moved in social circles which had relatively few people in common. And yet their enthusiasm for each other's work (despite Byron's mischievous dedication of the infamous *Cain* to Scott) is clearly genuine. And Scott's comments on Byron are amongst the most balanced and credible that we have. Perhaps things would have been different had they spent more time in each other's company.

Due to the poor quality of the original text the passage below has been reset.

CHARACTER OF LORD BYRON
&c. &c.

The following warm-hearted tribute to the memory of Lord
Byron, by an individual who ranked next to him as a poet, is a
proof how much liberality is allied to true genius:–
"Amidst the general calmness of the political atmosphere, we
have been stunned, from another quarter, by one of those
death-notes which are pealed at intervals, as from an arch-
angel's trumpet, to awaken the soul of a whole people at once.
Lord Byron, who has so long and so amply filled the highest
place in the public eye, has shared the lot of humanity. His
lordship died at Missolonghi on the 19th of April. That mighty
genius, which walked amongst men as something superior to
ordinary mortality, and whose powers were beheld with wonder, and something approaching to terror, as if we knew not
whether they were of good or of evil, is laid as soundly to rest as
the poor peasant whose ideas never went beyond his daily task.
The voice of just blame and of malignant censure are at once
silenced, and we feel almost as if the great luminary of heaven
had suddenly disappeared from the sky, at the moment when
every telescope was levelled for the examination of the spots
which dimmed its brightness. It is not now the question what
were Byron's faults, what his mistakes; but how is the blank
which he has left in British literature to be filled up? Not, we fear,
in one generation, which, among many highly gifted persons,
has produced none who approach Byron in ORIGINALITY, the
first attribute of genius. Only thirty-seven years old:—so much
already done for immortality—so much time remaining, as it

seems to us short-sighted mortals, to maintain and to extend his fame, and to atone for errors in conduct and levities in composition: who will not grieve that such a race has been shortened, though not always keeping the straight path; such a light extinguished, though sometimes flaming to dazzle and to bewilder? One word on this ungrateful subject ere we quit it for ever.

The errors of Lord Byron arose neither from depravity of heart,—for nature had not committed the anomaly of uniting to such extraordinary talents an imperfect moral sense,—nor from feelings dead to the admiration of virtue. No man had ever a kinder heart for sympathy, or a more open hand for the relief of distress; and no mind was ever more formed for the enthusiastic admiration of noble actions, providing he was convinced that the actors had proceeded on disinterested principles. Lord Byron was totally free from the curse and degradation of literature,— its jealousies we mean, and its envy. But his wonderful genius was of a nature which disdained restraint, even when restraint was most wholesome. When at school, the tasks in which he excelled were those only which he undertook voluntarily; and his situation as a young man of rank, with strong passions, and in the uncontrolled enjoyment of a considerable fortune, added to that impatience of strictures or coercion which was natural to him. As an author, he refused to plead at the bar of criticism; as a man, he would not submit to be morally amenable to the tribunal of public opinion. Remonstrances from a friend, of whose intentions and kindness he was secure, had often great weight with him; but there were few who could venture on a task so difficult. Reproof he endured with impatience, and reproach hardened him in his error,—so that he often resembled the gallant war-steed, who rushes forward on the steel that wounds him. In the most painful crisis of his private life, he evinced this irritability and impatience of censure in such a degree, as almost to resemble the noble victim of the bull-fight, which is more maddened by the squibs, darts, and petty annoyances of the unworthy crowds beyond the lists than by the lance of his nobler, and so to speak, his more legitimate antagonist. In a word, much of that in which he erred was in bravado and scorn of his censors, and was done with the motive of Dryden's despot, 'do show his arbitrary power.' It is needless to say that his was a false and prejudiced view of such a contest; and if the noble bard gained a sort of triumph, by compelling the world to read poetry, though mixed with baser matter, because it was *his*, he gave, in return, an unworthy triumph to the unworthy, besides deep sorrow to those whose applause, in his cooler moments, he most valued.

It was the same with his politics, which on several occasions assumed a tone menacing and contemptuous to the constitution of his country; while, in fact, Lord Byron was in his own heart sufficiently sensible, not only of his privileges as a Briton, but of the distinction attending his high birth and rank, and was peculiarly sensitive of those shades which constitute what is termed the manners of a gentleman. Indeed, notwithstanding his having employed epigrams, and all the petty war of wit, when such would have been much better abstained from, he would have been found, had a collision taken place between the aristocratic parties in the state, exerting all his energies in defence of that to which he naturally belonged. His own feeling on these subjects he has explained in the very last canto of Don Juan; and they are in entire harmony with the opinions which we have seen expressed in his correspondence, at a moment when matters appeared to approach a serious struggle in his native country:

> 'He was an independent—ay, much more,
>   Than those who were not paid for independence,
> As common soldiers, or a common——Shore,
>   Have in their several acts or parts ascendence
> O'er the irregulars in lust or gore,
>   Who do not give professional attendance,
> Thus on the mob all statesmen are as eager
> To prove their pride, as footmen to a beggar.

We are not, however, Byron's apologists, for *now*, alas! he needs none. His excellencies will *now* be universally acknowledged, and his faults (let us hope and believe) not remembered in his epitaph. It will be recollected what a part he has sustained in British literature since the first appearance of Childe Harold, a space of nearly sixteen years. There has been no reposing under the shade of his laurels, no living on the resource of past reputation; none of that *coddling* and petty precaution, which little authors call 'taking care of their fame.' Byron let his fame take care of itself. His foot was always in the arena, his shield hung always in the lists; and although his own gigantic renown increased the difficulty of the struggle, since he could produce nothing, however great, which exceeded the public estimates of his genius, yet he advanced to the honorable contest again and again and again, and came always off with distinction, almost always with complete triumph. As various in composition as Shakspeare himself (this will be admitted by all who are acquainted with his Don Juan), he has embraced every topic of human life, and sounded every string on the divine harp, from its slightest to its most powerful and heart-astounding tones. There is scarce a passion or a situation which has escaped his pen; and he might be drawn, like Garrick, between the weeping and the laughing muse, although his most powerful efforts have certainly been dedicated to Melpomene. His genius seemed as prolific as various. The most prodigal use did not exhaust his powers, nay, seemed rather to increase their vigor. Neither Childe Harold, nor any of the most beautiful of Byron's earlier tales contain more exquisite morsels of poetry than are to be found scattered through the Cantos of Don Juan, amidst verses which the author appears to have thrown off with an effort as spontaneous as that of a tree resigning its leaves to the wind.— But that noble tree will never more bear fruit or blossom! It has been cut down in its strength, and the past is all that remains to us of Byron. We can scarce reconcile ourselves to the idea— scarce think that the voice is silent for ever, which, bursting so often on our ear, was often heard with rapturous admiration, sometimes with regret, but always with the deepest interest:–

'All that's bright must fade,
The brightest still the fleetest.'

With a strong feeling of awful sorrow, we take leave of the subject. Death creeps on our most serious as well as on our most idle employments; and it is a reflection solemn and gratifying, that he found our Byron in no moment of levity, but contributing his fortune and hazarding his life, in behalf of a people only endeared to him by their past glories, and as fellow creatures suffering under the yoke of a heathen oppressor. To have fallen in a crusade for freedom and humanity, as in olden times it would have been an atonement for the blackest crimes, may in the present be allowed to expiate greater follies than even exaggerated calumny has propagated against Byron.

John Galt, *The Life of Lord Byron* (London, 1830)

The turgid prose and slipshod accuracy of Galt's *Life of Byron* did not prevent it from having a major impact on the formation of post-Regency Byronism; fortunately his literary style had improved by the time he wrote his famous novels to the extent that he became one of the handful of leading writers of his day. To the modern reader however the value of the memoir lies as much in its inability to stick to the facts of Galt's personal experience of Byron as in its containing especially surprising facts about the poet. Galt's is a faithful account only insofar as it reproduces a portrait of what Galt believed to be the real man: he was not prepared to let other people's protestations about the inaccuracy of his account get in the way of his impressionistic portrait. It is of course no less valuable a document for all that.

John Galt was born in Ayrshire in 1779, the son of a ship's captain. After starting life working in a customs house he began to write amateur poetry and plays, and developed a taste for the Tory politics that dominated the domestic political scene of his childhood. Although he entered Lincoln's Inn he was never called to the bar, and instead secured a job travelling Europe with the aim of discovering opportunities for the export of British goods during Napoleon's Continental Blockade. This led to the first in a series of business projects which bore ample witness to the utter inadequacy of his commercial judgement, when he dreamt up a scheme for smuggling British goods into French-held Spain – only for Wellington to invade the country and remove the entire point of the smuggling operation. Galt then decided to turn his hand to the precarious career of literary journeyman, and scraped a living producing plays, poetry and reviews for the next few years. His reward was almost universal ridicule and condemnation (Scott described his tragedies as 'the worst ever seen'): but with the persistence that was perhaps his chief virtue Galt continued in his chosen career, and even stepped up his rate of production in proportion to the amount of bad press he received. In 1820 he finally met his reward, when, with the publication of *The Ayrshire Legatees,* he found success as a novelist specializing in the post-Walter Scott market for novels about Scottish provincial life. In 1821 he published *The Annals of the Parish,* perhaps his most famous work (Scott this time thought it 'excellent') which he followed with a series of novels which made him a middle-ranking literary celebrity. He never earned, however, as much as his perpetual optimism had led him to expect, and he ended his days in relative poverty. He died in 1839.

Galt met Byron on 15 August 1809 in Gibraltar, and then travelled with him onwards to Malta. They were to meet again in February 1810 in Athens. Byron does not seem to have formed a very high opinion of his fellow passenger, and this may be reflected in Galt's slightly bitter account of the voyage. It is likely that Lady Blessington was for once accurate when she recorded Byron's comment that Galt lacked sufficient deference to his aristocratic rank. In fact Galt was clearly irked by Byron's snobbishness, and he makes obvious at several points in the *Life* how much Byron's aloofness annoyed him. Nevertheless Byron seems not to have taken an insuperable dislike to Galt, and determined to do him what favours lay in his power. In February 1812 he wrote to Francis Hodgson, an occasional reviewer for the *Monthly*, in a style jocularly referring to his recent celebrity as the chivalric Childe Harold. The occasion was the publication of Galt's *Voyages and Travels in the Years 1809, 1810, and 1811*, which Byron had rightly anticipated was about to be slated by the reviews for its pedantic and boring style:

> My dear Hodgson, – There is a book entituled 'Galt, his Travels in ye Archipelago,' daintily printed by Cadell and Davies, ye which I could desiderate might be criticised by you, inasmuch as ye author is a well-respected esquire of mine acquaintance, but I fear will meet with little mercy as a writer, unless a friend passeth judgment. Truth to say, ye boke is ye boke of a cock-brained man, and is full of devices crude and conceitede, but peradventure for my sake this grace may be vouchsafed unto him. Review him myself I can not, will not, and if you are likewise hard of heart, woe unto ye boke, ye which is a comely quarto.' (*BLJ* II, p. 164)

The 'cock-brained' Galt's encounter with the poet had not been lengthy, but he fleshed it out as much as he could when he published in 1830 his *Life of Byron*, which was intended to cash in on the boom in sales of Byroniana in the years after the poet's death. The book is packed with innacuracies of fact and judgement. It is long-winded and slow-paced, failing even to reflect much of Galt's character, which was described by those who knew him as easy-going, complacent and optimistic. Although the biography met a limited success, its value today lies not so much in its role in the formation of the Byron myth as in the evidence it provides of what the prospective market for Byronic biographies wanted and expected to hear. It is a second-hand interpretation of the life and significance of Byron, hung onto the peg of a personal reminiscence.

CHAPTER II.

Moral effects of local scenery; a peculiarity in taste.—Early love.—Impressions and traditions.

BEFORE I proceed to the regular narrative of the character and adventures of Lord Byron, it seems necessary to consider the probable effects of his residence, during his boyhood, in Scotland. It is generally agreed, that while a schoolboy in Aberdeen, he evinced a lively spirit, and sharpness enough to have equalled any of his schoolfellows, had he given sufficient application; and he was, undoubtedly, delicately susceptible of impressions from the beauties of nature, for he retained recollections of the scenes which interested his childish wonder, fresh and glowing, to his latest days. Nor have there been wanting plausible theories to ascribe the formation of his poetical character to the contemplation of those romantic scenes. But, whoever has attended to the influential causes of character, will reject such theories as shallow. Genius of every kind belongs to some innate temperament; it does not necessarily imply a particular bent, because that may possibly be the effect of circumstances; but, without question, the peculiar quality is inborn, and particular to the individual. All hear and see much alike; but there is an undefinable though wide difference between the ear of the musician, or the eye of the painter, compared with the hearing and seeing organs of ordinary men; and it is in something like that difference in which genius consists. Genius is, however, an ingredient of mind

more easily described by its effect than by its qualities.
It is as the fragrance, independent of the freshness
and complexion, of the rose; as the light on the cloud;
as the bloom on the cheek of beauty, of which the
possessor is unconscious until the charm has been seen
by its influence on others; it is the internal golden
flame of the opal; a something which may be ab-
stracted from the thing in which it appears, without
changing the quality of its substance, its form, or its
affinities. I am not, therefore, disposed to consider
the idle and reckless childhood of Byron, as unfavourable to the development of his genius; but on the
contrary, inclined to think that the indulgence of his
mother, leaving him so much to the accidents of un-
disciplined impression, was calculated to cherish associations which rendered them, in the maturity of
his powers, ingredients of the spell that ruled his
destiny.

It is singular, that with all his tender and impassioned apostrophes to love, Byron has in no instance,
not even in the freest passages of Don Juan, joined it
with sensual images, elegantly as he has described
voluptuous beauty. The extravagance of Shakspeare's
Juliet, when she speaks of Romeo being cut after
death into stars, that all the world may be in love
with night, is flame and ecstasy compared to the icy
metaphysical glitter of Byron's amorous allusions.
The verses beginning with

> She walks in beauty like the light
> Of eastern climes and starry skies,

is a perfect example of what I have conceived of
his bodiless admiration, and objectless enthusiasm.
The sentiment itself is unquestionably in the highest
mood of the intellectual sense of beauty; the simile
is, however, any thing but such an image as woman
would suggest. It is only the remembrance of some
impression or imagination of the loveliness of a twilight

applied to an object that awakened the same abstract general idea. The fancy which could conceive in its passion the charms of a female to be like the glow of the evening, or the general effect of the midnight stars, must have been enamoured of some beautiful abstraction, rather than aught of flesh and blood. Poets and lovers have compared the complexion of their mistresses to the hues of the morning or of the evening, and their eyes to the dew-drops and the stars; but it has no place in the feelings of man to think of female charms in the sense of admiration which the beauties of the morning or evening awaken. It is to make the simile the principal. Perhaps, however, it may be as well to defer the criticism to which this peculiar characteristic of Byron's amatory effusions gives rise, until we shall come to estimate his general powers as a poet. There is upon the subject of love, no doubt, much beautiful composition throughout his works; but not one line in all the thousands which shows a sexual feeling—all is vague and passionless, save in the delicious rhythm of the verse, and in pure voluptuousness.

But these remarks, though premature as criticisms, are not uncalled for here, even while we are speaking of a child not more than ten years old. Before Byron had attained that age, he describes himself as having felt the passion. Dante is said as early as nine years old to have fallen in love with Beatrice; Alfieri, who was himself precocious in the passion, considered such early sensibility to be an unerring sign of a soul formed for the fine arts; and Canova used to say that he was in love when but five years old. But these instances, however, prove nothing. Calf-love, as it is called in the country, is common; and in Italy it may arise earlier than in the bleak and barren regions of Lochynagar. This movement of juvenile sentiment is not, however, love—that strong masculine avidity, which, in its highest excitement, is unrestrained by the laws alike of God and man.

In truth, the feeling of this kind of love is the very
reverse of the irrepressible passion : it is a mean,
shrinking, stealthy awe, and in no one of its symptoms, at least in none of those which Byron describes,
has it the slightest resemblance to that bold energy
which has prompted men to undertake improbable adventures.

He was not quite eight years old when, according
to his own account, he formed an impassioned attachment to Mary Duff; and he gives the following account of his recollections of her, nineteen years afterwards :

" I have been thinking lately a good deal of Mary
Duff. How very odd that I should have been so
devotedly fond of that girl, at an age when I could
neither feel passion, nor know the meaning of the
word and the effect! My mother used always to
rally me about this childish amour, and at last, many
years after, when I was sixteen, she told me one day,
' O Byron, I have had a letter from Edinburgh, and
your old sweetheart, Mary Duff, is married to Mr.
C****.' And what was my answer? I really cannot
explain or account for my feelings at that moment,
but they nearly threw me into convulsions, and
alarmed my mother so much, that after I grew better
she generally avoided the subject—to me—and contented herself with telling it to all her acquaintance."
But was this agitation the effect of natural feeling, or
of something in the manner in which his mother may
have told the news? He proceeds to inquire. " Now
what could this be? I had never seen her since her
mother's *faux pas* at Aberdeen had been the cause of
her removal to her grandmother's, at Banff. We were
both the merest children. I had, and have been,
attached fifty times since that period ; yet I recollect all we said to each other, all our caresses, her
features, my restlessness, sleeplessness, my tormenting
my mother's maid to write for me to her, which she at

last did to quiet me. Poor Nancy thought I was
wild, and, as I could not write for myself, became my
secretary.   I remember too our walks, and the happiness of sitting by Mary, in the children's apartment,
at their house, not far from the Plainstones, at
Aberdeen, while her lesser sister, Helen, played
with the doll, and we sat gravely making love in our
own way.

" How the deuce did all this occur so early? where
could it originate? I certainly had no sexual ideas
for years afterwards, and yet my misery, my love for
that girl, were so violent, that I sometimes doubt, if I
have ever been really attached since. Be that as it
may, hearing of her marriage several years afterwards,
was as a thunderstroke. It nearly choked me, to the
horror of my mother, and the astonishment and almost
incredulity of every body ; and it is a phenomenon
in my existence, for I was not eight years old, which
has puzzled and will puzzle me to the latest hour of it.
And lately, I know not why, the *recollection* (*not* the
attachment) has recurred as forcibly as ever : I wonder
if she can have the least remembrance of it or me, or
remember pitying her sister Helen, for not having
an admirer too. How very pretty is the perfect image
of her in my memory. Her brown dark hair and hazel
eyes, her very dress—I should be quite grieved to see
her now. The reality, however beautiful, would destroy, or at least confuse, the features of the lovely
Peri, which then existed in her, and still lives in my
imagination, at the distance of more than sixteen
years."

Such precocious affections are, as already mentioned, common among children, and is something
very different from the love of riper years ; but the
extract is curious, and shows how truly little and vague
Byron's experience of the passion must have been. In
his recollection, be it observed, there is no circumstance noticed which shows, however strong the mutual

sympathy, the slightest influence of particular attraction. He recollects the colour of her hair, the hue of her
eyes, her very dress, and he remembers her as a Peri,
a spirit; nor does it appear that his sleepless restlessness, in which the thought of her was ever uppermost,
was produced by jealousy, or doubt, or fear, or any
other concomitant of the passion.

There is another most important circumstance in
what may be called the Aberdonian epoch of Lord
Byron's life.

That, in his boyhood, he was possessed of lively
sensibilities, is sufficiently clear ; that he enjoyed the
advantage of indulging his humour and temper without
restraint, is not disputable; and that his natural temperament made him sensible in no ordinary degree, to
the beauties of nature, is also abundantly manifest in
all his productions; but it is surprising that this admiration of the beauties of nature is but an ingredient
in Byron's poetry, and not its most remarkable characteristic. Deep feelings of dissatisfaction and disappointment are far more obvious; they constitute,
indeed, the very spirit of his works; and a spirit of
such qualities is the least of all likely to have arisen
from the contemplation of magnificent nature, or to
have been inspired by studying her storms or serenity.
Dissatisfaction and disappointment are the offspring
of moral experience, and have no natural association
with the forms of external things. The habit of asso-
ciating morose sentiments with any particular kind of
scenery, only shows that the sources of the sullenness
arose in similar visible circumstances. It is from these
premises I would infer, that the seeds of Byron's
misanthropic tendencies were implanted during the
" silent rages " of his childhood, and that the effect of
mountain scenery, which continued so strong upon
him after he left Scotland, producing the sentiments
with which he has imbued his heroes in the wild circumstances in which he places them, was mere remi-

niscence and association. For although the sullen
tone of his mind was not fully brought out until he
wrote Childe Harold, it is yet evident from his HOURS
OF IDLENESS, that he was tuned to that key before he
went abroad. The dark colouring of his mind was
plainly imbibed in a mountainous region, from sombre
heaths, and in the midst of rudeness and grandeur.
He had no taste for more cheerful images, and there is
neither rural objects nor village play in the scenes he
describes, but only loneness and the solemnity of
mountains.

To those who are acquainted with the Scottish
character, it is unnecessary to suggest how very probable it is that Mrs. Byron and her associates were
addicted to the oral legends of the district and of her
ancestors, and that the early fancy of the Poet was
nourished with the shadowy descriptions in the tales o'
the olden time:—at least this is manifest, that although
Byron shows little of the melancholy and mourning
of Ossian, he was yet evidently influenced by some
strong bias and congeniality of taste, to brood and
cogitate on topics of the same character as those of
that bard. Moreover, besides the probability of his
imagination having been early tinged with the sullen
hue of the local traditions, it is remarkable that the
longest of his juvenile poems is an imitation of the
manner of the Homer of Morven.

In addition to a natural temperament, kept in a
state of continual excitement, by unhappy domestic
incidents, and the lurid legends of the past, there
were other causes in operation around the young Poet,
that could not but greatly affect the formation of his
character.

Descended of a distinguished family, counting
among its ancestors the fated line of the Scottish kings,
and reduced almost to extreme poverty, it is highly
probable, both from the violence of her temper, and
the pride of blood, that Mrs. Byron would complain

of the almost mendicant condition to which she was
reduced, especially so long as there was reason to fear
that her son was not likely to succeed to the family
estates and dignity. Of his father's lineage, few traditions were perhaps preserved, compared with those
of his mother's family ; but still enough was known to
impress the imagination. Mr. Moore, struck with
this circumstance, has remarked, that " in reviewing
the ancestors, both near and remote, of Lord Byron, it
cannot fail to be remarked how strikingly he combined in his own nature some of the best and perhaps
worst qualities that lie scattered through the various
characters of his predecessors." But still it is to his
mother's traditions of her ancestors that should be
ascribed the conception of the dark and guilty beings
in which he delighted. And though it may be contended that there was little in her conduct to exalt
poetical sentiment, still there was a great deal in her
condition calculated to affect and impel an impassioned disposition. Few situations were more likely
to produce lasting recollections of affection than that
in which Mrs. Byron, with her only child, was placed
in Aberdeen. Whatever might have been the violence
of her temper, or the improprieties of her afterlife, the
fond and mournful caresses with which she used to
hang over her lame and helpless orphan, must have
greatly contributed to the formation of that morbid
sensibility which became the chief characteristic of his
life. The time he spent in Aberdeen can only be
contemplated with pity, mingled with sorrow, still it
must have been richly fraught with incidents of inconceivable value to the genius of the Poet.

☆ ★ ☆

Byron was, during the passage, in delicate health,
and upon an abstemious regimen. He rarely tasted
wine, nor more than half a glass, mingled with water,
when he did. He ate little; no animal food, but only
bread and vegetables. He reminded me of the gowl
that picked rice with a needle; for it was manifest,
that he had not acquired his knowledge of the world
by always dining so sparely. If my remembrance is
not treacherous, he only spent one evening in the cabin
with us—the evening before we came to anchor at
Cagliari; for, when the lights were placed, he made
himself a man forbid, took his station on the railing,
between the pegs on which the sheets are belayed and
the shrouds, and there, for hours, sat in silence, enamoured, it may be, of the moon. All these peculiarities, with his caprices, and something inexplicable in
the cast of his metaphysics, while they served to awaken
interest, contributed little to conciliate esteem. He

was often strangely rapt—it may have been from his genius; and, had its grandeur and darkness been then divulged, susceptible of explanation; but, at the time, it threw, as it were, around him the sackcloth of penitence. Sitting amidst the shrouds and rattlings, in the tranquillity of the moonlight, churming an inarticulate melody, he seemed almost apparitional, suggesting dim reminiscences of him who shot the albatros. He was as a mystery in a winding-sheet, crowned with a halo.

The influence of the incomprehensible phantasma which hovered about Lord Byron, has been more or less felt by all who ever approached him. That he sometimes came out of the cloud, and was familiar and earthly, is true; but his dwelling was amidst the murk and the mist, and the home of his spirit in the abysm of the storm, and the hiding-places of guilt. He was, at the time of which I am speaking, scarcely two-and-twenty, and could claim no higher praise than having written a clever satire; and yet it was impossible, even then, to reflect on the bias of his mind, as it was revealed by the casualties of conversation, without experiencing a presentiment, that he was destined to execute some ominous purpose. The description he has given of Manfred in his youth, was of himself.

My spirit walk'd not with the souls of men,
Nor look'd upon the earth with human eyes;
The thirst of their ambition was not mine;
The aim of their existence was not mine.
My joys, my griefs, my passions, and my powers,
Made me a stranger. Though I wore the form,
I had no sympathy with breathing flesh.
My joy was in the wilderness—to breathe
The difficult air of the iced mountain's top,
Where the birds dare not build, nor insect's wing
Flit o'er the herbless granite; or to plunge
Into the torrent, and to roll along
On the swift whirl of the new-breaking wave
Of river, stream, or ocean in their flow—
In these my early strength exulted; or

To follow through the night the moving moon,
The stars, and their development ; or catch
The dazzling lightnings till my eyes grew dim ;
Or to look listening on the scatter'd leaves
While autumn winds were at their evening song.
These were my pastimes—and to be alone.
For if the beings, of whom I was one—
Hating to be so—cross'd me in my path,
I felt myself degraded back to them,
And was all clay again.

☆ ★ ☆

CHAPTER XXIV.

Dispute with the ambassador.—Reflections on Byron's pride of rank.—Abandons his Oriental travels.—Re-embarks in the Salsette.—The dagger-scene.—Zea.—Returns to Athens—Tour in the Morea.—Dangerous illness.—Return to Athens.—The adventure on which the Giaour is founded.

ALTHOUGH Lord Byron remained two months in Constantinople, and visited every object of interest and curiosity, within and around it, he yet brought away with him fewer poetical impressions than from any other part of the Ottoman dominions; at least he has made less use in his works of what he saw and learned there, than of the materials he collected in other places.

From whatever cause it arose, the self-abstraction which I had noticed at Smyrna, was remarked about him while he was in the capital, and the same jealousy of his rank was so nervously awake, that it led him to attempt an obtrusion on the ambassadorial etiquettes—which he probably regretted.

It has grown into a custom at Constantinople, when the foreign ministers are admitted to audiences of ceremony with the sultan, to allow the subjects and travellers of their respective nations to accompany them, both to swell the pomp of the spectacle, and to gratify their curiosity. Mr. Adair, our ambassador, for whom the Salsette had been sent, had his audience of leave appointed soon after Lord Byron's arrival, and his Lordship was particularly anxious to occupy a station of distinction in the procession. The pretension was ridiculous in itself, and showed less ac-

quaintance with courtly ceremonies than might have
been expected in a person of his rank and intelligence. Mr. Adair assured him that he could obtain
no particular place; that in the arrangements for the
ceremonial, only the persons connected with the embassy could be considered, and that the Turks neithei
acknowledged the precedence, nor could be requested
to consider the distinctions of our nobility. Byron,
however, still persisted, and the minister was obliged
to refer him on the subject to the Austrian Internuncio,
a high authority in questions of etiquette, whose
opinion was decidedly against the pretension.

The pride of rank was indeed one of the greatest
weaknesses of Lord Byron, and every thing, even of
the most accidental kind, which seemed to come between the wind and his nobility, was repelled on the
spot. I recollect having some debate with him once
respecting a point of etiquette, which arose between
him and Sir William Drummond, somewhere in Portugal or Spain. Sir William was at the time an ambassador (not however, I believe, in the country where
the incident occurred), and was on the point of taking
precedence in passing from one room to another,
when Byron stepped in before him. The action was
undoubtedly rude on the part of his Lordship, even
though Sir William had presumed too far on his
ribbon: to me it seemed also wrong; for, by the custom of all nations from time immemorial, ambassadors
have been allowed their official rank in passing
through foreign countries, while peers in the same
circumstances claim no rank at all; even in our own
colonies it has been doubted if they may take precedence of the legislative counsellors. But the rights
of rank are best determined by the heralds, and I
have only to remark, that it is almost inconceivable
that such things should have so morbidly affected the
sensibility of Lord Byron; yet they certainly did so,
and even to a ridiculous degree. On one occasion,

when he lodged in St. James's-street, I recollect him rating the footman for using a double knock in accidental thoughtlessness.

These little infirmities are, however, at most only calculated to excite a smile, there is no turpitude in them, and they merit notice but as indications of the humour of character. It was his Lordship's foible to overrate his rank, to grudge his deformity beyond reason, and to exaggerate the condition of his family and circumstances. But the alloy of such small vanities, his caprice and feline temper, were as vapour compared with the mass of rich and rare ore which constituted the nucleus of his brilliancy.

He had not been long in Constantinople, when a change came over his intentions ; the journey to Persia was abandoned, and the dreams of India were dissolved. The particular causes which produced this change are not very apparent, but Mr. Hobhouse was, at the same time, directed to return home, and perhaps that circumstance had some influence on his decision, which he communicated to his mother, informing her, that he should probably return to Greece. As in that letter he alludes to his embarrassment on account of remittances, it is probably that the neglect of his agent, with respect to them, was the main cause which induced him to determine on going no farther.

Accordingly, on the 14th of July, he embarked with Mr. Hobhouse and the ambassador on board the Salsette. It was in the course of the passage to the island of Zea, where he was put on shore, that one of the most emphatic incidents of his life occurred; an incident which throws a remarkable gleam into the springs and intricacies of his character—more, perhaps, than any thing which has yet been mentioned.

One day, as he was walking the quarter-deck, he lifted an ataghan (it might be one of the midshipmen's weapons), and unsheathing it, said, contemplating the blade, " I should like to know how a person feels after committing murder."—By those who have inquiringly noticed the extraordinary cast of his metaphysical associations, this dagger-scene must be regarded as both impressive and solemn : the wish to know how a man felt after committing murder, does not imply any desire to perpetrate the crime. The feeling might be appreciated by experiencing any actual degree of guilt; for it is not the deed, the sentiment which follows it makes the horror. But it is doing injustice to suppose the expression of such a wish dictated by desire. Lord Byron has been heard to express, in the eccentricity of conversation, wishes for a more intense knowledge of remorse than murder itself could give. There is, however, a wide and wild difference between the curiosity that prompts the wish to know the exactitude of any feeling or idea, and the direful passions that instigate to guilty gratifications.

Being landed, according to his request, with his valet, two Albanians, and a Tartar, on the shore of Zea, it may be easily conceived that he saw the ship depart with a feeling before unfelt. It was the first time he was left companionless, and the scene around was calculated to nourish stern fancies, even though there was not much of suffering to be withstood.

The landing-place in the port of Zea I recollect distinctly. The port itself is a small land-locked gulf, or as the Scottish Highlander would call it, a loch. The banks are rocky and forbidding; the hills, which rise to the altitude of mountains, have, in a long course of ages, been always inhabited by a civilized people. Their precipitous sides are formed into innumerable artificial terraces, the aspect of which, austere, ruinous, and ancient, produces on the mind of the stranger a sense of the presence of a greater antiquity than the sight of monuments of mere labour and art. The town stands high upon the mountain; I

counted on the lower side of the road which leads to
it forty-nine of those terraces at one place under me,
and on the opposite hills, in several places, upwards
of sixty. Whether Lord Byron ascended to the town
is doubtful. I have never heard him mention that he
had ; and I am inclined to think that he proceeded at
once to Athens by one of the boats which frequent the
harbour.

At Athens he met an old fellow-collegian, the
Marquis of Sligo, with whom he soon after travelled as far as Corinth; the marquis turning off there
for Tripolizza, while Byron went forward to Patras,
where he had some needful business to transact
with the consul. He then made the tour of the Morea,
in the course of which he visited the vizier Velhi
Pashaw, by whom he was treated, as every other
English traveller of the time was, with great distinction and hospitality.

Having occasion to go back to Patras, he was
seized by the local fever there, and reduced to
death's door. On his recovery he returned to Athens,
where he found the marquis, with Lady Hester Stanhope, and Mr. Bruce, afterwards so celebrated for his
adventures in assisting the escape of the French general
Lavalette. He took possession of the apartments
which I had occupied in the monastery, and made
them his home during the remainder of his residence
in Greece; but when I returned to Athens, in October, he was not there. I found, however, his valet,
Fletcher, in possession.

There is no very clear account of the manner in
which Lord Byron employed himself after his return
to Athens, but various intimations in his correspondence show that during the winter his pen was not
idle. It would, however, be to neglect an important
occurrence, not to notice that during the time when
he was at Athens alone, the incident which he afterwards embodied in the impassioned fragments of the

Giaour came to pass; and to apprize the reader that the story is founded on an adventure which happened to himself: he was, in fact, the cause of the girl being condemned and sentenced to be sewn up in a sack and thrown into the sea.

One day as he was returning from bathing in the Piræus, he met the procession going down to the shore to execute the sentence which the waywode had pronounced on the girl; and learning the object of the ceremony, and who was the victim, he immediately interfered with great resolution; for, on observing some hesitation on the part of the leader of the escort to return with him to the governor's house, he drew a pistol and threatened to shoot him on the spot. The man then turned about, and accompanied him back, when, partly by bribery and entreaty, he succeeded in obtaining a pardon for her, on condition that she was sent immediately out of the city. Byron conveyed her to the monastery, and on the same night sent her off to Thebes, where she found a safe asylum.

With this affair, I may close his adventures in Greece; for, although he remained several months subsequently at Athens, he was in a great measure stationary. His health which was never robust, was impaired by the effects of the fever which lingered about him; perhaps, too, by the humiliating anxiety he suffered on account of the uncertainty in his remittances. But however this may have been, it was fortunate for his fame that he returned to England at the period he did, for the climate of the Mediterranean was detrimental to his constitution. The heat oppressed him so much as to be positive suffering, and scarcely had he reached Malta, on his way home, when he was visited again with a tertian ague.

☆ ★ ☆

CHAPTER XXVII.

Sketches of character.—His friendly dispositions.—Introduce Prince K——
to him —Our last interview.—His continued kindness towards me.—
Instance of it to one of my friends.

For some time after the publication of Childe
Harold, the noble author appeared to more advantage
than I ever afterwards saw him.   He was soothed by
success ; and the universal applause which attended
his poem seemed to make him think more kindly of
the world, of which he has too often complained,
while it would be difficult to discover, in his career
and fortunes, that he had ever received any cause
from it to justify his complaint.

At no time, I imagine, could it be said that Lord
Byron was one of those men who interest themselves
in the concerns of others.   He had always too much
to do with his own thoughts about himself, to afford
time for the consideration of aught that was lower in
his affections.   But still he had many amiable fits, and
at the particular period to which I allude, he evinced
a constancy in the disposition to oblige, which proved
how little self-control was wanting to have made
him as pleasant as he was uniformly interesting.
I felt this towards myself in a matter which had certainly the grace of condescension in it, at the expense
of some trouble to him.   I then lived at the corner
of Bridge-street, Westminster, and in going to the
House of Lords he frequently stopped to inquire if I
wanted a frank.   His conversation, at the same time,
was of a milder vein, and with the single exception of

one day, while dining together at the St. Alban's, it was light and playful, as if gaiety had become its habitude.

Perhaps I regarded him too curiously, and more than once it struck me that he thought so. For at times, when he was in his comfortless moods, he has talked of his affairs and perplexities as if I had been much more acquainted with them than I had any opportunity of being. But he was a subject for study, such as is rarely met with—at least, he was so to me; for his weaknesses were as interesting as his talents, and he often indulged in expressions which would have been blemishes in the reflections of other men, but which in him often proved the germs of philosophical imaginings. He was the least qualified for any sort of business of all men I have ever known; so skinless in sensibility as respected himself, and so distrustful in his universal apprehensions of human nature, as respected others. It was, indeed, a wild, though a beautiful error of nature, to endow a spirit with such discerning faculties, and yet render it unfit to deal with mankind. But these reflections belong more properly to a general estimate of his character, than to the immediate purpose before me, which was principally to describe the happy effects which the splendid reception of Childe Harold had on his feelings; effects which, however, did not last long. He was gratified to the fulness of his hopes; but the adulation was enjoyed to excess, and his infirmities were aggravated by the surfeit. I did not, however, see the progress of the change, as in the course of the summer I went to Scotland, and soon after again abroad. But on my return, in the following spring, it was very obvious.

I found him, in one respect, greatly improved; there was more of a formed character about him; he was evidently, at the first glance, more mannered, or endeavouring to be so, and easier with the proprieties of his rank; but he had risen in his own estimation above the honours so willingly paid to his genius, and was again longing for additional renown. Not content with being acknowledged as the first poet of the age, and a respectable orator in the House of Lords, he was aspiring to the eclat of a man of gallantry, so that many of the most ungracious peculiarities of his temper, though brought under better discipline, were again in full activity.

Considering how much he was then caressed, I ought to have been proud of the warmth with which he received me. I did not, however, so often see him as in the previous year ; for I was then on the eve of my marriage, and I should not so soon, after my return to London, have probably renewed my visits, but a foreign nobleman of the highest rank, who had done me the honour to treat me as a friend, came at that juncture to this country, and knowing I had been acquainted with Lord Byron, he requested me to introduce him to his Lordship. This rendered a visit preliminary to the introduction necessary, and so long as my distinguished friend remained in town, we again often met. But after he left the country my visits became few and far between ; owing to nothing but that change in a man's pursuits and associates which are among some of the evils of matrimony. It is somewhat remarkable, that of the last visit I ever paid him, he has made rather a particular memorandum. I remember well, that it was in many respects an occasion not to be at once forgotten ; for, among other things, after lighter topics, he explained to me a variety of tribulations in his affairs, and I urged him, in consequence, to marry, with the frankness which his confidence encouraged; subjoining certain items of other good advice concerning a *liaison* which he was supposed to have formed, and which Mr. Moore does not appear to have known, though it was much talked of at the time.

During that visit the youthful peculiarities of his

temper and character showed all their original blemish.
But, as usual, when such was the case, he was often
more interesting than when in his discreeter moods.
He gave me the copy of The Bride of Abydos, with a
very kind inscription on it, which I have already men‑
tioned; but, still there was an impression on my mind
that led me to believe he could not have been very
well pleased with some parts of my counselling.
This, however, appears not to have been the case; on
the contrary, the tone of his record breathes something
of kindness; and long after I received different reasons
to believe his recollection of me was warm and friendly.

When he had retired to Genoa, I gave a gentleman
a letter to him, partly that I might hear something of
his real way of life, and partly in the hope of grati‑
fying my friend by the sight of one of whom he had
heard so much. The reception from his Lordship was
flattering to me; and, as the account of it contains
what I think a characteristic picture, the reader will,
I doubt not, be pleased to see so much of it as may
be made public without violating the decorum which
should always be observed in describing the incidents
of private intercourse, when the consent of all parties
cannot be obtained to the publication.

"Dear Galt,   " *Edinburgh, June* 3, 1830.
"Though I shall always retain a lively general recollection of my agreeable interview with Lord Byron, at
Genoa, in May, 1823, so long a time has since elapsed
that much of the aroma of the pleasure has evaporated,
and I can but recall generalities. At that time there
was an impression in Genoa that he was averse to receive visits from Englishmen, and I was indeed advised not to think of calling on him, as I might run
the risk of meeting with a savage reception. However, I resolved to send your note, and to the surprise
of every one the messenger brought a most polite answer, in which, after expressing the satisfaction of

hearing of his old friend and fellow-traveller, he added
that he would do himself the honour of calling on me
next day, which he accordingly did ; but owing to the
officious blundering of an Italian waiter, who mentioned I was at dinner, his Lordship sent up his card
with his compliments that he would not *deranger* the
party. I was determined, however, that he should not
escape me in this way, and drove out to his residence
next morning, when, upon his English valet taking
up my name, I was immediately admitted.

"As every one forms a picture to himself of remarkable characters, I had depicted his Lordship in my
mind as a tall, sombre, Childe Harold personage, tinc-
tured somewhat with aristocratic hauteur. You may
therefore guess my surprise when the door opened,
and I saw leaning upon the lock, a light animated
figure, rather *petite* than otherwise, dressed in a nankeen hussar-braided jacket, trowsers of the same material, with a white waistcoat; his countenance pale,
but the complexion clear and healthful, with the hair
coming down in little curls on each side of his fine
forehead.

" He came towards me with an easy cheerfulness of
manner, and after some preliminary inquiries concerning yourself we entered into a conversation which
lasted two hours, in the course of which I felt myself
perfectly at ease, from his Lordship's natural and simple manners; indeed so much so, that forgetting all my
anticipations, I found myself conversing with him with
as fluent an intercourse of mind as I ever experienced,
even with yourself.

" It is impossible for me at present to overtake a detail of what passed, but as it produced a kind of
scene, I may mention one incident.

" Having remarked that in a long course of desultory
reading, I had read most of what had been said by
English travellers concerning Italy ; yet, on coming
to it I found there was no country of which I had less

accurate notions : that among other things I was much
struck with the harshness of the language.   He seemed
to jerk at this, and immediately observed, that perhaps in going rapidly through the country, I might not
have had many opportunities of hearing it politely
spoken. ' Now,' said he, ' there are supposed to be
nineteen dialects of the Italian language, and I shall
let you hear a lady speak the principal of them, who
is considered to do it very well.'   I pricked up my
ears at hearing this, as I considered it would afford
me an opportunity of seeing the far-famed Countess
Guiccioli.   His Lordship immediately rose and left the
apartment, returning in the course of a minute or two
leading in the lady, and while arranging chairs for the
trio, he said to me, ' I shall make her speak each of
the principal dialects, but you are not to mind how I
pronounce, for I do not speak Italian well.'   After
the scene had been performed he resumed to me,
' now what do you think?'   To which I answered,
that my opinion still remained unaltered.   He seemed
at this to fall into a little revery, and then said ab-
ruptly, ' Why 'tis very odd, Moore thought the same.'
' Does your Lordship mean Tom Moore?' ' Yes.' ' Ah,
then, my Lord, I shall adhere with more pertinacity to
my opinion, when I hear that a man of his exquisite
taste in poetry and harmony was also of that opinion.'
   " You will be asking what I thought of the lady ; I
had certainly heard much of her high personal attractions, but all I can say is, that in my eyes her graces
did not rank above mediocrity.   They were youth,
plumpness, and good-nature."

☆ ★ ☆

CHAPTER XLIII.

Lord Byron's conversations on religion with Dr. Kennedy.

WHILE Lord Byron was hesitating, in the island of Cephalonia, about proceeding to Greece, an occurrence took place, of which so much has been made, that I may not venture to cast it into the notes of the appendix. I allude to the acquaintance he formed with a Dr. Kennedy, the publication of whose conversations with him on religion, has attracted some degree of public attention

This gentleman was originally destined for the Scottish bar, but afterwards became a student of medicine, and entering the medical department of the army, happened to be stationed in Cephalonia when Lord Byron arrived. He appears to have been a man of kind dispositions, possessed of a better heart than judgment ; in all places wherever his duty bore him he took a lively interest in the condition of the inhabitants, and was active, both in his official and private capacity, to improve it. He had a taste for circulating pious tracts, and zealously co-operated in distributing copies of the Scriptures.

Firmly settled, himself, in a conviction of the truth of Christianity, he was eager to make converts to his views of the doctrines ; but whether he was exactly the kind of apostle to achieve the conversion of Lord Byron,

may, perhaps, be doubted. His sincerity and the disinterestedness of his endeavours would secure to him
from his Lordship an indulgent and even patient hearing. But I fear that without some more effectual calling, the arguments he appears to have employed were
not likely to have made Lord Byron a proselyte. His
Lordship was so constituted in his mind, and by his
temperament, that nothing short of regeneration could
have made him a Christian, according to the gospel
of Dr. Kennedy.
Lord Byron had but loose feelings in religion—
scarcely any. His sensibility and a slight constitu-
tional leaning towards superstition and omens showed
that the sense of devotion was, however, alive and
awake within him; but with him religion was a
sentiment, and the convictions of the understanding
had nothing whatever to do with his creed. That he
was deeply imbued with the essence of natural piety;
that he often felt the power and being of a God thrill-
ing in all his frame, and glowing in his bosom, I declare
my thorough persuasion; and that he believed in some
of the tenets and in the philosophy of Christianity;
as they influence the spirit and conduct of men, I
am as little disposed to doubt; especially if those
portions of his works which only trend towards the
subject, and which bear the impression of fervour
and earnestness, may be admitted as evidence. But
he was not a member of any particular church,
and, without a re-construction of his mind and temperament, I venture to say, he could not have become such;
not in consequence, as too many have represented, of
any predilection, either of feeling or principle, against
Christianity; but, entirely owing to an organic peculiarity of mind. He reasoned on every topic by instinct, rather than by induction or any process of logic;
and could never be so convinced of the truth or falsehood of an abstract proposition, as to feel it affect the
current of his actions. He may have assented to ar-

guments, without being sensible of their truth ; merely
because they were not objectionable to his feelings at the
time. And, in the same manner, he may have disputed
even fair inferences, from admitted premises, if the state
of his feelings happened to be indisposed to the subject.
I am persuaded, nevertheless, that to class him
among absolute infidels were to do injustice to his
memory, and that he has suffered uncharitably in
the opinion of " the rigidly righteous," who, because
he had not attached himself to any particular sect or
congregation, assumed that he was an adversary to
religion. To claim for him any credit, as a pious
man, would be absurd ; but, to suppose he had not
as deep an interest as other men, " in his soul's
health" and welfare, was to impute to him a nature which cannot exist. Being, altogether, a creature of impulses, he certainly could not be ever employed in doxologies, or engaged in the logomachy of
churchmen ; but he had the sentiment which at a tamer
age might have made him more ecclesiastical. There
was as much truth as joke in the expression, when he
wrote

I am myself a moderate Presbyterian.

A mind, constituted like that of Lord Byron, was
little susceptible of impressions from the arguments of
ordinary men. It was necessary that Truth, in visiting
him, should come arrayed in her solemnities, and
with Awe and Reverence for her precursors. Acknowledged superiority, yea, celebrated wisdom, were in-
dispensable, to bespeak his sincere attention ; and,
without disparagement, it may be fairly said, these
were not the attributes of Dr. Kennedy. On the contrary, there was a taint of cant about him—perhaps he
only acted like those who have it—but, still he was
not exactly the dignitary to command unaffected deference from the shrewd and irreverent author of Don

Juan. The result verified what ought to have been the anticipation. The doctor's attempt to quicken Byron to a sense of grace, failed ; but his Lordship treated him with politeness. The history of the affair will, however, be more interesting than any reflections which it is in my humble power to offer.

Some of Dr. Kennedy's acquaintances wished to hear him explain, in " a logical and demonstrative manner, the evidences and doctrines of Christianity ;" and Lord Byron, hearing of the intended meeting, desired to be present, and was accordingly invited. He attended ; but was not present at several others which followed ; he however intimated to the Doctor, that he would be glad to converse with him, and the invitation was accepted. " On religion," says the Doctor, " his Lordship was in general a hearer, proposing his difficulties and objections with more fairness than could have been expected from one under similar circumstances ; and with so much candour, that they often seemed to be proposed more for the purpose of procuring information, or satisfactory answers, than from any other motive."

At the first meeting, Dr. Kennedy explained, becomingly, his views of the subject, and that he had read every work against Christianity which fell in his way. It was this consideration which had induced him with such confidence to enter upon the discussion, knowing, on the one hand, the strength of Christianity, and, on the other, the weakness of its assailants. " To show you, therefore," said the Doctor, " the grounds on which I demand your attention to what I may say on the nature and evidence of Christianity, I shall mention the names of some of the authors whose works I have read or consulted." When he had mentioned all these names, Lord Byron asked if he had read Barrow's and Stillingfleet's works ? The Doctor replied, " I have seen them, but I have not read them."

After a disquisition, chiefly relative to the history of Christianity, Dr. Kennedy observed, " We must, on all occasions, but more particularly in fair and logical discussions with sceptics, or Deists, make a distinction between Christianity, as it is found in the Scriptures, and the errors, abuses, and imperfections of Christians themselves. To this his Lordship remarked, that he always had taken care to make that distinction, as he knew enough of Christianity to feel that it was both necessary and just. The Doctor remarked that the contrary was almost universally the case with those who doubted or denied the truth of Christianity, and proceeded to illustrate the statement. He then read a summary of the fundamental doctrines of Christianity ; but he had not proceeded far, when he observed signs of impatience in Lord Byron, who inquired if these sentiments accorded with the Doctor's ? and being answered they did, and with those of all sound Christians, except in one or two minor things, his Lordship rejoined, that he did not wish to hear the opinions of others, whose writings he could read at any time, but only his own. The Doctor then read on till coming to the expression " grace of God," his Lordship inquired, " what do you mean by grace ?" " The primary and fundamental meaning of the word," replied the Doctor, somewhat surprised at his ignorance (I quote his own language), " is favour ; though it varies according to the context to express that disposition of God, which leads him to grant a favour; the action of doing so, or the favour itself, or its effects on those who receive it." The arrogance of the use of the term ignorance here, requires no animadversion ; but to suppose the greatest master, then in existence, of the English language, not acquainted with the meaning of the word, when he asked to be informed of the meaning attached to it by the individual making use of it, gives us some insight into the true character of the teacher. The Doctor closed the book, as he

perceived that Lord Byron, as he says, had no distinct
conception of many of the words used; and his Lordship subjoined, " What we want is to be convinced
that the Bible is true; because if we can believe that,
it will follow as a matter of course, that we must
believe all the doctrines it contains."

The reply to this was to the effect, that the observa-
tion was partly just; but though the strongest evidence were produced of the Scriptures being the revealed will of God, they (his Lordship and others present)
would still remain unbelievers, unless they knew and
comprehended the doctrines contained in the Scriptures. This was not conclusive, and Lord Byron
replied, that they wished him to prove that the Scriptures were the word of God, which the Doctor, with
more than apostolic simplicity, said that such was his
object, but he should like to know what they deemed
the clearest course to follow with that object in view.
After some further conversation—" No other plan was
proposed by them," says the Doctor; and, he adds,
" They had violated their engagement to hear me for
twelve hours, for which I had stipulated." This
may, perhaps, satisfy the reader as to the quality of
the Doctor's understanding; but as the subject in its
bearings touches Lord Byron's character, I shall proceed a little further into the marrow of the matter.

The inculcation being finished for that evening,
Lord Byron said, that when he was young his mother
brought him up strictly; and that he had access to
a great many theological works, and remembered that
he was particularly pleased with Barrow's writings,
and that he also went regularly to church. He declared that he was not an infidel who denied the Scriptures and wished to remain in unbelief; on the contrary, he was desirous to believe, as he experienced
no happiness in having his religious opinions so un-
steady and unfixed. But he could not, he added,
understand the Scriptures. "Those people who con-

scientiously believe, I always have respected, and was always disposed to trust in them more than in others." A desultory conversation then ensued, respecting the language and translations of the Scriptures; in the course of which his Lordship remarked, that Scott, in his Commentary on the Bible, did not say that it was the devil who tempted Eve, nor does the Bible say a word about the devil. It is only said that the serpent spoke, and that it was the subtlest of all the beasts of the field.—Will it be said that truth and reason were served by Dr. Kennedy's* answer? "As beasts have not the faculty of speech, the just inference is, that the beast was only an instrument made use of by some invisible and superior being. The Scriptures accordingly tell us, that the devil is the father of lies—the lie made by the serpent to Eve being the first we have on record; they call him also a murderer from the beginning, as he was the cause of the sentence of death which was pronounced against Adam and all his posterity; and still further, to remove all doubt, and to indentify him as the agent who used the serpent as an instrument, he is called the serpent—the devil."

Lord Byron inquired what the Doctor thought of the theory of Warburton, that the Jews had no distinct idea of a future state? The Doctor acknowledged that he had often seen, but had never read The Divine Legation. And yet, he added, had Warburton read his Bible with more simplicity and attention, he would have enjoyed a more solid and honourable fame.

His Lordship then said, that one of the greatest difficulties he had met with was the existence of so much pure and unmixed evil in the world, and which he could not reconcile to the idea of a benevolent Creator. The Doctor set aside the question as to the origin of evil; but granted the extensive existence of

---

* The Doctor evidently makes a mistake in confounding Sir William Hamilton with Sir William Drummond.

evil in the universe; to remedy which, he said, the
Gospel was proclaimed; and, after some of the customary commonplaces, he ascribed much of the ex-
isting evil to the slackness of Christians in spreading
the Gospel.

" Is there not," said his Lordship, " some part of
the New Testament where it appears that the disciples
were struck with the state of physical evil, and made
inquiries into the cause?"—" There are two passages,"
was the reply. The disciples inquired, when they
saw a man who had been born blind, whether it was
owing to his own or his parents' sin?—and, after
quoting the other instance, he concludes, that moral
and physical evil in individuals are not always a judgment or punishment, but are intended to answer certain ends in the government of the world.

" Is there not," said his Lordship, " a prophecy in
the New Testament which it is alleged has not been
fulfilled, although it was declared that the end of the
world would come before the generation then exist-
ing should pass away?"—" The prediction," said Dr.
Kennedy, " related to the destruction of Jerusalem,
which certainly took place within the time assigned;
though some of the expressions descriptive of the
signs of that remarkable event are of such a nature
as to appear to apply to Christ's coming to judge the
world at the end of time."

His Lordship then asked, if the doctor thought that
there had been fewer wars and persecutions, and less
slaughter and misery, in the world since the introduction of Christianity than before? The Doctor
answered this by observing, that since Christianity
inculcates peace and good-will to all men, we must
always separate pure religion from the abuses of which
its professors are guilty.

Two other opinions were expressed by his Lordship
in the conversation. The Doctor, in speaking of the
sovereignty of God, had alluded to the similitude of

the potter and his clay; for his Lordship said, if he were broken in pieces, he would say to the potter, " Why do you treat me thus?" The other was an absurdity. It was—if the whole world were going to hell, he would prefer going with them than go alone to heaven.

Such was the result of the first council of Cephalonia, if one may venture the allusion. It is manifest, without saying much for Lord Byron's ingenuity, that he was fully a match for the Doctor, and that he was not unacquainted with the subject under discussion.

In the next conversation Lord Byron repeated " I have no wish to reject Christianity without investigation ; on the contrary, I am very desirous of believing. But I do not see very much the need of a Saviour, nor the utility of prayer. Devotion is the affection of the heart, and this I feel. When I view the wonders of creation, I bow to the Majesty of Heaven; and when I feel the enjoyments of life, I feel grateful to God for having bestowed them upon me." Upon this some discussion arose, turning chiefly on the passage in the third chapter of John, " Unless a man is converted, he cannot enter the kingdom of Heaven ;" which naturally led to an explanatory interlocutor concerning new birth, regeneration, &c.; and thence diverged into the topics which had been the subject of the former conversation.

Among other things, Lord Byron inquired, if the Doctor really thought that the devil appeared before God, as is mentioned in the book of Job, or is it only an allegorical or poetical mode of speaking ?"—The reply was, " I believe it in the strict and literal meaning."

" If it be received in a literal sense," said his Lordship, " it gives me a much higher idea of the majesty, power, and wisdom of God, to believe that the devils themselves are at his nod, and are subject to his control, with as much ease as the elements of nature fol-

low the respective laws which his will has assigned
them."

This notion was characteristic, and the poetica
feeling in which it originated, when the Doctor attempted to explain the doctrine of the Manicheans,
was still more distinctly developed; for his Lordship
again expressed how much the belief of the real appearance of Satan, to hear and obey the commands of
God, added to his views of the grandeur and majesty
of the Creator.

This second conversation was more desultory than
the first; religion was brought in only incidentally,
until his Lordship said, " I do not reject the doctrines
of Christianity; I want only sufficient proofs of it, to
take up the profession in earnest; and I do not believe
myself to be so bad a Christian as many of them who
preach against me with the greatest fury—many of
whom I have never seen nor injured."

" You have only to examine the causes which prevent you" (from being a true believer), said the Doctor, " and you will find they are futile, and only tend
to withhold you from the enjoyment of real happiness
which at present it is impossible you can find."

" What, then, you think me in a very bad way?"

" I certainly think you are," was the reply; " and
this I say, not on my own authority, but on that of
the Scriptures.—Your Lordship must be converted,
and must be reformed, before any thing can be said of
you, except that you are bad, and in a bad way."

" But," replied his Lordship, " I already believe
in predestination, which I know you believe, and in
the depravity of the human heart in general, and o
my own in particular; thus you see there are two points
in which we agree. I shall get at the others by-and-
by. You cannot expect me to become a perfect
Christian at once."

And further his Lordship subjoined:

" Predestination appears to me just; from my

own reflection and experience, I am influenced in a way which is incomprehensible, and am led to do things which I never intended; and if there is, as we all admit, a Supreme Ruler of the universe; and if, as you say, he has the actions of the devils, as well as of his own angels, completely at his command, then those influences, or those arrangements of circumstances, which lead us to do things against our will, or with ill-will, must be also under his directions. But I have never entered into the depths of the subject; I have contented myself with believing that there is a predestination of events, and that predestination depends on the will of God."

Dr. Kennedy, in speaking of this second conversation, bears testimony to the respectfulness of his Lordship's attention. "There was nothing in his manner which approached to levity, or any thing that indicated a wish to mock at religion; though, on the other hand, an able dissembler would have done and said all that he did, with such feelings and intentions.

Subsequent to the second conversation, Dr. Kennedy asked a gentleman who was intimate with Lord Byron, if he really thought his Lordship serious in his desire to hear religion explained. " Has he exhibited any contempt or ridicule at what I have said?" This gentleman assured him that he had never heard Byron allude to the subject in any way which could induce him to suspect that he was merely amusing himself. " But on the contrary, he always names you with respect. I do not, however, think you have made much impression on him; he is just the same fellow as before. He says, he does not know what religion you are of, for you neither adhere to creeds or councils."

It ought here to be noticed, as showing the general opinion entertained of his Lordship with respect to these polemical conversations, that the wits of the garrison made themselves merry with what was going

on.   Some of them affected to believe, or did so, that
Lord Byron's wish to hear Dr. Kennedy proceeded
from a desire to have an accurate idea of the opinions
and manners of the Methodists, in order that he might
make Don Juan become one for a time, and so be
enabled to paint their conduct with greater accuracy.

The third conversation took place soon after this
comment had been made on Lord Byron's conduct.
The Doctor inquired if his Lordship had read any of
the religious books he had sent.   "I have looked,"
replied Byron, "into Boston's Fourfold State, but I
have not had time to read it far : I am afraid it is too
deep for me."

Although there was no systematic design, on the
part of Lord Byron, to make Dr. Kennedy subser-
vient to any scheme of ridicule ; yet, it is evident that
he was not so serious as the Doctor so meritoriously
desired.

"I have begun," said his Lordship, "very fairly ;
I have given some of your tracts to Fletcher (his valet)
who is a good sort of man, but still wants, like myself,
some reformation ; and I hope he will spread them
among the other servants, who require it still more.
Bruno, the physician, and Gamba, are busy, reading
some of the Italian tracts ; and, I hope it will have a
good effect on them.   The former is rather too decided against it at present ; and too much engaged
with a spirit of enthusiasm for his own profession, to
attend to other subjects ; but we must have patience, and we shall see what has been the result.   I
do not fail to read, from time to time, my Bible,
though not, perhaps, so much as I should."

"Have you begun to pray that you may understand it ?"

"Not yet.   I have not arrived at that pitch of
faith yet ; but it may come by-and-by.   You are in
too great a hurry."

His Lordship then went to a side-table, on which a

great number of books were ranged; and, taking hold of an octavo, gave it to the Doctor. It was " Illustrations of the Moral Government of God;" by E. Smith, M. D., London. " The author," said he, " proves that the punishment of hell is not eternal; it will have a termination."

" The author," replied the Doctor, " is, I suppose, one of the Socinians; who, in a short time, will try to get rid of every doctrine in the Bible. How did your Lordship get hold of this book?"

" They sent it out to me from England, to make a convert of me, I suppose. The arguments are strong, drawn from the Bible itself; and, by showing that a time will come, when every intelligent creature shall be supremely happy, and eternally so, it expunges that shocking doctrine, that sin and misery will for ever exist under the government of God, whose highest attribute is love and goodness. To my present apprehension, it would be a most desirable thing, could it be proved that, alternately, all created beings were to be happy. This would appear to be most consistent with the nature of God.—I cannot yield to your doctrine of the eternal duration of punishment.—This author's opinion is more humane; and, I think, he supports it very strongly from Scripture."

The fourth conversation was still more desultory, being carried on at table amidst company; in the course of it Lord Byron, however, declared "that he was so much of a believer as to be of opinion that there is no contradiction in the Scriptures, which cannot be reconciled by an attentive consideration and comparison of passages."

It is needless to remark that Lord Byron, in the course of these conversations, was incapable of preserving a consistent seriousness. The volatility of his humour was constantly leading him into playfulness, and he never lost an opportunity of making a pun or saying a quaint thing. " Do you know," said he to the Doctor, " I am nearly reconciled to St. Paul, for he says there is no difference between the Jews and the Greeks, and I am exactly of the same opinion, for the character of both is equally vile."

Upon the whole it must be conceded, that whatever was the degree of Lord Byron's dubiety as to points of faith and doctrine, he could not be accused of gross ignorance, nor described as animated by any hostile feeling against religion.

In this sketch of these conversations, I have restricted myself chiefly to those points which related to his Lordship's own sentiments and belief. It would have been inconsistent with the concise limits of this work to have detailed the controversies. A fair summary of what Byron did not believe, what he was disposed to believe but had not satisfied himself with the evidence, and what he did believe, seemed to be the task I ought to undertake. The result confirmed the statement of his Lordship's religious condition, given in the preliminary remarks; which, I ought to mention, were written before I looked into Dr. Kennedy's book; and the statement is not different from the estimate which the conversations warrant. It is true that Lord Byron's part in the conversations is not very characteristic; but the integrity of Dr. Kennedy is a sufficient assurance that they are substantially correct.*

---

* Connected with this subject there is a letter in the Appendix, from Fletcher to the Doctor, concerning his master's religious opinions, well worthy of preservation on its own account, as affording a tolerably fair specimen of what persons in his condition of life think of religion. I fear poor Dr. Kennedy must have thought of the proverb "like master like man."

☆ ★ ☆

CHAPTER XLIX.

─────────

The character of Lord Byron.

My endeavour, in the foregoing pages, has been to give a general view of the intellectual character of Lord Byron; with only the most influential incidents of his life, aud such occurrences as might make the book interesting   It did not accord with this plan to enter minutely into the details of his private life, which I suspect was not greatly different from that of any other person of his rank, not distinguished for particular severity of manners.   In some respects his Lordship was, no doubt, peculiar.   He possessed a vivacity of sensibility not common, and talents of a very extraordinary k nd.   He was also distinguished for superior personal elegance, particularly in his bust.   The style and character of his head was universally admired; but perhaps the beauty of his physiognomy has been more highly spoken of than it really merited.   Its chief grace consisted, when he was in a gay humour, of a liveliness which gave a joyous meaning to every articulation of the muscles and features: when he was less agreeably disposed, the expression was morose to a very repulsive degree.   It is, however, unnecessary to describe his personal character here.   I have already said enough, incidentally, to explain my full opinion of it.   In the mass, I do not think it was calculated to attract much permanent affection or esteem.   In the

detail it was the reverse : few men possessed more
companionable qualities than Lord Byron did occasionally; and seen at intervals in those felicitous moments, I imagine it would have been difficult to have
said, that a more interesting companion had been
previously met with. But he was not always in that
fascinating state of pleasantry : he was as often otherwise; and no two individuals could be more distinct
from each other than Byron in his gaiety and in
his gloom. This antithesis was the great cause of
that diversity of opinion concerning him, which has
so much divided his friends and adversaries. Of
his character as a poet there can be no difference
of opinion, but only a difference in the degree of
admiration.

Excellence in talent, as in every other thing, is
comparative; but the universal republic of letters
will acknowledge, that in energy of expression and
liveliness of imagery Byron had no equal in his own
time. Doubts, indeed, may be entertained, if in
these high qualities even Shakspeare himself was his
superior.

I am not disposed to think with many of those who
rank the genius of Byron almost as supreme, that he
has shown less skill in the construction of his plots,
and the development of his tales, than might have
been expected from one so splendidly endowed ; for
it has ever appeared to me that he has accomplished
in them every thing he proposed to attain, and that in
this consists one of his great merits. His mind, fervid
and impassioned, was in all his compositions, except
Don Juan, eagerly fixed on the catastrophe. He ever
held the goal full in view, and drove to it in the most immediate manner. By this straightforward simplicity all
the interest which intricacy excites was of necessity dis-
regarded. He is therefore not treated justly when it is
supposed that he might have done better had he shown
more art: the wonder is that he should have pro-

duced such magnificent effects with so little. He could not have made the satiated and meditative Harold so darkling and excursive, had he treated him as the hero of a scholastic epic. The might of the poet in such creations lay in the riches of his diction, and in the felicity with which he described feelings in relation to the aspect of scenes and the reminiscences with which the scenes themselves were associated.

If in language and plan he be so excellent, it may be asked why should he not be honoured with that pre-eminent niche in the temple which so many in the world have by suffrage assigned to him? Simply because with all the life and beauty of his style, the vigour and truth of his descriptions, the boldness of his conceptions, and the reach of his vision in the dark abysses of passion, Lord Byron was but imperfectly acquainted with human nature. He looked but on the outside of man. No characteristic action distinguishes one of his heroes from another, nor is there much dissimilarity in their sentiments; they have no individuality; they stalk and pass in mist and gloom, grim, ghastly, and portentous, mysterious shadows, entities of the twilight, weird things like the sceptred effigies of the unborn issue of Banquo.

Combined with vast power, Lord Byron possessed, beyond all question, the greatest degree of originality of any poet of this age. In this rare quality he has no parallel in any age. All other poets and inventive authors are measured in their excellence by the accuracy with which they fit sentiments appropriate not only to the characters they create, but to the situations in which they place them : the works of Lord Byron display the opposite to this and with the most extraordinary splendour. He endows his creations with his own qualities; he finds in the situations in which he places them only opportunities to express what he has himself felt or suffered; and yet he

mixes so much probability in the circumstances, that
they are always eloquently proper. He does every
thing, as it were, the reverse of other poets; in the air
and sea, which have been in all times the emblems of
change and the similitudes of inconstancy, he has discovered the very principles of permanency. The
ocean in his view, not by its vastness, its unfathom-
able depths, and its limitless extent, becomes an image
of deity, but by its unchangeable character!

The variety of his productions present a prodigious
display of power. In his short career he has entitled
himself to be ranked in the first class of the British
poets for quantity alone. By Childe Harold, and his
other poems of the same mood, he has extended the
scope of feeling, made us acquainted with new trains
of association, awakened sympathies which few suspected themselves of possessing; and he has laid open
darker recesses in the bosom than were previously
supposed to exist. The deep and dreadful caverns
of remorse had long been explored; but he was the
first to visit the bottomless pit of satiety.

The delineation of that Promethean fortitude which
defied conscience, as he has shown it in Manfred, is
his greatest achievement. The terrific fables of Mar-
lowe, and of Goëthe, in their respective versions of
the legend of Faustus, had disclosed the utmost
writhings which remorse, in the fiercest of its tor-
ments, can express; but what are those Laocoon
agonies to the sublime serenity of Manfred. In the
power, the originality, and the genius combined, of
that unexampled performance, Lord Byron has placed
himself on an equality with Milton. The Satan of
the Paradise Lost is animated by motives, and dignified by an eternal enterprise. He hath purposes of
infinite prospect to perform, and an immeasurable
ambition to satisfy. Manfred hath neither purpose,
nor ambition, nor any desire that seeks gratification.
He hath done a deed which severs him from hope, as

everlastingly as the apostacy with the angels has done Satan. He acknowledges no contrition to bespeak commiseration, he complains of no wrong to justify revenge, for he feels none; he despises sympathy, and almost glories in his perdition. He is like the spirit of one who, after crimes, having committed self-slaughter, stands calm in the bucket as he is lowered down the hatchway of hell.

The creation of such a character is in the sublimest degree of originality; to give it appropriate thoughts and feelings required powers worthy of the conception; and to make it susceptible of being contemplated as within the scope and range of human sympathy, places Byron above all his contemporaries and antecedents. Milton has described in Satan the greatest of human passions, supernatural attributes, directed to immortal intents, and stung with inextinguishable revenge; but Satan is only a dilatation of man. Manfred is loftier, and worse than Satan; he has conquered punishment, having within himself a greater than hell can inflict. There is a fearful mystery in this conception; it is only by solemnly questioning the spirits that lurk within the dark metaphors in which Manfred expresses himself, that the hideous secrets of the character can be conjectured.

But although in intellectual power, and in creative originality, Byron is entitled to stand on the highest peak of the mountain, his verse is often so harsh, and his language so obscure, that in the power of delighting he is only a poet of the second class. He had all the talent and the means requisite to imbody his conceptions in a manner worthy of their might and majesty; his treasury was rich in every thing rare and beautiful for illustration, but he possessed not the instinct requisite to guide him in the selection of the things necessary to the inspiration of delight;—he could give his statue life and beauty, and warmth, and motion, and eloquence, but not a tuneful voice.

Some curious metaphysicians, in their subtle criticism, have said that Don Juan was but the bright side of Childe Harold, and that all its most brilliant imagery was similar to that of which the dark and the shadows were delineated in his other works. It may be so. And, without question, a great similarity runs through every thing that has come from the poet's pen; but it is a family resemblance, the progeny are all like one another; but where are those who are like them? I know of no author in prose or rhyme, in the English language, with whom Byron can be compared. Imitators of his manner there will be often and many, but he will ever remain one of the few whom the world acknowledges are alike supreme, and yet unlike each other—epochal characters, who mark extraordinary periods in history.

Raphael is the only man of pre-eminence whose career can be compared with that of Byron, at an age when the genius of most men is but in the dawning, they had both attained their meridian of glory, and they both died so early, that it may be said they were lent to the world only to show the height to which the mind may ascend when time shall be allowed to accomplish the full cultivation of such extraordinary endowments.

NOTE

p. 23, l. 19: Sir William Drummond (1770?-1828). Orientalist and diplomat. His radically sceptical mythography was highly appealing to Byron – especially his *Oedipus Judaicus* (1811) which attempts to prove that large parts of the Old Testament are in fact astronomical allegories.

Thomas Moore, *The Life of Byron* (London, 1832)

Thomas Moore's account of the life of his great friend Byron is by far the most extensive memoir written by a close friend of the poet. As any modern reader of Byron's correspondence will know, Moore played the most prominent role in the posthumous censorship of Byron's letters, and this was a process he carried into his biography of the poet. Moore's *Life* is an almost entirely uncritical celebration of a great poet by one of his closest friends, and represents faithfully the side of Byron admired by his personal friends and his political sympathisers in Holland House. It falls into the category of eulogy typified by Southey's *Life of Nelson*, and is no less enjoyable to read for that.

Thomas Moore shared with John Cam Hobhouse the claim to be Byron's most consistently valued friend; but in the later years of Byron's life there was little doubt that Moore was the man whom he saw and respected the most. Moore was born in Dublin in 1779 and was educated at Trinity College, where he began to write poetry, and was briefly and tangentially involved in the aftershocks of the 1798 Irish Revolution. He soon moved to England, and with the publication of *The Poetry of Thomas Little* began a career of writing and singing the light, often erotic, lyrical poetry for which he is most often remembered today. Although he could lay claim to being one of the most widely-read of the English Romantics, his erotic poetry, along with his occasional Whig-inspired satires, endeared him above all to Whig members of the aristocracy, who stood at a distance from the tide of moralistic political correctness (or 'cant' as Byron was to call it) that was to gain momentum throughout the Romantic period. In 1817 he published, in *Lalla Rookh*, one of the most important poems of the Romantic Period in England, an oriental epic which was to achieve instant success and earn its author the magnificent sum of £3000. The success of the poetry was such as to make it difficult today to recover a sense of Moore's place in the literary world of Regency England. He was not, as his modest reputation today might lead the reader to expect, an impossibly minor figure living parasitically off the poetical energy of Byron. Still less was he regarded solely as an exotic Irish import, tolerated only so long as he sang to accompany the parties of the powerful. He was instead one of the pre-eminent poets of his day; his appeal was wide, and admiration of him was almost universal.

Moore was also the most celebrated Irish poet of his day, although after a Nationalist backlash he was not to maintain his foothold on the Irish Parnassus for long. Instead he was regarded as having sold out the Irish cause to the English. He had abandoned his Dublin friends – many of whom had connections with the revolutionary movement – in favour of an English aristocracy to whom he sold a tame version of Irish grievances. Moore had commercialized the Irish cause, and profited from it, and would never be worthy of the Irish laureateship.

Moore was one of the most sanguine of the English romantic poets; his immense popularity in the dinners and parties of the English aristocracy may have been in large part owing to this 'sunshiny' character (in the words of Elizabeth Rennie). In part this was made possible by the stability of his married life (which earned him the epithet 'ultra-uxorious' from Croker): but he seems in addition to have possessed the most remarkably buoyant nature. And this was despite setbacks which included severe financial embarrassment and the premature deaths of all of his children. He had an almost uncanny ability to get on with people – and in particular people who could be useful to him in some way. In practice this meant the aristocracy, and it was as a parasite of the aristocracy that Moore was most often satirized by contemporary critics (hence Byron's often-repeated claim 'Tommy loves a lord'). And for writers like Hazlitt this was the worst of his crimes. Moore, he claimed, was a vain, pretentious, snobbish would-be dandy who had forgotten that his presence in aristocratic circles was by sufferance and not by right.

For all his apparent confidence, Moore was deeply insecure, and painfully vulnerable to attacks like these. But if his social climbing made him anathema to a radical like Hazlitt, his rather fawning admiration for anyone with a title would hardly have had the same affect on Byron, who was throughout his life almost embarrassingly 'diffident' on the score of his rank. The friendship could hardly, however, have had a less auspicious start. In his *English Bards and Scotch Reviewers* Byron had satirized an abortive duel Moore had had with the critic Francis Jeffrey after Jeffrey's *Edinburgh Review* had lambasted Moore's *Poetry of Thomas Little*. On the appointed morning the duel was disrupted by the authorities, who examined the pistols and discovered that one of them did not contain a bullet. Both Moore and Jeffrey were instantly subject to universal ridicule, and Byron's reference to 'Little's leadless pistol' may have been one insult too many. Moore fired off a furious note to Byron demanding an explanation, in terms that would have made a duel between the two men inevitable. As luck would have it, the note failed to reach Byron, and after the publication of *Childe Harold's Pilgrimage* the two men became steadfast friends, meeting for the first time for dinner at the house of Samuel Rogers in November 1811. There were obvious reasons for the remarkable affinity between the two. They shared a similar outlook on life and politics – both had formed part of the favoured Holland House circle – and held similar views on the state of poetry in their time. Moore, of course, was happy to supply the mixture of deference and inspiration that Byron demanded in his friends, and Byron probably valued him – as he had valued Hobhouse – as a loyal and stabilizing element throughout the latter part of his turbulent social life.

In the event Moore was Byron's only friend from his early days in London to see a significant amount of him in Italy. An anecdote from Moore's account of the first evening the two men shared together in Venice illustrates vividly the intense friendship that existed between them. As they stood together on the balcony of Byron's house, Moore, overcome by an excess of his trademark sentimentality, began to talk of 'that peculiar rosy hue' of Italian sunsets. Byron's response was immediate, and equally characteristic of him at the time – 'Come, damn it, Tom,' he replied – 'don't be poetical'. The response is of course especially amusing coming from the poet who for an English literary audience virtually invented the Venetian sunset. But for our purposes Byron's words have an even greater significance; there were very few amongst Byron's male acquaintance whom he condescended to address by their first name.

While this may have made Moore one of the best qualified of Byron's friends to write his biography, for the reader of this book he may figure as more the villain of the piece than the friend of Byron. For it was to Moore that Byron entrusted the publication of his *Memoirs*, and it was Moore that allowed himself to be persuaded by Hobhouse and Kinnaird to burn them in John Murray's parlour fire. For this, of course, he will never be forgiven by Byron's many biographers – even if his apologists might feel relieved that what the *Memoirs* had to reveal of Byron's peculiar brand of morality is now unlikely ever to emerge. As a consolation, however, we are left with Moore's biography of Byron, which is amongst the most informative documents we possess in respect of the poet's life and nature. Moore clearly felt guilty about his betrayal of Byron's trust in burning the *Memoirs*: we can only assume he attempted to compensate for it by making the best job he could of his *Life*.

At the beginning of the month of December,
being called up to town by business, I had opportunities, from being a good deal in my noble friend's
society, of observing the state of his mind and feelings,
under the prospect of the important change he was
now about to undergo; and it was with pain I found
that those sanguine hopes * with which I had sometimes looked forward to the happy influence of marriage, in winning him over to the brighter and
better side of life, were, by a view of all the circumstances of his present destiny, considerably diminished; while, at the same time, not a few doubts and

* I had frequently, both in earnest and in jest, expressed
these hopes to him; and, in one of my letters, after touching
upon some matters relative to my own little domestic circle, I
added, " This will all be unintelligible to you; though I sometimes cannot help thinking it within the range of possibility,
that even *you*, volcano as you are, may, one day, cool down
into something of the same *habitable* state.   Indeed, when one
thinks of lava having been converted into buttons for Isaac
Hawkins Browne, there is no saying what such fiery things
may be brought to at last."

misgivings, which had never before so strongly occurred to me, with regard to his own fitness, under
any circumstances, for the matrimonial tie, filled me
altogether with a degree of foreboding anxiety as to
his fate, which the unfortunate events that followed
but too fully justified.

The truth is, I fear, that rarely, if ever, have men
of the higher order of genius shown themselves fitted
for the calm affections and comforts that form the
cement of domestic life.   " One misfortune (says
Pope) of extraordinary geniuses is, that their very
friends are more apt to admire than love them."   To
this remark there have, no doubt, been exceptions,—
and I should pronounce Lord Byron, from my own
experience, to be one of them,—but it would not be
difficult, perhaps, to show, from the very nature and
pursuits of genius, that such must generally be the
lot of all pre-eminently gifted with it; and that the
same qualities which enable them to command admiration are also those that too often incapacitate
them from conciliating love.

The very habits, indeed, of abstraction and self-
study to which the occupations of men of genius
lead, are, in themselves, necessarily, of an unsocial
and detaching tendency, and require a large portion
of indulgence from others not to be set down as
unamiable.   One of the chief sources, too, of sympathy and society between ordinary mortals being
their dependence on each other's intellectual resources, the operation of this social principle must
naturally be weakest in those whose own mental
stores are most abundant and self-sufficing, and who,

rich in such materials for thinking within themselves, are rendered so far independent of any aid from others.   It was this solitary luxury (which Plato called " banqueting his own thoughts") that led Pope, as well as Lord Byron, to prefer the silence and seclusion of his library to the most agreeable conversation. — And not only too, is the necessity of commerce with other minds less felt by such persons, but, from that fastidiousness which the opulence of their own resources generates, the society of those less gifted than themselves becomes often a restraint and burden, to which not all the charms of friendship, or even love, can reconcile them.   " Nothing is so tiresome (says the poet of Vaucluse, in assigning a reason for not living with some of his dearest friends) as to converse with persons who have not the same information as one's self."

But it is the cultivation and exercise of the imaginative faculty that, more than any thing, tends to wean the man of genius from actual life, and, by substituting the sensibilities of the imagination for those of the heart, to render, at last, the medium through which he feels no less unreal than that through which he thinks.   Those images of ideal good and beauty that surround him in his musings soon accustom him to consider all that is beneath this high standard unworthy of his care ; till, at length, the heart becoming chilled as the fancy warms, it too often happens that, in proportion as he has refined and elevated his theory of all the social affections, he has unfitted himself for the practice of them. *   Hence so frequently it arises that, in persons of this temperament, we see some bright but artificial idol of the brain usurp the place of all real and natural objects of tenderness. The poet Dante, a wanderer away from wife and children, passed the whole of a restless and detached life in nursing his immortal dream of Beatrice; while Petrarch, who would not suffer his only daughter to reside beneath his roof, expended thirty-two years of poetry and passion on an ideal‑ised love.

It is, indeed, in the very nature and essence of genius to be for ever occupied intensely with Self, as the great centre and source of its strength. Like the sister Rachel, in Dante, sitting all day before her mirror,

" mai non si smaga
Del suo ammiraglio, e siede tutto giorno."

To this power of self-concentration, by which alone all the other powers of genius are made avail-able, there is, of course, no such disturbing and fatal

---

* Of the lamentable contrast between sentiments and con-duct, which this transfer of the seat of sensibility from the heart to the fancy produces, the annals of literary men afford unluckily too many examples.   Alfieri, though he could write a sonnet full of tenderness to his mother, never saw her (says Mr. W. Rose) but once after their early separation, though he frequently passed within a few miles of her residence.   The poet Young, with all his parade of domestic sorrows, was, it appears, a neglectful husband and harsh father; and Sterne (to use the words employed by Lord Byron) preferred " whining over a dead ass to relieving a living mother."

enemy as those sympathies and affections that draw the mind out actively towards others*; and, accordingly, it will be found that, among those who have felt within themselves a call to immortality, the greater number have, by a sort of instinct, kept aloof from such ties, and, instead of the softer duties and rewards of being amiable, reserved themselves for the high, hazardous chances of being great. In looking back through the lives of the most illustrious poets, — the class of intellect in which the characteristic features of genius are, perhaps, most strongly marked, — we shall find that, with scarcely one exception, from Homer down to Lord Byron, they have been, in their several degrees, restless and solitary spirits, with minds wrapped up, like silk-worms, in their own tasks, either strangers, or rebels to domestic ties, and bearing about with them a deposit for posterity in their souls, to the jealous watching and enriching of which almost all other thoughts and considerations have been sacrificed.

" To follow poetry as one ought (says the authority † I have already quoted), one must forget father and mother and cleave to it alone." In these few words is pointed out the sole path that leads genius to greatness. On such terms alone are the high

---

* It is the opinion of Diderot, in his Treatise on Acting, that not only in the art of which he treats, but in all those which are called imitative, the possession of real sensibility is a bar to eminence; — sensibility being, according to his view, " le caractère de la bonté de l'ame et de la médiocrité du génie."

† Pope.

places of fame to be won ; — nothing less than the sacrifice of the entire man can achieve them. However delightful, therefore, may be the spectacle of a man of genius tamed and domesticated in society, taking docilely upon him the yoke of the social ties, and enlightening without disturbing the sphere in which he moves, we must nevertheless, in the midst of our admiration, bear in mind that it is not thus smoothly or amiably immortality has been ever struggled for, or won. The poet thus circumstanced may be popular, may be loved ; for the happiness of himself and those linked with him he is in the right road, — but not for greatness. The marks by which Fame has always separated her great martyrs from the rest of mankind are not upon him, and the crown cannot be his. He may dazzle, may captivate the circle, and even the times in which he lives, but he is not for hereafter.

To the general description here given of that high class of human intelligences to which he belonged, the character of Lord Byron was, in many respects, a signal exception. Born with strong affections and ardent passions, the world had, from first to last, too firm a hold on his sympathies to let imagination altogether usurp the place of reality, either in his feelings, or in the objects of them. His life, indeed, was one continued struggle between that instinct of genius, which was for ever drawing him back into the lonely laboratory of Self, and those impulses of passion, ambition, and vanity, which again hurried him off into the crowd, and entangled him in its interests ; and though it may be granted that he

would have been more purely and abstractedly the
poet, had he been less thoroughly, in all his pursuits
and propensities, the *man*, yet from this very mixture and alloy has it arisen that his pages bear so
deeply the stamp of real life, and that in the works
of no poet, with the exception of Shakspeare, can
every various mood of the mind — whether solemn
or gay, whether inclined to the ludicrous or the sublime, whether seeking to divert itself with the follies
of society or panting after the grandeur of solitary
nature — find so readily a strain of sentiment in accordance with its every passing tone.

But while the naturally warm cast of his affections
and temperament gave thus a substance and truth to
his social feelings which those of too many of his
fellow votaries of Genius have wanted, it was not to
be expected that an imagination of such range and
power should have been so early developed and unrestrainedly indulged without producing, at last, some
of those effects upon the heart which have invariably
been found attendant on such a predominance of this
faculty. It must have been observed, indeed, that
the period when his natural affections flourished
most healthily was before he had yet arrived at the
full consciousness of his genius, — before Imagination had yet accustomed him to those glowing pictures, after gazing upon which all else appeared cold
and colourless. From the moment of this initiation
into the wonders of his own mind, a distaste for the
realities of life began to grow upon him. Not even
that intense craving after affection, which nature had
implanted in him, could keep his ardour still alive in

a pursuit whose results fell so short of his " imaginings ; " and though, from time to time, the combined
warmth of his fancy and temperament was able to
call up a feeling which to his eyes wore the semblance
of love, it may be questioned whether his heart had
ever much share in such passions, or whether, after
his first launch into the boundless sea of imagination,
he could ever have been brought back and fixed by
any lasting attachment. Actual objects there were,
in but too great number, who, as long as the illusion
continued, kindled up his thoughts and were the
themes of his song. But they were, after all, little
more than mere dreams of the hour ;— the qualities
with which he invested them were almost all ideal,
nor could have stood the test of a month's, or even
week's, cohabitation. It was but the reflection of his
own bright conceptions that he saw in each new
object ; and while persuading himself that they furnished the models of his heroines, he was, on the
contrary, but fancying that he beheld his heroines
in them.

There needs no stronger proof of the predominance of imagination in these attachments than his
own serious avowal, in the Journal already given,
that often, when in the company of the woman he
most loved, he found himself secretly wishing for
the solitude of his own study. It was *there*, indeed,—
in the silence and abstraction of that study, — that
the chief scene of his mistress's empire and glory
lay. It was there that, unchecked by reality, and
without any fear of the disenchantments of truth, he
could view her through the medium of his own fer-

vid fancy, enamour himself of an idol of his own creating, and out of a brief delirium of a few days or weeks, send forth a dream of beauty and passion through all ages.

While such appears to have been the imaginative character of his loves, (of all, except the one that lived unquenched through all,) his friendships, though, of course, far less subject to the influence of fancy, could not fail to exhibit also some features characteristic of the peculiar mind in which they sprung.   It was a usual saying of his own, and will be found repeated in some of his letters, that he had " no genius for friendship," and that whatever capacity he might once have possessed for that sentiment had vanished with his youth.   If in saying thus he shaped his notions of friendship according to the romantic standard of his boyhood, the fact must be admitted: but as far as the assertion was meant to imply that he had become incapable of a warm, manly, and lasting friendship, such a charge against himself was unjust, and I am not the only living testimony of its injustice.

To a certain degree, however, even in his friendships, the effects of a too vivid imagination, in disqualifying the mind for the cold contact of reality, were visible.   We are told that Petrarch (who, in this respect, as in most others, may be regarded as a genuine representative of the poetic character,) abstained purposely from a too frequent intercourse with his nearest friends, lest, from the sensitiveness he was so aware of in himself, there should occur any thing that might chill his regard for them * ; and though Lord Byron was of a nature too full of social and kindly impulses ever to think of such a precaution, it is a fact confirmatory, at least, of the principle on which his brother poet, Petrarch, acted, that the friends, whether of his youth or manhood, of whom he had seen least, through life, were those of whom he always thought and spoke with the most warmth and fondness. Being brought less often to the touchstone of familiar intercourse, they stood naturally a better chance of being adopted as the favourites of his imagination, and of sharing, in consequence, a portion of that bright colouring reserved for all that gave it interest and pleasure. Next to the dead, therefore, whose hold upon his fancy had been placed beyond all risk of severance, those friends whom he but saw occasionally, and by such favourable glimpses as only renewed the first kindly impression they had made, were the surest to live unchangingly, and without shadow, in his memory.

To this same cause, there is little doubt, his love for his sister owed much of its devotedness and fervour. In a mind sensitive and versatile as his, long habits of family intercourse might have estranged, or at least dulled, his natural affection for her ; — but their separation, during youth, left this feeling

* See Foscolo's Essay on Petrarch. On the same principle, Orrery says, in speaking of Swift, " I am persuaded that his distance from his English friends proved a strong incitement to their mutual affection."

fresh and untried.* His very inexperience in such ties made the smile of a sister no less a novelty than a charm to him ; and before the first gloss of this newly awakened sentiment had time to wear off, they were again separated, and for ever.

If the portrait which I have here attempted of the general character of those gifted with high genius be allowed to bear, in any of its features, a resemblance to the originals, it can no longer, I think, be matter of question whether a class so set apart from the track of ordinary life, so removed, by their very elevation, out of the influences of our common atmosphere, are at all likely to furnish tractable subjects for that most trying of all social experiments, matrimony. In reviewing the great names of philosophy and science, we shall find that all who have most distinguished themselves in those walks have, at least, virtually admitted their own unfitness for the marriage tie by remaining in celibacy ; — Newton, Gassendi, Galileo, Descartes, Bayle, Locke, Leibnitz, Boyle, Hume, and a long list of other illustrious sages, having all led single lives. †

---

* That he was himself fully aware of this appears from a passage in one of his letters already given : — " My sister is in town, which is a great comfort; for, never having been much together, we are naturally more attached to each other."

† Wife and children, Bacon tells us in one of his Essays, are " impediments to great enterprises ; " and adds, " Certainly, the best works, and of greatest merit for the public, have proceeded from the unmarried or childless men." See, with reference to this subject, chapter xviii. of Mr. D'Israeli's work on " The Literary Character."

The poetic race, it is true, from the greater susceptibility of their imaginations, have more frequently
fallen into the ever ready snare. But the fate of the
poets in matrimony has but justified the caution of
the philosophers. While the latter have given
warning to genius by keeping free of the yoke, the
others have still more effectually done so by their
misery under it ; — the annals of this sensitive race
having, at all times, abounded with proofs, that genius
ranks but low among the elements of social happiness, — that, in general, the brighter the gift, the
more disturbing its influence, and that in married
life particularly, its effects have been too often like
that of the " Wormwood Star," whose light filled
the waters on which it fell with bitterness.

Besides the causes already enumerated as leading
naturally to such a result, from the peculiarities by
which, in most instances, these great labourers in
the field of thought are characterised, there is also
much, no doubt, to be attributed to an unluckiness
in the choice of helpmates, — dictated, as that
choice frequently must be, by an imagination accustomed to deceive itself. But from whatever
causes it may have arisen, the coincidence is no
less striking than saddening, that, on the list of
married poets who have been unhappy in their
homes, there should already be found four such
illustrious   names   as   Dante,   Milton *,   Shaks-

* Milton's first wife, it is well known, ran away from him,
within a month after their marriage, disgusted, says Phillips,
" with his spare diet and hard study ; " and it is difficult to
conceive a more melancholy picture of domestic life than is

MOORE: LORD BYRON   69

peare *, and Dryden; and that we should now have to add, as a partner in their destiny, a name worthy of being placed beside the greatest of them, — Lord Byron.

I have already mentioned my having been called up to town in the December of this year. The opportunities I had of seeing Lord Byron during my stay were frequent; and, among them, not the least memorable or agreeable were those evenings we passed together at the house of his banker, Mr. Douglas Kinnaird, where music, — followed by its accustomed sequel of supper, brandy and water, and

---

disclosed in his nuncupative will, one of the witnesses to which deposes to having heard the great poet himself complain, that his children " were careless of him, being blind, and made nothing of deserting him."

* By whatever austerity of temper or habits the poets Dante and Milton may have drawn upon themselves such a fate, it might be expected that, at least, the " gentle Shakspeare" would have stood exempt from the common calamity of his brethren. But, among the very few facts of his life that have been transmitted to us, there is none more clearly proved than the unhappiness of his marriage. The dates of the birth of his children, compared with that of his removal from Stratford, — the total omission of his wife's name in the first draft of his will, and the bitter sarcasm of the bequest by which he remembers her afterwards, — all prove beyond a doubt both his separation from the lady early in life, and his unfriendly feeling towards her at the close of it.

In endeavouring to argue against the conclusion naturally to be deduced from this will, Boswell, with a strange ignorance of human nature, remarks: — " If he had taken offence at any part of his wife's conduct, I cannot believe that he would have taken this petty mode of expressing it."

not a little laughter, — kept us together, usually, till
rather a late hour. Besides those songs of mine which
he has himself somewhere recorded as his favourites,
there was also one to a Portuguese air, " The song
of war shall echo through our mountains," which
seemed especially to please him ; — the national
character of the music, and the recurrence of the
words " sunny mountains," bringing back freshly to
his memory the impressions of all he had seen in
Portugal.   I have, indeed, known few persons more
alive to the charms of simple music ; and not unfre-
quently have seen the tears in his eyes while listening to the Irish Melodies.   Among those that
thus affected him was one beginning " When first
I met thee warm and young," the words of which,
besides the obvious feeling which they express,
were intended also to admit of a political application.   He, however, discarded the latter sense
wholly from his mind, and gave himself up to the
more natural sentiment of the song with evident
emotion.

☆ ★ ☆

" My first acquaintance with Byron began in a
manner rather doubtful.   I was so far from having

any thing to do with the offensive criticism in the
Edinburgh, that I remember remonstrating against
it with our friend, the editor, because I thought the
' Hours of Idleness' treated with undue severity.
They were written, like all juvenile poetry, rather
from the recollection of what had pleased the author
in others than what had been suggested by his own
imagination ; but, nevertheless, I thought they contained some passages of noble promise. I was so
much impressed with this, that I had thoughts of
writing to the author ; but some exaggerated reports
concerning his peculiarities, and a natural unwilling-
ness to intrude an opinion which was uncalled for,
induced me to relinquish the idea.

" When Byron wrote his famous Satire, I had my
share of flagellation among my betters. My crime
was having written a poem (Marmion, I think) for a
thousand pounds ; which was no otherwise true than
that I sold the copy-right for that sum. Now, not to
mention that an author can hardly be censured for
accepting such a sum as the booksellers are willing
to give him, especially as the gentlemen of the trade
made no complaints of their bargain, I thought the
interference with my private affairs was rather beyond the limits of literary satire. On the other hand,
Lord Byron paid me, in several passages, so much
more praise than I deserved, that I must have been
more irritable than I have ever felt upon such
subjects, not to sit down contented, and think no
more about the matter.

" I was very much struck, with all the rest of the
world, at the vigour and force of imagination dis-

played in the first Cantos of Childe Harold, and the other splendid productions which Lord Byron flung from him to the public with a promptitude that savoured of profusion. My own popularity, as a poet, was then on the wane, and I was unaffectedly pleased to see an author of so much power and energy taking the field. Mr. John Murray happened to be in Scotland that season, and as I mentioned to him the pleasure I should have in making Lord Byron's acquaintance, he had the kindness to mention my wish to his Lordship, which led to some correspondence.

" It was in the spring of 1815 that, chancing to be in London, I had the advantage of a personal introduction to Lord Byron. Report had prepared me to meet a man of peculiar habits and a quick temper, and I had some doubts whether we were likely to suit each other in society. I was most agreeably disappointed in this respect. I found Lord Byron in the highest degree courteous, and even kind. We met, for an hour or two almost daily, in Mr. Murray's drawing-room, and found a great deal to say to each other. We also met frequently in parties and evening society, so that for about two months I had the advantage of a considerable intimacy with this distinguished individual. Our sentiments agreed a good deal, except upon the subjects of religion and politics, upon neither of which I was inclined to believe that Lord Byron entertained very fixed opinions. I remember saying to him, that I really thought, that if he lived a few years he would alter his sentiments. He answered, rather sharply, ' I suppose you are one of those who prophesy I will turn Methodist.' I replied, ' No — I don't expect your conversion to be of such an ordinary kind. I would rather look to see you retreat upon the Catholic faith, and distinguish yourself by the austerity of your penances. The species of religion to which you must, or may, one day attach yourself must exercise a strong power on the imagination.' He smiled gravely, and seemed to allow I might be right.

" On politics, he used sometimes to express a high strain of what is now called Liberalism ; but it appeared to me that the pleasure it afforded him as a vehicle of displaying his wit and satire against individuals in office was at the bottom of this habit of thinking, rather than any real conviction of the political principles on which he talked. He was certainly proud of his rank and ancient family, and, in that respect, as much an aristocrat as was consistent with good sense and good breeding. Some disgusts, how adopted I know not, seemed to me to have given this peculiar and, as it appeared to me, contradictory cast of mind : but, at heart, I would have termed Byron a patrician on principle.

" Lord Byron's reading did not seem to me to have been very extensive either in poetry or history. Having the advantage of him in that respect, and possessing a good competent share of such reading as is little read, I was sometimes able to put under his eye objects which had for him the interest of novelty. I remember particularly repeating to him the fine poem of Hardyknute, an imitation of the old Scottish Ballad, with which he was so much affected, that some one who was in the same apartment asked me what I could possibly have been telling Byron by which he was so much agitated.

" I saw Byron, for the last time, in 1815, after I returned from France. He dined, or lunched, with me at Long's in Bond Street. I never saw him so full of gaiety and good-humour, to which the presence of Mr. Mathews, the comedian, added not a little. Poor Terry was also present. After one of the gayest parties I ever was present at, my fellow-traveller, Mr. Scott, of Gala, and I set off for Scotland, and I never saw Lord Byron again. Several letters passed between us — one perhaps every half year. Like the old heroes in Homer, we exchanged gifts: — I gave Byron a beautiful dagger mounted with gold, which had been the property of the redoubted Elfi Bey. But I was to play the part of Diomed, in the Iliad, for Byron sent me, some time after, a large sepulchral vase of silver. It was full of dead men's bones, and had inscriptions on two sides of the base. One ran thus: — ' The bones contained in this urn were found in certain ancient sepulchres within the land walls of Athens, in the month of February, 1811.' The other face bears the lines of Juvenal :

" Expende — quot libras in duce summo invenies.
— Mors sola fatetur quantula hominum corpuscula."
JUV. X.

" To these I have added a third inscription, in these words —' The gift of Lord Byron to Walter Scott.' *

* Mr. Murray had, at the time of giving the vase, suggested to Lord Byron, that it would increase the value of the

There was a letter with this vase more valuable to me than the gift itself, from the kindness with which the donor expressed himself towards me. I left it naturally in the urn with the bones, — but it is now missing. As the theft was not of a nature to be practised by a mere domestic, I am compelled to suspect the inhospitality of some individual of higher station, — most gratuitously exercised certainly, since, after what I have here said, no one will probably choose to boast of possessing this literary curiosity.

" We had a good deal of laughing, I remember, on what the public might be supposed to think, or say, concerning the gloomy and ominous nature of our mutual gifts.

" I think I can add little more to my recollections of Byron. He was often melancholy, — almost gloomy. When I observed him in this humour, I used either to wait till it went off of its own accord, or till some natural and easy mode occurred of leading him into conversation, when the shadows almost always left his countenance, like the mist rising from a landscape. In conversation he was very animated.

---

gift to add some such inscription ; but the feeling of the noble poet on this subject will be understood from the following answer which he returned : —

" April 9. 1815.

" Thanks for the books. I have great objection to your proposition about inscribing the vase, — which is, that it would appear *ostentatious* on my part ; and of course I must send it as it is, without any alteration.

" Yours," &c.

" I met with him very frequently in society ; our mutual acquaintances doing me the honour to think that he liked to meet with me. Some very agreeable parties I can recollect, — particularly one at Sir George Beaumont's, where the amiable landlord had assembled some persons distinguished for talent. Of these I need only mention the late Sir Humphry Davy, whose talents for literature were as remarkable as his empire over science. Mr. Richard Sharpe and Mr. Rogers were also present.

" I think I also remarked in Byron's temper starts of suspicion, when he seemed to pause and consider whether there had not been a secret, and perhaps offensive, meaning in something casually said to him. In this case, I also judged it best to let his mind, like a troubled spring, work itself clear, which it did in a minute or two. I was considerably older, you will recollect, than my noble friend, and had no reason to fear his misconstruing my sentiments towards him, nor had I ever the slightest reason to doubt that they were kindly returned on his part. If I had occasion to be mortified by the display of genius which threw into the shade such pretensions as I was then supposed to possess, I might console myself that, in my own case, the materials of mental happiness had been mingled in a greater proportion.

" I rummage my brains in vain for what often rushes into my head unbidden, — little traits and sayings which recall his looks, manner, tone, and gestures; and I have always continued to think that a crisis of life was arrived in which a new career of fame was opened to him, and that had he been permitted to start upon it, he would have obliterated the memory of such parts of his life as friends would wish to forget."

☆ ★ ☆

A person who was of these parties has thus described to me one of their evenings:—" When the *bise* or north-east wind blows, the waters of the Lake are driven towards the town, and with the stream of the Rhone, which sets strongly in the same direction, combine to make a very rapid current towards the harbour. Carelessly, one evening, we had yielded to its course, till we found ourselves almost driven on the piles; and it required all our rowers' strength to master the tide. The waves were high and in-spiriting—we were all animated by our contest with the elements. ' I will sing you an Albanian song,' cried Lord Byron; ' now, be sentimental and

* Childe Harold, Canto iii.

give me all your attention.' It was a strange, wild howl that he gave forth; but such as, he declared, was an exact imitation of the savage Albanian mode, — laughing, the while, at our disappointment, who had expected a wild Eastern melody."

Sometimes the party landed, for a walk upon the shore, and, on such occasions, Lord Byron would loiter behind the rest, lazily trailing his sword-stick along, and moulding, as he went, his thronging thoughts into shape. Often too, when in the boat, he would lean abstractedly over the side, and surrender himself up, in silence, to the same absorbing task.

The conversation of Mr. Shelley, from the extent of his poetic reading, and the strange, mystic speculations into which his system of philosophy led him, was of a nature strongly to arrest and interest the attention of Lord Byron, and to turn him away from worldly associations and topics into more abstract and untrodden ways of thought. As far as contrast, indeed, is an enlivening ingredient of such intercourse, it would be difficult to find two persons more formed to whet each other's faculties by discussion, as on few points of common interest between them did their opinions agree; and that this difference had its root deep in the conformation of their respective minds needs but a glance through the rich, glittering labyrinth of Mr. Shelley's pages to assure us.

In Lord Byron, the real was never forgotten in the fanciful. However Imagination had placed her whole realm at his disposal, he was no less a man of this world than a ruler of hers; and, accordingly,

through the airiest and most subtile creations of
his brain still the life-blood of truth and reality
circulates.   With Shelley it was far otherwise ; —
his fancy (and he had sufficient for a whole generation
of poets) was the medium through which he saw all
things, his facts as well as his theories ; and not only
the greater part of his poetry, but the political and
philosophical speculations in which he indulged,
were all distilled through the same over-refining
and unrealising alembic.   Having started as a
teacher and reformer of the world, at an age when
he could know nothing of the world but from fancy,
the persecution he met with on the threshold of this
boyish enterprise but confirmed him in his first paradoxical views of human ills and their remedies ;
and, instead of waiting to take lessons of authority
and experience, he, with a courage, admirable had
it been but wisely directed, made war upon both.
From this sort of self-willed start in the world, an
impulse was at once given to his opinions and powers
directly contrary, it would seem, to their natural
bias, and from which his life was too short to allow
him time to recover.   With a mind, by nature,
fervidly pious, he yet refused to acknowledge a
Supreme Providence, and substituted some airy
abstraction of " Universal Love " in its place.   An
aristocrat by birth and, as I understand, also in appearance and manners, he was yet a leveller in
politics, and to such an Utopian extent as to be,
seriously, the advocate of a community of property.
With a delicacy and even romance of sentiment,
which lends such grace to some of his lesser poems,

he could notwithstanding contemplate a change in the relations of the sexes, which would have led to results fully as gross as his arguments for it were fastidious and refined; and though benevolent and generous to an extent that seemed to exclude all idea of selfishness, he yet scrupled not, in the pride of system, to disturb wantonly the faith of his fellow-men, and, without substituting any equivalent good in its place, to rob the wretched of a hope, which, even if false, would be worth all this world's best truths.

Upon no point were the opposite tendencies of the two friends,—to long-established opinions and matter of fact on one side, and to all that was most innovating and visionary on the other,—more observable than in their notions on philosophical subjects; Lord Byron being, with the great bulk of mankind, a believer in the existence of Matter and Evil, while Shelley so far refined upon the theory of Berkeley as not only to resolve the whole of Creation into spirit, but to add also to this immaterial system some pervading principle, some abstract non-entity of Love and Beauty, of which — as a substitute, at least, for Deity — the philosophic bishop had never dreamed. On such subjects, and on poetry, their conversation generally turned; and, as might be expected, from Lord Byron's facility in receiving new impressions, the opinions of his companion were not altogether without some influence on his mind. Here and there, among those fine bursts of passion and description that abound in the third Canto of Childe Harold, may be discovered traces of that mysticism of meaning, — that sublimity, losing itself in its own vagueness, — which so much characterised the writings of his extraordinary friend; and in one of the notes we find Shelley's favourite Pantheism of Love thus glanced at : — " But this is not all : the feeling with which all around Clarens and the opposite rocks of Meillerie is invested, is of a still higher and more comprehensive order than the mere sympathy with individual passion ; it is a sense of the existence of love in its most extended and sublime capacity, and of our own participation of its good and of its glory : it is the great principle of the universe, which is there more condensed, but not less manifested; and of which, though knowing ourselves a part, we lose our individuality, and mingle in the beauty of the whole."

Another proof of the ductility with which he fell into his new friend's tastes and predilections, appears in the tinge, if not something deeper, of the manner and cast of thinking of Mr. Wordsworth, which is traceable through so many of his most beautiful stanzas. Being naturally, from his love of the abstract and imaginative, an admirer of the great poet of the Lakes, Mr. Shelley omitted no opportunity of bringing the beauties of his favourite writer under the notice of Lord Byron ; and it is not surprising that, once persuaded into a fair perusal, the mind of the noble poet should — in spite of some personal and political prejudices which unluckily survived this short access of admiration — not only feel the influence but, in some degree, even reflect the hues of one of the very few real and original poets that this age (fertile as it is in rhymers *quales ego et Clu-vienus*) has had the glory of producing.

Robert Dallas, *Recollections of the Life of Lord Byron, from the Year 1808 to the End of 1814* (London, 1824)

The Reverend Robert Charles Dallas was born in 1754, the son of a doctor living in Kingston, Jamaica. After a legal training he entered the Inner Temple, before taking religious orders and returning to Jamaica on the death of his father to take possession of his inheritance. He remained in the West Indies for the next three years, before returning to England just long enough to be married, after which he returned to Jamaica. A combination of war and his wife's ill health, however, persuaded him to move for good to Britain, where he abandoned his legal practice in favour of literary work. By 1808, when he first sought Byron's acquaintance, his novels, poetry and tragedy had made him an extremely minor celebrity on the literary scene, though he did possess the advantage of a slight family connection with the moderately famous young Lord. Over the next few years he was to act as Byron's agent for the publication of *English Bards and Scotch Reviewers* and the first two cantos of *Childe Harold's Pilgrimage,* a service for which he was rewarded handsomely by Byron with financial support including the gift of the copyrights of the two poems. In later years he became disgruntled when the stream of Byron's generosity began to dry up, and took to accusing Byron of miserliness – a common accusation amongst those on the receiving end of Byron's considerable financial generosity. In fact, as Byron was ready to inform his correspondents, Dallas had benefited from Byron's charity to the tune of £1,400 – by any standards an extraordinary amount to receive by way of casual handouts from a distant relation. In 1824 he attempted to publish the letters Byron had given to him, and which the poet had written to his mother during the travels which made up the subject matter of *Childe Harold's Pilgrimage.* In this he was prevented by Hobhouse and Kinnaird, who took out an injunction in case Dallas's letters should reflect badly on Byron. A disappointed man, Dallas published the *Recollections* without the letters, making it very clear as he did so that his book resembled, as Byron would have said, the play of *Hamlet* with the part of Hamlet omitted by particular request. (for an explanation of this favoured theatrical reference of Byron's see Marchand, IV, pp. 368–9). He died shortly afterwards in Paris.

The relation between Byron and Dallas was never close, and certainly was not one about which Byron seems at any stage of his career to have worried greatly. Dallas's principal function resulted entirely from Byron's initial reluctance to profit from the extraordinary financial success of his early writing. By channelling the profits to Dallas he was able to maintain the requisite aristocratic disdain for working for a living – while at the same time avoiding handing the entirety of the proceeds of his writing back to the publisher. Dallas understood the relationship perfectly and, on the one occasion that Byron was falsely accused of profiting from his early poems, was quick to write to the national press to announce that it was he and not Byron who had been on the receiving end of the proceeds. His acumen in this respect, however, did not fully compensate the irritation he caused Byron at other times – for example when attempting to convert the poet (and modify the poetry) in favour of his own Anglicanism. Or when vainly trying to rein in Byron's expenditure (Dallas's nephew being the poet's heir). In Byron's eyes Dallas was, as he told Hobhouse in 1813, 'a *damned* nincom. assuredly' – a sentiment which sounds more understandable in the light of Dallas's attempts to have *English Bards and Scotch Reviewers* retitled 'The Parish Poor of Parnassus'. Amongst Byron's friends Dallas was satirized as a 'half-witted' sycophant, to quote a Leigh Hunt who would have been anxious to avoid the accusation himself (see Hunt, *Recollections*, p. 94). Reading Dallas's letters to Byron, however, tends to make one sympathize for once with Hunt's assessment. In his first fawning letter to Byron, for example, we read

> I feel myself irresistibly impelled to pay you a tribute on the effusions of a noble mind in strains so truly poetic... Your Poems, my Lord, are not only beautiful as compositions; – they bespeak a heart glowing with honour, and attuned to virtue, which is infinitely the higher praise...(Dallas, *Recollections of the Life of Lord Byron*, pp. 3–4)

The letter is a good example of Dallas's style – verbose, moralistic, and above all servile. But what may have irritated Byron more than any of this was his egotism; it did not take Dallas long, for example, to suggest that Byron include some of Dallas's own poetry in *English Bards and Scotch Reviewers*. And reading his *Recollections of the Life of Byron* involves wading through a disproportionate quantity of Dallas's own turgid letters to Byron, which are reproduced verbatim. If he was to be prevented from publishing Byron's letters, Dallas appears to have thought, then perhaps the public would be just as interested in his own.

Today Dallas – whose name Hobhouse transformed with little effort into 'Dull ass' and 'Damn'd ass' – is as famous amongst Byronists for his sponging as for his abject flattery. Although in neither of these respects was he unique amongst Byron's friends, the tone of his letters, and in particular his dedication to Byron of his *Miscellaneous Works* of 1813, reaches new heights ('It will be more than mortal self-denial, my Lord, not to take a public pride in having been the first to appreciate a production of genius, now so generally and fully stamped with the approbation of the best judges...'). (see *Miscellaneous Works and Novels of Robert Charles Dallas*, vol. 1, 'Dedication'). His *Recollections*, however, were written after the death of Byron, and it is in them that we may hope to find Dallas at his most unbiassed. He is by no means the least accurate of those who wrote memoirs about Byron: but he was as personally involved in the Byron story as any.

CHAPTER III.

TAKING HIS SEAT IN THE HOUSE OF LORDS—
SECOND EDITION OF THE SATIRE—DEPAR-
TURE FROM ENGLAND.

I NOW saw Lord Byron daily. It was
about this time that Lord Falkland was
killed in a duel, which suggested some lines
as the Satire was going through the press.
Nature had endowed Lord Byron with very
benevolent feelings, which I have had opportunities of discerning, and I have seen
them at times render his fine countenance
most beautiful. His features seemed formed
in a peculiar manner for emanating the
high conceptions of genius, and the work-
ings of the passions. I have often, and
with no little admiration, witnessed these

effects. I have seen them in the glow of poetical inspiration, and under the influence of strong emotion; on the one hand amounting to virulence, and on the other replete with all the expression and grace of the mild and amiable affections. When under the influence of resentment and anger, it was painful to observe the powerful sway of those passions over his features: when he was impressed with kindness, which was the natural state of his heart, it was a high treat to contemplate his countenance. I saw him the morning after Lord Falkland's death. He had just come from seeing the lifeless body of the man with whom he had a very short time before spent a social day; he now and then said, as if it were to himself, but aloud, " Poor Falkland!" He looked more than he spoke—" But his wife, it is she who is to be pitied." I saw his mind teeming with benevolent intentions— and they were not abortive. If ever an

action was pure, that which he then meditated was so; and the spirit that conceived,
the man that performed it, was at that time
making his way through briers and bram-
bles to that clear but narrow path which
leads to heaven. Those, who have taken
pains to guide him from it, must answer
for it!

The remembrance of the impression produced on Lord Byron by Lord Falkland's
death, at the period I am retracing, has excited this slight, but sincere and just, effusion; and I am sensible that the indulgence
of it needs no apology.

The Satire was published about the middle of March, previous to which he took
his seat in the House of Lords, on the 13th
of the same month. On that day, passing
down St. James's-street, but with no intention of calling, I saw his chariot at his
door, and went in. His countenance, paler
than usual, showed that his mind was agi-

tated, and that he was thinking of the nobleman to whom he had once looked for a
hand and countenance in his introduction
to the House. He said to me—" I am glad
you happened to come in; I am going to
take my seat, perhaps you will go with
me."   I expressed my readiness to attend
him; while, at the same time, I concealed
the shock I felt on thinking that this young
man, who, by birth, fortune, and talent,
stood high in life, should have lived so unconnected and neglected by persons of his
own rank, that there was not a single member of the senate to which he belonged, to
whom he could or would apply to introduce him in a manner becoming his birth.
I saw that he felt the situation, and I fully
partook his indignation.   If the neglect he
had met with be imputed to an untoward
or vicious disposition, a character which
he gave himself, and which I understood
was also given to him by others, it is

natural to ask, how he came by that disposition, for he got it not from Nature ? Had
he not been left early to himself, or rather
to dangerous guides and companions, would
he have contracted that disposition ? Or
even, had nature been cross, might it not
have been rectified ? During his long minority, ought not his heart and his intellect
to have been trained to the situation he
was to fill ? Ought he not to have been
saved from money-lenders, and men of
business ? And ought not a shield to have
been placed over a mind so open to impressions, to protect it from self-sufficient free-
thinkers, and witty sophs ? The wonder
is, not that he should have erred, but that
he should have broken through the cloud
that enveloped him, which was dispersed
solely by the rays of his own genius.

After some talk about the Satire, the
last sheets of which were in the press, I accompanied Lord Byron to the House. He

was received in one of the antechambers
by some of the officers in attendance, with
whom he settled respecting the fees he had
to pay.   One of them went to apprize the
Lord Chancellor of his being there, and
soon returned for him.   There were very
few persons in the House.   Lord Eldon
was going through some ordinary business.
When Lord Byron entered, I thought he
looked still paler than before; and he certainly wore a countenance in which mortification was mingled with, but subdued
by, indignation.   He passed the woolsack
without looking round, and advanced to the
table where the proper officer was attending to administer the oaths.   When he had
gone through them, the Chancellor quitted
his seat, and went towards him with a
smile, putting out his hand warmly to welcome him; and, though I did not catch his
words, I saw that he paid him some compliment.   This was all thrown away upon

Lord Byron, who made a stiff bow, and put the tips of his fingers into a hand, the amiable offer of which demanded the whole of his. I was sorry to see this, for Lord Eldon's character is great for virtue, as well as talent; and, even in a political point of view, it would have given me inexpressible pleasure to have seen him uniting heartily with him. The Chancellor did not press a welcome so received, but resumed his seat; while Lord Byron carelessly seated himself for a few minutes on one of the empty benches to the left of the throne, usually occupied by the Lords in opposition. When, on his joining me, I expressed what I had felt, he said: "If I had shaken hands heartily, he would have set me down for one of his party—but I will have nothing to do with any of them, on either side; I have taken my seat, and now I will go abroad." We returned to St. James's-street, but he did not recover his spirits.

☆ ★ ☆

At this period of his life his mind was full
of bitter discontent.   Already satiated with
pleasure, and disgusted with those companions who have no other resource, he had resolved on mastering his appetites ; he broke
up his harams; and he reduced his palate
to a diet the most simple and abstemious ;
but the passions of the heart were too
mighty, nor did it ever enter his mind to

overcome *them:* resentment, anger, and
hatred held full sway over him, and his
greatest gratification at that time was in
overcharging his pen with gall, which
flowed in every direction against individuals, his country, the world, the universe,
creation, and the Creator. He might have
become, he ought to have been, a different
creature ; and he but too well accounts for
the unfortunate bias of his disposition in
the following lines :—

> E'en I—least thinking of a thoughtless throng,
> Just skill'd to know the right and choose the wrong,
> Freed at that age when Reason's shield is lost,
> To fight my course through Passion's countless host;
> Whom every path of Pleasure's flowery way
> Has lured in turn, and all have led astray.

I took leave of him on the 10th of June,
1809, and he left London the next morning:
his objects were still unsettled; but he
wished to hear from me particularly on the
subject of the Satire, and promised to inform

me how to direct to him when he could so with certainty;—it was, however, long before I heard from him. After some time I wrote to him; directing, at a chance, to Malta, informing him of the success of his Poem.

Leaving England with a soured mind, disclaiming all attachments, and even belief in the existence of friendship, it will be no wonder if it shall be found that Lord Byron, during the period of his absence, kept up little correspondence with any persons in England. A letter, dated at Constantinople, is the only one I received from him, till he was approaching the shores of England in the Volage frigate. To his mother he wrote by every opportunity. Upon her death, which happened very soon after his arrival, and before he saw her, I was conversing with him about Newstead, and expressing my hope that he would never be persuaded to part with it; he assured me he would not, and promised to give me a letter which he had written to his mother to that effect, as a pledge that he never would. His letters to her being at Newstead, it was some time before he performed his promise ; but in doing it he made me a present of all his letters to her on his leaving England and during his absence ; saying, as he put them into my hands, " Some day or other they will be curiosities." They are written in an easy style, and if they do not contain all that is to be expected from a traveller, what they do contain of that nature is pleasant ; and they strongly mark the character of the writer.

☆ ★ ☆

CHAPTER VIII.

RETROSPECT—MAIDEN SPEECH.

———

As I was now near Lord Byron, for he was at this time seldom absent from town, our personal communications were frequent; and, except a few queries addressed to him on the proofs, his work went smoothly on through the press during the months of January and February, without further solicitation on my part, till we came to the shorter Poems, when I urged him to omit the one entitled " Euthanasia," which he was kind enough to consent to do; but which, I must add, he had not resolution enough to persist in suppressing, and it was inserted in the succeeding editions.

Lord Byron had excited in my heart a warm affection ; I felt, too, some pride in the part I took in combating his errors, as well as in being instrumental to his reputation, and I anxiously wished to see a real change of mind effected in him. Though I could not flatter myself that I had made any successful invasion on his philosophical opinions, and was almost hopeless on the subject, I was still very desirous to keep as much as possible of his free-thinking in a latent state, being as solicitous that he should acquire the esteem and affection of men, as I was eager in my anticipation of the admiration and fame that awaited his genius. It was with this view I wished, and sometimes prevailed upon him, to suppress some passages in his compositions : and it was with this view that I often spoke to him of the superior and substantial fame, the way to which lay before him through the House of Lords, expressing my hope of one day seeing him an active and eloquent statesman. He was alive to this ambition; and I looked accordingly for great enjoyment in the session of 1812, now approaching.

In spite of these prospects—in spite of genius—in spite of youth—Lord Byron often gave way to a depression of spirits, which was more the result of his peculiar position than of any gloomy tendency received from nature. The fact is, he was out of his sphere, and he felt it. By the death of his cousin William, who was killed at a siege in the Mediterranean, he unexpectedly became presumptive heir to his grand uncle, and not long after succeeded to the barony, at a very early period of his minority. His immediate predecessor had long given up society; and, after his fatal duel with Mr. Chaworth, had never appeared either at Court or in Parliament, but shut himself up in Newstead Abbey, the monastic mansion of an estate bestowed upon one of his ancestors by Henry VIII. at the suppression of the religious houses; or, if compelled to go to London on business, he travelled with the utmost privacy, taking the feigned name of Waters. From him, therefore, no connexion could spring. His brother, the Admiral, was a man very highly respected; but he too, after distinguishing his courage and ability, had been unfortunate in his professional career, and equally avoided society. The elder son of the admiral was an officer of the guards; who, after the death of his first wife, Lady Conyers, by whom he had only one daughter, married Miss Gordon, of Gight, a lady related to a noble family in Scotland, of whom Lord Byron was born, and whom his lordship took a pleasure in stating to be a descendant of King James II. of Scotland, through his daughter, the princess Jane Stuart, who married the Marquis of Huntley. But neither did she bring connexion.   At the death of her husband, she found her finances in an impoverished state, and she consequently by no means associated in a manner suitable to the situation of a son who was one day to take a seat among the Peers of Great Britain. Captain George Anson Byron, whom I have mentioned in the first chapter, the brother of her husband, had, a little before she became a widow, obtained the command of a frigate stationed in the East Indies, where, while engaged in a particular service, he received a blow which caused a lingering disorder and his death*.

---

* I cannot resist the impulse I feel to introduce here the memorial of him, which was published in most of the public papers and journals at the time of his death.

" George Anson Byron was a Captain in the British navy, and second son of the late Admiral, the Honourable John Byron, by whom he was introduced very early into the service ; in which, having had several opportunities of exerting personal bravery and professional skill, he

This was the greatest loss Lord Byron, however unconscious of it, ever sustained. His uncle George not only stood high in his

attained a great degree of glory. In the war with France, previous to its revolution, he commanded the Proserpine, of 28 guns, in which he engaged the Sphinx, a French frigate, assisted by an armed ship; and some time after the Alcmene, another French frigate, both of which severally struck to his superior conduct and gallantry. In the course of the war he was appointed to the command of the Andromache, of 32 guns. He was present at Lord Howe's relief of Gibraltar, and at Lord Rodney's victory over Count de Grasse, to the action of which he was considerably instrumental; for, as it was publicly stated at the time, being stationed to cruise off the Diamond Rock, near Martinico, he kept the strictest watch upon the enemy, by sailing into the very mouth of their harbour, and gave the Admiral such immediate notice of their motions, that the British squadron, then lying off St. Lucia, were enabled to intercept and bring them to battle. In consequence of that important victory, he was selected by Lord Rodney to carry home Lord Cranstoun, with the account of it. In the despatches, Byron's services were publicly and honourably noticed, and he had the gratification of being personally well received by his Majesty.

" Desirous of serving in the East Indies, and applying

profession, but was generally beloved, and personally well connected. Had he returned from India with health, he would

for a ship going to that quarter of the globe, he was appointed to the command of the Phœnix, of 36 guns, and sailed with a small squadron under the Hon. William Cornwallis, early in the year 1789. Ever active, he sought the first occasion of being serviceable in the war against Tippoo Saib, and at the very outset intercepted the Sultan's transports, loaded with military stores. After this he distinguished himself by landing some of his cannon, and leaving a party of his men to assist in reducing one of the enemy's fortresses on the coast of Malabar. Unfortunately he fell a victim to his alacrity in that war.

" When General Abercrombie was on his march towards Seringapatam, the ship which Byron commanded lay off the mouth of a river, on which his assistance was required to convey a part of the army, and it was necessary that he should have an interview with the General. At the time that the interview was to take place, it blew fresh, and there was a heavy sea on the bar of the river; but the service required expedition, and danger disappeared before his eagerness. A sea broke upon the boat, and overset it: in rising through the waves the gunwale struck him twice violently upon the breast, and when he was taken up, it was not supposed that he could survive the shock he had sustained. He was, however, for a time

have made amends for the failure resulting
from the supineness or faults of other parts
of the family; and his nephew would have
grown up in society that would have given
a different turn to his feelings. The Earl
of Carlisle and his family would have acted

restored to life, but he was no more to be restored to his
country. The faculty did what could be done to preserve
him, and then ordered him to England, rather hoping
than believing that he could escape so far with life.

" In England he lived above twelve months; during
which he suffered the misery of witnessing the dissolution
of a beautiful, amiable, and beloved wife, who died at
Bath, on the 26th of February, 1793, at the age of twenty-
nine years; upon which he fled with his children to
Dawlish, and there closed his eyes upon them, just three
months and a fortnight after they had lost their mother.

" In his public character he was brave, active, and
skilful; and by his death his Majesty lost an excellent
and loyal officer. In his private character, he was devout
without ostentation, fond of his family, constant in friendship, generous and humane. The memory of many who
read this will bear testimony to the justice of the praise;
the memory of him who writes it will, as long as that
memory lasts, frequently recall his virtues, and dwell
with pleasure on his friendship."

a different part. They received his sister
kindly as a relation; and there could have
been no reason why their arms should not
have been open to him also, had he not been
altogether unknown to them personally, or
had not some suspicion of impropriety
in the mode of his being brought up
attached to him or his mother. Be this as
it may, certain it is, his relations never
thought of him nor cared for him; and he
was left both at school and at college to
the mercy of the stream into which circumstances had thrown him. Dissipation was
the natural consequence; and imprudencies
were followed by enmity which took pains
to blacken his character. His Satire had
in some degree repelled the attacks that
had been made upon him, but he was still
beheld with a surly awe by his detractors;
and that poem, though many were extolled
in it, brought him no friends. He felt himself ALONE. The town was now full;

but in its concourse he had no intimates whom he esteemed, or wished to see. The Parliament was assembled, where he was far from being dead to the ambition of taking a distinguished part; there he was, if it may be said, still more *alone*.

In addition to this his affairs were involved, and he was in the hands of a lawyer,— a man of business. To these combined circumstances, more than either to nature, or sensibility on the loss of a mistress, I imputed the depressed state of mind in which I sometimes found him. At those times he expressed great antipathy to the world, and the strongest misanthropic feelings, particularly against women. He did not even see his sister, to whom he afterwards became so attached. He inveighed more particularly against England and Englishmen; talked of selling Newstead, and of going to reside at Naxos, in the Grecian Archipelago, to adopt the

eastern costume and customs, and to pass
his time in studying the Oriental languages
and literature.   He had put himself upon a
diet, which other men would have called
starving, and to which some would have
attributed his depression.   It consisted of
thin plain biscuits, not more than two, and
often one, with a cup of tea, taken about one
o'clock at noon, which he assured me was
generally all the nourishment he took in the
four-and-twenty hours.   But he declared,
that, far from sinking his spirits, he felt him
self lighter and livelier for it; and that it
had given him a greater command over himself in every other respect.   This great abstemiousness is hardly credible, nor can I
imagine it a literal fact, though doubtless
much less food is required to keep the
body in perfect health than is usually
taken.   He had a habit of perpetually
chewing mastic, which probably assisted
his determination to persevere in this mea-

gre regimen; but I have no doubt that his principal auxiliary was an utter abhorrence of corpulence, which he conceived to be equally unsightly and injurious to the intellect; and it was his opinion that great eaters were generally passionate and stupid.

As the printing of Childe Harold's Pilgrimage drew towards a conclusion, his doubt of its success and of its consequences was renewed; he was occasionally agitated at the thought, and more than once talked of suppressing it. But while this was passing in his mind, the poem had begun to work its way by report; and the critical junto were prepared, probably through Mr. Gifford, for something extraordinary. I now met more visitors, new faces, and some fashionable men at his lodgings; among others, Mr. Rogers, and even Lord Holland himself. Soon after the meeting of Parliament, a Bill was introduced into the House of Lords in consequence of Riots in Nottinghamshire, for the prevention of those riots, in which the chief object of the rioters was the destruction of the manufacturing frames throughout the country, so as to compel a call for manual labour. Lord Byron's estate lying in that county, he felt it incumbent upon him to take a part in the debate upon the Bill, and he resolved to make it the occasion of his first speech in the House. But this Nottingham Frame-breaking Bill, as it was called, was also interesting to the Recorder of Nottingham, Lord Holland, who took the lead in opposing it. Lord Byron's interest in the county, and his intention respecting the Bill were made known to Mr. Rogers, who, I understood, communicated it to Lord Holland, and soon after made them acquainted. In his Satire, Mr. Rogers ranked, among the eulogized, next to Gifford; and Lord Holland, among the lashed, was just not on a par with Jeffrey. The introduction took place at

Lord Byron's lodgings, in St. James's-street —I happened to be there at the time, and I thought it a curious event. Lord Byron evidently had an awkward feeling on the occasion, from a conscious recollection, which did not seem to be participated by his visitors. Lord Holland's age, experience, and other acquired distinctions, certainly, in point of form, demanded that the visit should have been paid at his house. This I am confident Lord Byron at that time would not have done; though he was greatly pleased that the introduction took place, and afterwards waved all ceremony. It would be useless to seek a motive for Lord Holland's condescension, unless it could be shown that it was to overcome evil with good. Whether that was in his mind or not, the new acquaintance improving into friendship, or something like it, had a great influence in deciding the fate of a new edition of English Bards and Scotch Reviewers, which the publisher, Cawthorn, was now actively preparing, to accompany the publication of the Hints from Horace, that was still creeping on in the press.

Meanwhile, the Poem that was to be the foundation of Lord Byron's fame, and of the events of his future days, retarded nearly a month longer than was proposed, was now promised to the public for the end of February. The debate on the Notting-ham Frame-Breaking Bill was appointed for the 27th of the same month. It was an extraordinary crisis in his life. He had before him, the characters of a Poet and of an Orator to fix and to maintain. For the former, he depended still upon his Satires, more than upon Childe Harold's Pilgrimage, which he contemplated with considerable dread; and, for the latter, he not only meditated, but wrote an oration, being afraid to trust his feelings in the assembly he was to address, with an extemporaneous effusion at first. He occasionally spoke parts of it when we were alone; but his delivery changed my opinion of his power as to eloquence, and checked my hope of his success in Parliament. He altered the natural tone of his voice, which was sweet and round, into a formal drawl, and he prepared his features for a part—it was a youth declaiming a task. This was the more perceptible, as in common conversation, he was remarkably easy and natural; it was a fault contracted in the studied delivery of speeches from memory, which has been lately so much attended to in the education of boys. It may wear off, and yield to the force of real knowledge and activity, but it does not promise well; and they who fall into it are seldom prominent characters in stations where eloquence is required. By the delay of the printer, Lord Byron's maiden speech preceded the appearance of his poem. It produced a considerable effect in the House of Lords, and he received many compliments from the Opposition Peers. When he left the great chamber, I went and met him in the passage; he was glowing with success, and much agitated. I had an umbrella in my right hand, not expecting that he would put out his hand to me—in my haste to take it when offered, I had advanced my left hand —" What," said he, " give your friend your left hand upon such an occasion ?" I showed the cause, and immediately changing the umbrella to the other hand, I gave him my right hand, which he shook and pressed warmly. He was greatly elated, and re-peated some of the compliments which had been paid him, and mentioned one or two of the Peers who had desired to be intro-duced to him. He concluded with saying, that he had, by his speech, given me the best advertisement for Childe Harold's Pilgrimage.

☆ ★ ☆

If his affection, his confidence, nay I
will boldly say his preference, on difficult
occasions, were but flattery or an illusion
lasting for years, the remembrance of
it is too agreeable to be parted with at
the closing period of my life, especially
as that remembrance is accompanied with
a recollection of my anxiety, and of my
efforts to exalt him as high in wisdom as
nature and education had raised him on
the standard of genius.   But it was no illusion; and at the very moment of his quit-

ting his country for ever, I received one more proof of his remembrance and of his confidence. I had returned to the Continent. Whatever was the cause of the breach between him and his lady, it appears to have been irreparable, and it attracted public notice and animadversion. All the odium fell on him, and his old enemies were glad of another opportunity of assailing him. Tale succeeded tale, and he was painted hideously in prose and verse, and tittle-tattle. Publicly and privately he was annoyed and goaded in such a manner, that he resolved to go abroad. On taking this resolution, he sent a note to my son, who was then in London, requesting to see him. He immediately waited upon him. Lord Byron said to him, he was afraid that I thought he had slighted me ; told him of his intention to go to Switzerland and Italy, and invited him to accompany him. This invitation doubly pleased

me : it showed that I still possessed a place
in his memory and regard; and I saw in it
advantages for my son in travelling which
he might not otherwise enjoy; but, upon
reflection, I was not sorry he did not avail
himself of the opportunity, and that the
proposal fell to the ground.

Lord Byron left England in the year
1816, and I trace him personally no farther. I continued to read his new poems
with great pleasure, as they appeared, till
he published the two first cantos of Don
Juan, which I read with a sorrow that admiration could not compensate. His muse,
his British muse, had disdained licentiousness and the pruriency of petty wits; but
with petty wits he had now begun to amal-
gamate his pure and lofty genius. Yet he
did not long continue to alloy his golden
ore with the filthy dross of impure metal:
whatever errors he fell into, whatever sins
lie at his door, he occasionally burst through

his impurities, as he proceeded in that wonderful and extraordinary medley, in which
we at once feel the poet and see the man :
no eulogy will reach his towering height in
the former character ; no eulogy dictated
by friendship and merited for claims which
truth can avow, will, I fear, cover the—I
have no word, I will use none—that has
been fastened upon him in the latter.   The
fact is, that he was like most men, a mixed
character ; and that, on either side, mediocrity was out of his nature.   If his pen
were sometimes virulent and impious, his
heart was always benevolent, and his sentiments sometimes apparently pious.   Nay,
he would have been pious,—he would have
been a christian, had he not fallen into the
hands of atheists and scoffers.

*   *   *   *   *   *

*   *   *   *   *   *

There was something of a pride in him
which carried him beyond the common

sphere of thought and feeling. And the
excess of this characteristic pride bore
away, like a whirlwind, even the justest
feelings of our nature; but it could not
root them entirely from his heart. In vain
did he defy his country and hold his countrymen in scorn; the choice he made of
the motto for Childe Harold evinces that
patriotism had taken root in his mind. The
visions of an Utopia in his untravelled
fancy deprived reality of its charm; but
when he awakened to the state of the
world, what said he? "I have seen the
most celebrated countries in the world,
and have learned to prefer and to love my
own." In vain too was he led into the defiance of the sacred writings; there are
passages in his letters and in his works
which show that religion might have been
in his soul. Could he cite the following
lines and resist the force of them? It is
true that he marks them for the beauty of

the verse, but no less for the sublimity of the conceptions; and I cannot but hope that had he lived he would have proved another instance of genius bowing to the power of truth :

> Dim as the borrow'd beams of moon and stars,
> To lonely, wandering, weary travellers,
> Is reason to the soul.—And as on high
> Those rolling fires discover but the sky,
> Not light us here ; so reason's glimmering ray
> Was lent, not to assure our doubtful way,
> But guide us upward to a better day.
> And as those nightly tapers disappear,
> When day's bright lord ascends our hemisphere ;
> So pale grows reason at religion's sight,
> So dies,—and so dissolves—in supernatural light.
>
> DRYDEN—quoted in the *Liberal.*

* * *

To return to the original character of
Lord Byron. Whoever has read these
pages attentively, or has seen the original
documents from whence they are drawn,
cannot fail to have perceived, that in his
Lordship's early character there were the
seeds of all the evil which has blossomed
and borne fruit with such luxuriance in
his later years   Nor will it be attempted
here, to shew that in any part of his life
he was without those seeds; but I think
that a candid observer will also be ready
to acknowledge, after reading this work,
that there was an opposing principle of

good acting in his mind, with a strength which produced opinions that were afterwards entirely altered. The coterie into which he unfortunately fell at Cambridge familiarized him with all the sceptical arguments of human pride. And his acquaintance with an unhappy atheist—who was suddenly summoned before his outraged Maker, while bathing in the streams of the Cam, was rendered a severe trial, by the brilliancy of the talent which he possessed, and which imparted a false splendour to the principles which he did not scruple to avow. Yet, when Lord Byron speaks of this man, as being an atheist, he considers it offensive;—when he remarks on the work of Mr. Townsend, who had attempted in the sketch of an intended poem to give an idea of the last judgment, he considered his idea as *too daring*;—in opening his heart to his mother he shows that he believed that *God knew, and did all things for the best;*—after having seen mankind in many nations and characters, he unrestrainedly conveys his opinion, that human nature is every where corrupt and despicable. These points are the more valuable, because they flowed naturally and undesignedly from the heart; while, on the contrary, his sceptical opinions were expressed only when the subject was before him, and as it were by way of apology.

When, in this period of his life, there is any thing like argument upon this subject, advanced by him in his correspondence, it is miserably weak and confused. The death of his atheistical friend bewildered him: he thought there was the stamp of immortality in all this person said and did— that he seemed a man created to display what the Creator could make —and yet, such as he was, he had been gathered into corruption, before the maturity of a mind that might have been the pride of posterity.

And this bewildered him! If his opinion of
his friend were a just one, ought not this
reasoning rather to have produced the
conviction, that such *a mind* could not be
gathered into the corruption which awaited
the perishable body? Accordingly, Lord
Byron's inference did not lead him to produce this death as a support to the doctrine
of annihilation; but his mind being tinc-
tured previously with that doctrine, he
confesses that it bewildered him.

When about to publish *Childe Harold's
Pilgrimage*, containing sceptical opinions,
the *decided* expression of which he was
then induced to withdraw, he wrote a note
to accompany them, which has been inserted in this work. Its main object is to
declare, that his was not sneering, but desponding scepticism—and he grounds his
opinions upon the most unlogical deduction
that could be formed: that, because he had
found many people abuse and disgrace

the religion they professed, that therefore religion was not true. This is like saying, that because a gamester squanders his guineas for his own destruction, they are therefore not gold, nor applicable for good purposes. Weak as this was, he called it *an apology* for his scepticism.

It cannot be said, that up to this period, Lord Byron was decidedly an unbeliever; but, on the contrary, I think it may be said, that there was a capability in his mind for the reception of Divine Truth,—that he had not closed his eyes to the light which therefore forced its way in with sufficient power to maintain some contest with the darkness of intellectual pride; and this opinion is strengthened, by observing the effects of that lingering light, in the colouring which it gave to vice and virtue in his mind. His conduct had been immoral and dissipated; but he knew it to be such, and acknowledged it in its true colours. He regretted the indulgence of his passions as producing criminal acts, and bringing him under their government. He expressed these feelings;—he did more, he strove against them. He scrupled not publicly to declare his detestation of the immorality which renders the pages of Mr. Moore inadmissible into decent society; and he severely satirizes the luxurious excitements to vice which abound in our theatrical importation of Italian manners*. When a circumstance occurred in which one of his tenants had given way to his passions, Lord Byron's opinion and decision upon the subject were strongly expressed, and his remarks upon that occasion are particularly worthy of notice. He thought our first

* Then let Ausonia, skilled in every art
    To soften manners, but corrupt the heart,
    Pour her exotic follies o'er the town,
    To sanction vice, and hunt decorum down.
                    ENGLISH BARDS.

duty was not to do evil, though he felt that was impossible.   The next duty was to repair the evil we have done, if in our power. He would not afford his tenants a privilege he did not allow himself.—He knew he had been guilty of many excesses, but had laid down a resolution to reform, and latterly kept it.

I mention these circumstances to call to the reader's mind the general tenor of Lord Byron's estimate of moral conduct, as it appears in the present work; because I think it may be said that he had a lively perception of what was right, and a strong desire to follow it; but he wanted the regulating influence of an acknowledged standard of sufficient purity, and, at the same time, established by sufficient authority in his mind.   The patience of God not only offered him such a standard in religion, but kept his heart in a state of capability for receiving it.   In spite of his many grievings of God's spirit, still, it would not absolutely desert him as long as he allowed a struggle to continue in his heart.

But the publication of *Childe Harold* was followed by consequences which seemed to have closed his heart against the long-tarrying spirit of God, and at once to have ended all struggle. Never was there a more sudden transition from the doubtings of a mind to which Divine light was yet accessible, to the unhesitating abandonment to the blindness of vice. Lord Byron's vanity became the ruling passion of his mind. He made himself his own god; and no eastern idol ever received more abject or degrading worship from a bigotted votary.

The circumstances which have been detailed in this work respecting the publication of *Childe Harold,* prove sufficiently how decided and how lamentable a turn they gave to a character, which, though

wavering and inconsistent for want of the
guide I have referred to, had not yet passed
all the avenues which might take him
from the broad way that leadeth to destruction, into the narrow path of life.   But
Lord Byron's unresisting surrender to the
first temptation of intrigue, from which all
its accompanying horrors could not affright
him, seems to have banished for ever from
his heart the Divine influence which could
alone defend him against the strength of
his passions and the weakness of his nature
to resist them ; and it is truly astonishing
to find the very great rapidity with which
he was involved in all the trammels of
fashionable vice.

With proportionable celerity his opinions
of moral conduct were changed ; his power
of estimating virtue at any thing like its
true value ceased ; and his mind became
spiritually darkened to a degree as great
perhaps as has ever been known to take

place from the results of one step.   Witness
the course of his life at this time, as detailed in the conversations lately published,
to which I have before alluded.   Witness
the fact of his being capable of detailing
such a course of life in familiar conversation to one almost a stranger.

What must have been the change in that
man who could at one time write these
lines,—

> Grieved to condemn, the muse must still be just,
> Nor spare melodious advocates of lust ;
> Pure is the flame that o'er her altar burns,
> From grosser incense with disgust she turns ;
> Yet kind to youth, this expiation o'er,
> She bids thee mend thy line, and sin no more—

and at another become the author of *Don
Juan*, where grosser, more licentious, more
degrading images are produced, than could
have been expected to have found their
way into any mind desirous merely of preserving a decent character in society ;—than

could have been looked for from any
tongue not habituated to the conversation
of the most abandoned of the lowest order
of society? What must have been the
change in him who, from animadverting
severely upon the licentiousness of a village
intrigue, could glory in the complication of
crimes which give zest to fashionable adultery; and even in the excess of his glorying
could forego his title to be called a *man of
honour* or a *gentleman*, for which the
merest coxcomb of the world will commonly
restrain himself within some bounds after
he has overstepped the narrower limits of
religious restraint! For who can venture to
call Lord Byron either one or the other after
reading the unrestrained *disclosures* he is
said, in his published Conversations, to have
made, "without any injunctions to secrecy."
Who could have imagined that the same man
who had observed upon the offensiveness
of the expression of another's irreligious

principles, should ever be capable of offending the world with such awfully fearless
impiety as is contained in the latter
Cantos of *Don Juan*, and boldly advanced
in *Cain?* Who can read, in his own hand-
writing, the opinion that a sublime and
well intentioned anticipation of the Last
Judgment is too daring, and puts him in
mind of the line—

" And fools rush in where Angels fear to tread,"

and conceive that the same hand wrote his
Vision of Judgment?

Yet such a change did take place, as any
one may be convinced of, who will take the
trouble to read the present work, and the
Conversations to which I have alluded, and
compare them together. For, let it be observed, that the few pages in the latter
publication which refer to Lord Byron's
religious opinions, state only his old weak
reasoning, founded upon the disunion of

professing christians, some faint, and, I may say, childish wishes; and a *disowning* of the principles of Mr. Shelley's school. So also that solitary reference to a preparation for death, when death stood visibly by his bed-side ready to receive him, which is related by his servant,* and upon which I have known a charitable hope to be hung, amounts to just as much—*an assertion*. It can only be the most puerile ignorance of the nature of religion, which can receive assertion for proof in such a matter. The very essence of real religion is to let itself be seen in the life, when it is really sown in the heart; and a man who appeals to his assertions to establish his religious character, may be his own dupe, but can never dupe any but such as are like him—just as the lunatic in Bedlam may call himself a king,

* Lord Byron is stated to have said to his servant, " I am not afraid of dying—I am more fit to die than people think."

and believe it; but it is only those who
are as mad as himself who will think themselves his subjects.   There is no possibility
of hermetically sealing up religion in the
heart; if it be there it cannot be confined,—
it must extend its influence over the principle of thought, of word, and of action.

When we see wonderful and rapid
changes take place in the physical world,
we naturally seek for the cause ; and it
cannot but be useful to trace the cause of
so visible a change in the moral world, as
that which appears upon the comparison I
have pointed out.   It will not, I think, be
too much to say, that it took place immediately that the resistance against evil
ceased in Lord Byron's mind.   Temptation
certainly came upon him in an overpower-
ing manner; and the very first temptation
was perhaps the worst, yet he yielded to it
almost immediately.   I refer to the circum-

stance recorded in these pages, which took place little more than a week after the first appearance of Childe Harold's Pilgrimage, when he received an extraordinary anonymous letter, which led immediately to the most disgraceful *liaison* of which he has not scrupled to boast. There was something so disgusting in the forwardness of the person who wrote, as well as deterring in the enormity of the criminal excesses of which this letter was the beginning, that he should have been roused against such a temptation at the first glance. But the sudden gust of public applause had just blown upon him, and having raised him in its whirlwind above the earth, he had already began to deify himself in his own imagination; and this incense came to him as the first offered upon his altar. He was intoxicated with its fumes; and, closing his mind against the light that had so long crept in at crevices, and endeavoured to shine through every transparent part, he called the darkness light, and the bitter sweet, and said Peace when there was no Peace.

As long as Lord Byron continued to re- sist his temptations to evil, and to refrain from exposing publicly his tendency to in- fidelity, so long he valued the friendship of the author of the foregoing chapters, who failed not to seize every opportunity of supporting the struggle within him, in the earnest hope that the good might ul- timately be successful. The contents of this book may give some idea of the nature and constancy of that friendship, and cannot fail of being highly honourable to its au- thor, as well as of reflecting credit on Lord Byron, who, on so many occasions, gave way to its influence. But it is a strong proof of the short-sightedness of man's judgment, that upon the most remarkable occasion on which this influence was excited, by inducing him to publish Childe Harold instead of the Hints from Horace, though the best intentions guided the opinion, it was made the step by which Lord Byron was lost; and he who, in a literary point of view, had justly prided himself upon having withheld so extraordinary a mind from encumbering its future efforts with the dead weight of a work which might have altogether prevented its subsequent buoyancy, and who was alive to the glory of having discerned the neglected merit of the real poem, and of having spread out the wings which took such an eagle flight— having lived to see the rebellious presumption which that towering flight occasioned, and to anticipate the destruction that must follow the audacity, died deeply regretting that he had, even though unconsciously,

ever borne such a part in producing so lamentable a loss.   One of the last charges
which he gave me upon his death-bed, but
a few days before he died, and with the
full anticipation of his end, was, not to let
this work go forth into the world without
stating his sincere feeling of sorrow that
ever he had been instrumental in bringing
forward *Childe Harold's Pilgrimage* to the
public, since the publication of it had produced such disastrous effects to one whom
he had loved so affectionately, and from
whom he had hoped so much good—effects
which the literary satisfaction the poem
may afford to all the men of taste in the
present and future generations, can never,
in the slightest degree, compensate.

NOTES

p. 108, l. 15: William Gifford (1756–1826) was the editor of the *Quarterly Review*. A Tory and noted writer of satires, he was hugely respected by Byron, and was used by Byron's publisher John Murray as a referee for much of Byron's work.

Samuel Rogers (1763–1855) the noted Whig poet and banker. His *Voyage of Columbus*, which was published in 1810, was popular and influential. Although none of his work is read today he was greatly respected in Regency England, and was at one time rated by Byron as second only to Scott amongst the writers of his day. His penny-pinching temperament, however, did not always make him an easy companion for Byron.

Henry Fox, third Lord Holland (1773–1840) was a leader of the Parliamentary Whigs and a correspondent of Byron's in 1812 and 1813. He lived in Holland House, the focus for much of London's artistic, social and political life, and which was satirized in Lady Caroline Lamb's *Glenarvon*.

p. 109, l. 22: Francis Jeffrey, first Baron Jeffrey, was a founding member and editor of the leading Whig journal *The Edinburgh Review*. His reputation in Regency England was damaged by his farcical aborted duel with Thomas Moore, and Byron blamed him personally for Henry Brougham's lacerating review of his own *Hours of Idleness*. A trained lawyer, he later in life pursued a distinguished legal career.

p. 121, l. 17: George Townsend (1788–1857). Vicar, third-rate poet, and anti-catholic. Byron owned his uncompleted jingoistic epic poem *Armageddon* (1816).

John Cam Hobhouse, *Recollections of a Long Life* (London, 1909)

Hobhouse's *Recollections* have been invaluable in the construction of the Byron believed by most Byronists to have been the 'real man'. Not only are they the memoir of one of Byron's two closest friends, but they are also the highly lucid production of perhaps the most eloquent of Byron's prose memoirists. The space they devote to Hobhouse's recollections of Byron is moderate – Hobhouse had after all plenty of other topics to discuss – and they possess none of the whiff of commercialism that would have been so repugnant to Byron himself. There was simply no question of Hobhouse having had a financial motive in publishing his memoirs of Byron: the *Recollections* were published decades after Byron's death, and at a time in Hobhouse's career when he could afford a degree of carelessness of the impact they might have on his standing in public opinion. The lucidity of his memoir, in other words, is matched by its candour.

John Cam Hobhouse was born in 1786, the elder son of Sir Benjamin Hobhouse, a wealthy Bristol trader and baronet. He was educated at Cambridge, where he was one of the founders of the University Whig Club, and became a staunch friend of the young Lord Byron, who shared his political sympathies. After graduating in 1809 the two young men set out together on the nearest approximation to a Grand Tour that the Napoleonic occupation of Europe would allow, and got as far as Albania before their forceful personalities began to jar and they separated (amicably) for the rest of the tour. On his return to England, Hobhouse set to work on his massive *Journey to Albania*, which he eventually published in 1813 to a critical acclaim that helped compensate for the failure of his earlier poetry. A period serving in the militia in Ireland helped calm his stormy relations with his father, and he spent most of the early 1810s living in London Whig society, where he continued his friendship with Byron and made the acquaintance of many of the leading politicians of his day. He was Byron's 'groomsman' at his ill-fated wedding to Annabella Milbanke. A fervent admirer of Napoleon, Hobhouse travelled to Paris in 1815 during the so-called 'Hundred Days' of the Emperor's return from Elba, and published his *Last Reign of the Emperor Napoleon*. This was an immediate success amongst the often pro-Napoleonic aristocratic Whigs in England, and confirmed the growing opinion that Hobhouse was a man whose political views needed taking seriously.

In 1817 he visited Byron, toured Italy, and returned to commence a career in Parliamentary politics – eventually being elected as the radical candidate for the seat of Westminster. Before long his radical politics had earned him a stay in Newgate gaol, for demanding in his *Trifling Mistake in Thomas Lord Erskine's Recent Preface* (1819) 'what prevents the people from walking down to the House, and pulling out the members by the ears, and locking up their doors, and flinging the key into the Thames?'. He was soon released, however, and after visiting Byron at Pisa in September 1822, settled into a more orthodox Parliamentary career. In 1823 he joined the London Greek Committee (which was supporting Byron's cause in the Greek war of Independence) and the following year had the distressing task of organizing the transportation of Byron's remains back to England. It was Hobhouse who arranged for their burial in Hucknall Torkard church, near Newstead Abbey, after the Dean of Westminster Abbey had refused them a resting place.

In 1831 Hobhouse succeded to his father's title, and in the following year achieved Cabinet rank as Secretary of War. His political career after this, however, was chequered, and, despite sitting in several cabinets he, occasionally failed entirely to win election to the House. Over time his politics mellowed until he rejoined the mainstream of Whig politics, and in 1851 he was made first Baron Broughton de Gyfford. Never a particularly effective speaker in the House of Commons, his most lasting contribution to British politics was probably his invention of the phrase 'His Majesty's Opposition'. He died in 1869.

Hobhouse was close to Byron for longer than anyone bar Augusta, the poet's half-sister, and pettishly disputed with Thomas Moore the title of having been Byron's best friend. After the death of the poet he wrote to Thomas Moore to say 'I know more about Byron than anyone else, and much more than I should wish any body else to know' (quoted in *Joyce*, p. 102). The friendship had bloomed in Cambridge once Hobhouse learnt that Byron shared his passion for poetry (he claimed earlier to have been put off by Byron's manner and clothes) and for much of Byron's life Hobhouse was a source of level-headed common sense that proved a much-needed foil to Byron's wilfulness. The only serious interruption in the friendship occured in 1819, when Byron sent his publisher John Murray some verses he had written on Hobhouse's incarceration – in the full knowledge that Murray, a vehement Tory and therefore radically opposed to Hobhouse's politics, would circulate them with relish amongst his acquaintances. Although Byron's own politics were by this time well on the way to the radicalism that was to flower briefly in the middle cantos of *Don Juan*, he felt little but contempt for what he saw to be Hobhouse's flirtation with the politics of the mob, and his poem is witheringly satirical of his friend's radical martyrdom:

> When to the mob you make a speech,
> My boy Hobbie O,
> How do you keep with out their reach
> The watch within you fobby O?...
>
> But never mind such petty things
> My boy Hobbie O;
> God save the people – damn all Kings,
> So let us crown the Mobby O!

Hobhouse, who had only just escaped receiving the verses while still in prison, was devastated. 'Oh you shabby fellow,' he upbraided Byron, 'so you strike a fellow when he is down do you?' And his journal shows exactly how wounded he felt; the poem was 'a melancholy proof of want of feeling. It has at any rate affected the mirage through which I have long looked at this singular man, and I know not that it is in the power of any suite of circumstances hereafter to make me think of him again exactly as I thought of him before.' Before long, however, the two men were once again friends – Hobhouse's indignation did not last, and Byron sent a feeble half-apology; and when they met in 1822 things were as good as they ever were. When they parted company for the last time Byron told his friend, 'Hobhouse, you should never have come, or you should never go.' And after Byron had died in 1824 Hobhouse wrote poignantly – and rather curiously – that he had loved Byron as though he had been a favourite sister.

As one of the most egregious hero-worshippers of his age, Hobhouse was particularly well-suited to be the intimate of Byron. He was intensely loyal, and almost over-jealous in his relationship with the poet, which led him at times into a strained self-pity whenever he felt his feelings were not reciprocated. His comments in the *Recollections* of Byron's dedication to him of *The Siege of Corinth* are in this respect typical:

> Byron's 'Siege of Corinth' and 'Parisina' I bought today. It is to be published on Tuesday. He showed me that the first was dedicated to John Hobhouse, Esq. The poem is inscribed by his *friend*. He thought this sublime. I should have like it better if he had not dedicated 'Parisina' to S. B. Davies. I told him this. (Hobhouse, I, p. 331)

Yet it should not be thought that Hobhouse was a loner who happened to strike it lucky in becoming the friend of Byron before he was famous. Like Thomas Moore, he was in almost every respect a highly successful man, and was if anything even more clubbable than the Irish poet. But Hobhouse's relationship with Byron transcended (in his view) what anyone else could lay claim to. This possessiveness was inevitably going to bring disappointment when it was directed at someone like Byron. Besides, although Hobhouse shared the poet's sceptical, irreverent and to an extent hedonistic disposition, he had also a substratum of priggishness – Marchand calls him 'too much the embodiment of the British conscience' – which as his politics matured brought him increasingly into conflict with the libertine poetry of Byron's later years (see Marchand, p. 89). And of course he could never forgive Byron's giving his famous *Memoirs* to Moore rather than himself, a transaction which Hobhouse described as 'this most extraordinary agreement (by which Lord Byron made a present of himself to Mr. Moore, and Mr. Moore sold his Lordship to the booksellers)' (Hobhouse, IV, p. 331). It would be less than surprising if Hobhouse's pique at being spurned had played a part in his insistence on the burning of the *Memoirs*.

In the event the *Recollections* are amongst the most valuable traces that remain of Byron's character. Hobhouse is not an entirely reliable witness – as no-one is – but nor was he blind to the deficiencies in the personality of his friend. Perhaps more than anyone else (with the possible exception of Lady Byron) he knew what a 'difficult person to live with' Byron was, to use his own words. Today Hobhouse remains what the Earl of Rosebery called him in his preface to *Recollections of a Long Life* – the 'high priest of the Byron mystery'.

☆ ★ ☆

CHAPTER VI

DIARY. *December* 24, 1814.—I rode up to London, and at twelve set off with Lord Byron on his matrimonial scheme. . . . 1814.

At Chesterford we parted, he for Sixmile Bottom, and I for Cambridge. I found S. B. Davies and all my friends out of college.

December 25.—Dined in Trinity College. Heard they have been throwing a collector of the property tax out of the window at St. Ives. . . .

December 26.—Byron did not arrive until three, when we set off and went three stages to Wansford (in Northants), a capital inn. . . . Never was lover less in haste. . . .

December 27.—Off at twelve. . . . Went as far as Newark in snow and rain. . . . Read the new Gibbon [1]—delightful. . . . The bridegroom more and more *less* impatient. . . . Never was lover less in haste. . . .

As to Gibbon, this reading miscellaneously gave me a literary ardour and infused a sort

[1] The completion of the Miscellaneous Works of Edward Gibbon, with Memoirs of his Life and Writings by himself. Edited by the Earl of Sheffield.

1814. of philosophic calm over me to which I have long been a stranger. . . . The pursuits and attainments of Gibbon are, though very noble and extensive, not absolutely beyond the reach of any lover of literature.

The researches of Newton and the brilliancy of Voltaire are objects of admiration, but of despair. . . .

December 28.—We travelled to and slept at Ferrybridge. I read La Bruyère, who is a base flatterer of Louis XIV., and a bigot, or a pretended bigot. . . . He actually praises the King for his persecution of the Huguenots. . . .

December 29.—We went as far as Thirsk to-day. . . .

December 30.—At eight o'clock in the evening we arrived at Seaham, Sir Ralph Milbanke's. . . . Miss Milbanke came to me when alone in the library, and with great frankness took me by the hand at once. . . . Presently in tottered her father. . . . Miss Milbanke is rather dowdy-looking, and wears a long and high dress (as Byron had observed), though she has excellent feet and ankles. . . . The lower part of her face is bad, the upper, expressive, but not handsome, yet she gains by inspection. . . .

She heard Byron coming out of his room, ran to meet him, threw her arms round his neck and burst into tears. She did this *not before us*. . . . Lady Milbanke was so much agitated that she had

gone to her room . . . our delay the cause. . . .
Indeed, I looked foolish in finding out an excuse
for our want of expedition. . . .

Miss Milbanke, before us, was silent and
modest, but very sensible and quiet, and inspiring
an interest which it is easy to mistake for love.
With me, she was frank and open, without little
airs and affectations. . . .

Of my friend she seemed dotingly fond, gazing
with delight on his bold and animated face . . .
this regulated, however, with the most entire
decorum. Byron appears to love her personally,
when in her company. . . .

Old Sir Ralph Milbanke is an honest, red-faced
spirit, a little prosy, but by no means devoid of
humour. . . . My lady, who has been a dasher
in her day, and has ridden the grey mare, is
pettish and tiresome, but clever. . . . Both are
dotingly fond of Miss Milbanke.

There were in the house a family of Mr. Hoare
of Durham, confidential counsel and agent of Sir
Ralph Milbanke, and the Rev. Thomas Noel,
rector of Kirkby Mallory, and illegitimate son of
Lord Wentworth. . . . Byron won his heart by
his kindness and open manners. . . .

Sir Ralph and Co. told stories. . . . Sir Ralph
said that Moore, Archbishop of Canterbury, informed him that he had changed the Archiepis-
copal signature from *Cant.* to Cantuar. . . .

Of the Bishop of Durham, Shute, he told
that the Bishop, when a tutor at Oxford, said to

1814. Lord Hampden . . . "The friendship which I have for my Lord, your father; my respect for my Lord, the Bishop, your uncle; and the peculiar situation in which I stand with my Lord God, etc."

Also that Shute desired some young man not to call his task an imposition. "You're a man of family, I'm a man of family; call it a literary transaction between two men of fashion."

A gentleman, who has lately seen Napoleon, told Hoare that Napoleon said to him, "There are but three generals in the world: myself, Lord Wellington, and that drunkard Blücher."

Byron told me that one day at dinner, Lady C. Lamb said to George Lamb, "George, what's the seventh commandment?" "*Thou shalt not bother* . . ."

December 31.—I walked on the seashore, which is close to the Mansion House of Seaham. The sight of the waters had an indescribable effect upon me. It was a fine, sunshiny day.

I had some private talk with Hoare and Miss Milbanke on Lord Byron's affairs, and I began to entertain doubts of Hanson's probity.

The young lady is most attractive.

We had dinner at six, and had a little jollity upon the signing of the settlements, which was done in the morning. I put my name to a deed which is to provide for the younger children of the marriage; my coadjutor is Sir T. Liddell.

I talked and talked in the evening, which concluded jollily with a mock marriage, I being Lady B., Noel parsonifying, and Hoare giving me away. Shook hands for New Year.

January 1.—Walked on the shore; the Hoares left us. We had not quite so jolly a dinner as yesterday, but fair, considering.

Byron at night said, " Well, Hobhouse, this is our last night; to-morrow I shall be Annabella's." (*Absit omen.*)

January 2.—I dressed in full-dress, with white gloves, and found Byron up and dressed, with Noel in canonicals. Lady Milbanke and Sir Ralph soon came, also dressed. Her Ladyship could not make tea, her hand shook.

Miss Milbanke did not appear. The Rev. Wallace came in, also in canonicals. At half-past ten we parted company; Byron and I went into his room, the others upstairs.

In ten minutes we walked up into the drawing-room, and found kneeling-mats disposed for the couple and the others. The two clergymen, the father and mother, and myself, were in waiting when Miss Milbanke came in, attended by her governess, the respectable Mrs. Clermont.

She was dressed in a muslin gown trimmed with lace at the bottom, with a white muslin curricle jacket, very plain indeed, with nothing on her head.

Noel was decent and grave. He put them, Byron and Miss Milbanke, on their cushions. Lady

1815. Milbanke placed Sir Ralph next to his daughter; I stood next to Sir Ralph; my Lady and Mrs. Clermont were rather opposite in the corner.

Wallace read the responses.

Miss Milbanke was as firm as a rock, and, during the whole ceremony, looked steadily at Byron. She repeated the words audibly and well. Byron hitched at first when he said, " I, George Gordon," and when he came to the words, " With all my worldly goods I thee endow," looked at me with a half-smile. They were married at eleven.

I shook Lady Byron by the hand after the parson, and embraced my friend with unfeigned delight. He was kissed by my Lady Milbanke. Lady Milbanke and Mrs. Clermont were much affected.

Lady Byron went out of the room, but soon returned to sign the register, which Wallace and I witnessed.

She again retired hastily, her eyes full of tears when she looked at her father and mother, and completed her conquest, her innocent conquest.

She came in her travelling-dress soon after, a slate-coloured satin pelisse trimmed with white fur, and sat quietly in the drawing-room. Byron was calm and as usual. I felt as if I had buried a friend.

I put a complete collection of Byron's Poems, bound in yellow morocco, into the carriage for Lady Byron as a wedding gift. It was inscribed thus :

"To the Right Honourable Lady Byron. 1815.

"These volumes, the production of a poet, the admiration of his countrymen, the delight of his associates, and the approved choice of her understanding and her heart, are presented, as a sincere token of congratulation, on her union with his best friend, by her faithful and devoted servant,

"John C. Hobhouse."

At a little before twelve I handed Lady Byron downstairs and into her carriage. When I wished her many years of happiness, she said, "If I am not happy it will be my own fault."

Of my dearest friend I took a melancholy leave. He was unwilling to leave my hand, and I had hold of his out of the window when the carriage drove off.

I left Seaham at twelve. Lady Milbanke asked me if she had not behaved well, as if she had been the mother of Iphigenia. It is not wonderful that the marriage of an only daughter and child, born seventeen years after marriage, should cause a pang at parting. . . .

The little bells of Seaham church struck up after the wedding, and half a dozen fired muskets in front of the house.

The couple went to Halnaby, Sir R. Milbanke's estate in Yorkshire. . . .

I arrived, on January 6, in London; there drove down to Whitton, where I found all my lovely sisters well, and in eager welcome.

CHAPTER II

FROM BOOK, " RECOLLECTIONS."

AT the close of the session of 1823, and the early part of 1824, I was much employed on the affairs of Greece, and became one of the most active members of the Greek Committee. The Greeks had sent two Deputies to negotiate a loan in England, and with these our Committee was in constant communication. But our chief duty was to correspond with the illustrious poet, who had left Genoa for Greece, and was our agent, or rather representative, in Greece. Whatever there was of Government in that country resided at Missolonghi; and in that floating capital Lord Byron, after staying some time in Cefalonia, resided, and devoted all his energies to the good cause. The readers of Moore's Life of him are aware of his exertions. Strange to say, whilst others, and more particularly Colonel Leicester Stanhope, a soldier by profession, were occupied in drawing up constitutions and devising forms of government, Byron was bent upon fighting, and had actually resolved upon an attack of the Castle of Lepanto, so soon as he could collect a sufficient body of troops on whom he could depend.

1824.

1824. Colonel Stanhope studied Bentham, and consulted the "Springs of Action" of that great writer; whilst Byron was providing arms for his soldiers, and concerting schemes for drilling and fitting them for actual war.

The Greek Committee were duly informed of his proceedings, and resolved to second them to the utmost of their power. They had the satisfaction of knowing that Mr. Secretary Canning regarded their efforts with far more favour than those of the Spanish patriots. Indeed, the feeling was universal; and there seemed little doubt that the Greek Deputies would accomplish their mission, and negotiate the projected loan on reasonable terms.

FROM DIARY.

April 12.—Letters from Greece stating that Lord Byron had been attacked by a serious convulsion fit at Missolonghi on February 15th. He lost his senses for a time, and his face was distorted, but he has since recovered, though he is so much shaken that Stanhope says he must retire from Greece, of which he is the life and soul. The Suliotes have behaved very ill, extorting all Lord Byron's money, and then refusing to march, which they were to have done, under Lord Byron, against Lepanto. A Suliote being struck by a Captain Says, shot him dead. Stanhope attributes Byron's illness to these disappointments. I do not. Stanhope says Byron behaved

with great firmness. He always does on emergen-   1824.
cies. The news made me very nervous. I could
hardly sleep.

May 14.—This morning at a little after eight
o'clock I was awakened by a loud tapping at
my bedroom door, and on getting up had a
packet of letters put into my hand, signed
" Sidney Osborne."   On the outside were the
words " By Express "; there was also a short
note from Kinnaird.

I anticipated some dreadful news, and on
opening Kinnaird's note found that Lord Byron
was dead.   In an agony of grief such as I have
experienced only twice before in my life—once
when I lost my dear friend, Charles Skinner
Matthews in 1811, and afterwards when at Paris
I heard my brother Benjamin had been killed
at Waterloo, Quatre-Bras—I opened the dis-
patches from Corfu, and there saw the details
of the fatal event.

The letters were from Lord Sidney Osborne
to me, from Count Gamba (Lord Byron's companion) to me, from Count Gamba to Lord
Sidney Osborne, and from the Count to the
English Consul at Zante.   Besides these there
were letters from Fletcher, Byron's valet, to
Fletcher's wife, to Mrs. Leigh, and to Captain
George (now Lord) Byron.   Also there were
four copies of a Greek proclamation by the
Provisional Government of Missolonghi, with a
translation annexed.

1824. The whole of these documents spoke the intense grief of everybody at this great calamity. The proclamation described my dear departed friend's illness of ten days—the public anxiety during those days of hope and fear—his death—the universal dejection and almost despair of the Greeks around him. The proclamation next decreed that the Easter festival should be suspended; that all the shops should be closed for three days; that a general mourning for twenty days should be observed; and that at sunrise next morning, the twentieth of April, thirty-seven minute-guns should be fired from the batteries of the town to indicate the age of the deceased. He was in his 37th year.

I read this proclamation over and over again, in order to find some consolation in the glorious conclusion of his life for the loss of such a man, but in vain. All our ancient and most familiar intercourse, the pleasure I had enjoyed in looking back to the days of our amusements at home and our travels abroad, the fond hope with which I had contemplated our again—in our own country —renewing the more than brotherly union which had bound us together, all our tokens of regard, nay, even our trifling differences,—all burst upon me and rendered me alive only to the deprivation I was now doomed to endure.

Afterwards I saw the account of his last illness by Fletcher in a letter to Mrs. Leigh, which letter she copied for me. The reading this letter tore my heart to pieces. It showed the boundless and tender attachment of all about him to my dear, dear friend. I shall keep it for ever. It seems he had but imperfectly recovered from the violent epileptic fit which had seized him on the 15th February; he had even had a slight return of it; but his death was owing to his being caught in a hard shower of rain when riding near Missolonghi. A fever ensued; he refused to be bled, and his physicians, young men, did not press him much, but put it off from day to day. Fletcher says he went on his knees with tears in his eyes and implored him to be bled. At last he consented, but Fletcher says it was then too late. He became delirious, and then for the last twenty-four hours neither spoke nor moved. He died on the nineteenth of April at six o'clock in the evening.

It is most afflicting to think that with good care he might have recovered, and yet it is possible that in his very reduced state he might not have been able to bear bleeding. To fancy that he *might* have been saved, and was not, doubles our regret. I shall take some calmer moment for recording some of the particulars of this calamity.

I went for Sir Francis Burdett and Mr. Kinnaird, both of whom were much affected. The former kindly undertook the painful duty of informing Mrs. Leigh of the event. The latter transmitted other letters from Lord Sidney

1824.   Osborne to various correspondents, and went to
the evening newspaper office to make the intelligence public by the speediest means.

After the first access of grief was over, I
determined to lose no time in doing my duty
by preserving all that was left to me of my friend
—his fame.

I called on Kinnaird, it being agreed that
Burdett and I should dine with him. We had
a melancholy evening, recalling to mind the
various excellencies of our dear friend. I shall
never forget this dreadful day.

I should have mentioned, at Mrs. Leigh's desire
I called on her; she was in an afflicting condition.
She gave me Fletcher's letter to read, and I could
not restrain my sorrow, but again burst out into
uncontrollable lamentation; but when recovered
I thought right to engage Mrs. Leigh not to
communicate to any but the nearest friends one
part of the letter, which mentioned that since
Lord Byron's fit on February 15th he had placed
on his breakfast table a Bible every morning.
This circumstance, which pleased his valet
Fletcher, I was afraid might be mistaken for
cowardice or hypocrisy, and I was anxious that
no idle stories to his discredit should get abroad.
I daresay that the Bible was on his table. I
have long recollected his having one near him;
it was a volume given to him by his sister, and
I remember well seeing it on his table at Pisa in
1822, but unless his mind was shaken by disease

I am confident he made no superstitious use of it.
That is to say, I am confident that although he
might have a general belief in its contents, he
was not overcome by any religious terrors.

He often said to me, " It may be true. It is,
as d'Alembert said, a ' grand peut-être ' " ; but I
own that I think he was rather inclined to take
the opposite line of thinking when I saw him at
Pisa, for when I remonstrated with him on the
freedom of some of his latter writings in that
respect, he said, " What, are *you* canting ? " He
then protested he would tell his opinions boldly,
let what would be the consequences.

Both Burdett and Kinnaird were anxious, as
well as myself, that no rumours prejudicial to
his fame respecting his last moments should get
abroad, and we therefore resolved to know the
contents of Fletcher's letters to Mr. Murray and
to Fletcher's wife. This we accomplished by
giving those letters to the parties ourselves. Mr.
Murray read the letter from him to me, and
Mrs. Fletcher did the same to Kinnaird. They
contained nothing but the expression that my
Lord died a good Christian.

Mrs. Leigh seemed to view the subject in the
same point of view as myself, and promised to
be discreet. Captain George Byron—now, alas,
Lord Byron—went down this evening to Becken-
ham in Kent to communicate the tidings to
Lady Byron.

May 15.—I called on Mrs. Leigh. . . . Captain

1824. G. Byron came in to us; he was much affected. He had seen Lady Byron, and told me she was in a distressing state. She had said she had no right to be considered by Lord Byron's friends, but she had her feelings. She wished to see any accounts that had come of his last moments. I agreed to send my letters down to her by Captain Byron, and I did so.

May 16.—Moore and Kinnaird called. Moore talked of Lord Byron's friendships, and said he had told him in his last letter that he never felt safe when absent from him; that he feared stones might be suddenly generated in the higher regions of his fancy, and even in the serenest sky might drop down and crush him, Moore. Byron's answer to this was pettish. I told Moore that Byron did not like being suspected.

Sir F. Burdett called. My dear sisters Matilda[1] and Sophia[2] came. When Burdett was gone I showed them a copy of Fletcher's letter to Mrs. Leigh, and went upstairs. On coming down I found them in floods of tears, such had been the effect of this simple narrative of the last moments of my dear friend on their tender hearts. They continued weeping during their visit. Indeed, I see by the papers that the regret is universal; the loss is felt to be a national loss. Party feeling is suspended in the contemplation

---

[1] Married Marchese Buancaleoni of Gubbio, Umbria, Italy.
[2] Married Boyd Alexander, Esq., of Ballochmyle, Ayrshire, Scotland.

of the genius of our fellow-countryman, and of 1824. sympathy with him for the great cause to promote which he may fairly be said to have died.

The *Times* of yesterday announced his death in a manner which is, I think, a fair sample of the general opinion on this event. The writer is, however, mistaken in saying that others may have *been more tenderly beloved* than *Lord Byron*, for no man ever lived who had such devoted friends. His power of attaching those about him to his person was such as no one I ever knew possessed. No human being could approach him without being sensible of this magical influence. There was something commanding, but not overawing in his manner. He was neither grave nor gay out of place, and he seemed always made for that company in which he happened to find himself. There was a mildness and yet a decision in his mode of conversing, and even in his address, which are seldom united in the same person. He appeared exceedingly free, open, and unreserved with everybody, yet he contrived at all times to retain just as much self-restraint as to preserve the respect of even his most intimate friends, so much so that those who lived most with him were seldom, if ever, witnesses to any weakness of character or conduct that could sink him in their esteem.

He was full of sensibility, but he did not suffer his feelings to betray him into absurdities. There never was a person who by his air, deportment,

1824. and appearance, altogether more decidedly persuaded you at once that he was well born and
well bred. He was, as Kinnaird said of him,
" a gallant gentleman."

FROM BOOK, " RECOLLECTIONS."

How much soever the Greeks of that day may
have differed on other topics, there was no difference of opinion in regard to the loss they had
sustained by the death of Byron. Those who
have read Colonel Leicester Stanhope's interesting volume " Greece in 1823 and 1824," and
more particularly Colonel Stanhope's " Sketch "
and Mr. Finlay's " Reminiscences " of Byron,
will have seen him just as he appeared to me
during our long intimacy. I liked him a great
deal too well to be an impartial judge of his
character; but I can confidently appeal to the
impressions he made upon the two above-men-
tioned witnesses of his conduct, under very trying
circumstances, for a justification of my strong
affection for him—an affection not weakened by
the forty years of a busy and chequered life that
have passed over me since I saw him laid in his
grave.

The influence he had acquired in Greece was
unbounded, and he had exerted it in a manner
most useful to her cause. Lord Sidney Osborne,
writing to Mrs. Leigh, said that if Byron had
never written a line in his life, he had done
enough, during the last six months, in Greece,

to immortalise his name. He added that no one unacquainted with the circumstances of the case could have any idea of the difficulties he had overcome: he had reconciled the contending parties, and had given a character of humanity and civilisation to the warfare in which they were engaged, besides contriving to prevent them from offending their powerful neighbours in the Ionian Islands. I heard that Sir F. Adam, in a dispatch to Lord Bathurst, bore testimony to his great qualities, and lamented his death as depriving the Ionian Government of the only man with whom they could act with safety. Mavrocordato, in his letter to Dr. Bowring, called him " a great man," and confessed that he was almost ignorant how to act when deprived of such a coadjutor.

FROM DIARY.

His friend Gamba says in his letter to me that, though cut off in the flower of his age, in the midst of his hopes, Byron will always be regarded as the saviour of Greece, *always !*

May 22.—This morning I was called up to Lady C. Lamb, whom I found waiting for me in my room. She had written to me saying she was perfectly satisfied if her letters were in my hands ; she now added that she could not give up Byron's letters to her, but she would leave them under seal directed to me in case of her dying before me, and she *was* dying, she said. I found

1824. her in a sad state ; but I could not consent to give up any of her letters, the only guarantee against her making a novel out of Byron's letters. I shall give the same answer about Lady Melbourne's letters, and all to whom I have spoken agree with me in the propriety of this measure.

May 24.—Went to Crown and Anchor. Numbers at dinner 320, 9 M.P.'s. All dreadfully put to it for speeches. The Greek Deputies were what Canning called the American Minister at Liverpool, a Godsend ; but I could not allude to Greece as I otherwise would, the very name stuck in my throat. Burdett, in giving the memory of my dear Byron, introduced it by a moving and eloquent address. The Greeks performed what they had to do well. Orlando was in the Greek dress.

May 25.—Lambton and I walked to the House together ; fought the Islington Improvement Bill. Lambton brought on the question of Buckingham's treatment in India, did it very well. Canning tried to joke. Called Wellesley and Hastings *candid souls,* out of Horace. Came poorly off. Lambton's reply very good and ready. He is certainly a very neat, and indeed finished, Parliamentary speaker.

May 27.—Mrs. Leigh and I talking over Lord Byron agreed that his principal failing was a wish to mystify those persons with whom he lived, especially if they were in an inferior condition and of inferior intellect to himself.

NOTES

p. 143, l. 5: Scrope Berdmore Davies (1782–1852) was a Fellow of King's College Cambridge, and one of Byron's circle during the time he was at the university. His brilliant mind and cutting wit endeared him to many, but his addiction to gambling left him a ruined man in 1820. He escaped his creditors by fleeing to the Continent, where he survived on his fellowship until his death.

p. 144, l. 18: Annabella Milbanke (1792–1860) first met Byron during the first year of his celebrity following the publication of *Childe Harold's Pilgrimage*. She appears to have been considered attractive, but her intelligence was often masked behind a prim and rather selfish sense of moral righteousness. She was not the ideal partner for Byron, but the two married on the second of January 1815. Almost exactly a year later they separated when she failed to return from a visit to her parents' house; the exact cause of the split remains a mystery, and investigations have not been helped by her claims that Byron was guilty of almost every crime one can imagine, and his equally incredible assertion that he could imagine no reason for the split. Lady Byron devoted her later life to tormenting Byron's half-sister Augusta, with whom she thought Byron had had an affair, and to attempting to justify her own conduct. Historians have tended not to judge her character favourably.

p. 146, l. 14: Lady Caroline Lamb (1785–1828) had a tumultous and scandalous affair with Byron during 1812, which she fictionalized out of all recognition in her novel *Glenarvon* (1816).

p. 152, l. 26: William Fletcher was Byron's personal servant. He was at Byron's side for most of his life, and was one of the few familiar faces at the poet's deathbed.

Augusta Leigh (1783–1851) was Byron's half-sister, though he did not meet her until the two had reached adulthood. She was a life-long confidante, and it is likely that the two had an affair in 1814 and 1815. It may have been fear of the consequences of this affair that drove Byron into an unsuitable marriage with Annabella Milbanke. Augusta, whom Byron occasionally called 'Goose', was not the most intelligent of his circle, but was thought by the poet to understand his character better than anyone.

p. 154, l. 27: Sir Francis Burdett, fifth Baronet (1770–1844) – an early radical MP who in later life found his politics mellowing to the extent that he became an ardent supporter of the Conservatives.

p. 160, l. 13: Aléxandros Mavrokordátos (Mavrocordato, 1791–1865) was a key figure in the movement for the liberation of Greece from Turkey. He was later to become Greek Prime Minister on more than one occasion.

Leigh Hunt, *Lord Byron and Some of His Contemporaries* (London, 1828)

Leigh Hunt holds a unique and uneviable place amongst those who wrote memoirs of Byron. Yet his memoir, for all its failings, is a masterpiece of its kind: the most sustained and unscrupulous piece of vituperative fiction to be written in the Romantic period under the guise of a memoir. It sounded the first great blast of the onslaught of Victorian hypocrisy that was to consign Byron's reputation to the outer limits of literary acceptability.

Hunt was born in 1784. His parents were American immigrants, his father a Tory lawyer turned clergyman who was to bequeath to his son little more than his devastating financial ineptitude. After an education at Christ's Hospital, Hunt published *Juvenilia* which enjoyed immediate if limited success, and determined the young man to pursue a career in letters. In the following years, despite a series of debilitating nervous complaints and a habit of extravagance that kept him eternally in debt, Hunt became editor of the *Examiner*, and was soon recognised as one of the most brilliant political journalists of his day. However his radical politics (in 1811 he had met a young and admiring Shelley) were soon to land him in trouble (see the headnote to *Lord Byron and some his Contemporaries* in the Shelley volume of this edition.) In *The Examiner* of 22 March 1812 he published his article 'The Prince on St. Patrick's Day', in which the Prince Regent was branded 'a libertine over head and ears in debt and disgrace', and was immediately and unsurprisingly sentenced to two years in Surrey Gaol. Here, despite the relative luxuriousness of his rooms, the 'martyr to liberty' became a cause célèbre, and was visited by the cream of London's Opposition society – including, in May 1813, Byron himself.

Leigh Hunt's enthusiasm for Byron was immediate; he wrote breathlessly to his wife Marianne about the virtues of the fashionable young Lord, concluding 'It strikes me that he and I shall become *friends* '. Byron, on the other hand, was less enthusiastic. He regarded with distaste the whingeing Hunt's appetite for political martyrdom, calling him a 'bigot of virtue', and was irritated by "Sir Oracle's" predilection for speaking *ex cathedra*. (quoted in Blainey, p. 102). It was perhaps predictable that when the 'wren and eagle' (as Shelley called Hunt and Byron) met in Italy nine years later they would not become the very best of friends. In the event the encounter was little short of disastrous. Hunt, who had been invited by Shelley, arrived with his wife and six small children to find that Shelley had drowned while sailing back after meeting him. Byron was willing to put them up on the ground floor of his mansion, but the confrontational attitude of Hunt's wife, combined with his uncontrollable offspring, soon drove Byron out of his own house. Not, however, before lending the chronically impecunious Hunt several hundred pounds – a gesture which, he told Thomas Moore, was like trying to save a drowning man who persists in throwing himself back into the water. The two men were not to meet again, and the *Liberal*, the journal Hunt had started with the contributions of Byron and Shelley, became an unfortunate casualty of the breakdown in relations. Hunt continued with his family for some years in Italy, before moving back to England and ultimately gaining a favoured place in the literary affections of the Victorians. He was eventually to die aged 75 in 1859.

Of course the dynamics of Hunt's relations with Byron are of far less consequence than the version of them which he was to publish in 1828, in the form of *Lord Byron and Some of His Contemporaries*. The book was to hurl Hunt into the arms of notoriety, earning him an instant reputation as the least savoury literary character in the Romantic period, and excluding him from polite society for several years. Of course the hypocrisy of this reaction on the part of a Victorian society which was itself only too quick to condemn Byron chimes nicely with modern conceptions of the public morality of the mid-nineteenth century. The book – which a shame-faced Hunt was years later to revise in his autobiography – purports to be an account of the character of Byron based on Hunt's personal experience of the poet. Its relation, however, to what was usually and still is recognised as the truth about Byron's character is blatantly distorted by Hunt's envy, his rankling sense of inferiority, and his resentment that Byron did not send more money after him. Despite Hunt's claim that the book contained not a 'shadow of untruth', it was so obviously a tissue of falsehood that even Byron's Tory critics came out against its author (Hunt, *Recollections*, p. v). Even until as recently as 1933 it has succeeded in sending critics into paroxysms of vicarious rage. Hunt's book, wrote the unknown amateur Romanticist Henry Harper in Boston,

> recalls the story of the kind-hearted boy who on finding a reptile, stiff with cold, took it home and warmed it before the fire, after which it bit him and killed him... the viperous breath of this particular book is calculated to dry up the milk of human kindness, in that it presents a striking example of ingratitude that might well cause charitably disposed persons to become wary of helping really worthy people who are in need. (Harper, *Byron's Malach Hamoves*, p. 12)

However it is clearly inadequate as a critical response to suggest that the distortions of *Lord Byron and Some of His Contemporaries* were made possible simply by envy or personal dislike. It is likely that there were clear

motives for his clumsy character assassination, some of them possibly political, and others probably financial; Hunt's debt situation in 1827 was worse
than ever and his publisher Colburn may well have hinted that to provoke a
succes de scandale would be to ensure the rapid sale of the book. In the event
Colburn was right; but the condemnation the book received clearly preyed
on Hunt's conscience (such as it was) and he was later to retract much of
what he had said. He had of course unwittingly exemplified the motto he
had originally chosen from Montaigne ('It is for slaves to lie, and for
freedmen to speak truth') and in his *Autobiography* he attempted to cover
this up. The result, even for a Byronist not favourably disposed towards
Hunt, is painful. 'I am not naturally a teller of truth,' he admits, and
confesses 'Impulse and fancy would tend to make me the reverse... I am at
once the sickliest and most sanguine of my race... naturally hasty and jealous'
– before descending into a bathetic and stupendously egotistical 'I am not a
courageous man... But I have great moral courage... I have, indeed, something of the Hamlet in me.' (Hunt, *Autobiography*, II, pp. 254–6).

His assessment of Byron in his *Autobiography* is not a great deal more
favourable than it had been the first time round (he condemns Byron's
'misanthropy' and 'effeminate wailings') but in his confession of the original
motivation behind *Lord Byron and Some of His Contemporaries* we may at
least move towards a productive reading of the earlier work. Of it he claims
'I do not mean that I ever wrote any fictions about him [Byron]. I wrote
nothing which I did not feel to be true, or think so.' The reader need only
make a 'little allowance for provocation' in order to see the value of his work
(Hunt, *Autobiography*, II, pp. 91–2). And this is the heart of the affair. Hunt
was a member of the so-called 'Cockney School' – the group of London-
based writers which included Keats, Lamb and Hazlitt and which was
characterized amongst other things by a shared lower-middle class background. This group has been seen by historians as important above all for
the role they played in the formation of a voice addressing for the first time
a unified middle class consciousness by the mid 1820s. It is this background
that may be of most help for understanding the perspective from which
Leigh Hunt wrote his book. Byron was lambasted because Hunt, conscious-
ly or not, was in the business of class formation – a process which defined
itself by reaction against the aristocracy rather than against the working
classes. Although much of his animosity against Byron did undoubtedly
result from personal incompatibility, the predisposition to this reaction was
probably in place long before the two men met in Italy. *Lord Byron and
Some of His Contemporaries* may seem a distasteful libel of a great man: but
it is also part of a wider assault on a class.

Ironically, the sheer malice and inaccuracy of Hunt's accusations did
succeed in the short term in casting light on Byron's personality when they

persuaded Hobhouse and Murray to lend Thomas Moore their Byron letters to assist him in his biography. Today, however, Hunt occupies a place of unrivalled infamy in the demonology of Byron's detractors. It will be most appropriate to conclude this introduction by quoting a verse from Thomas Moore's satire on Hunt's treatment of Byron, 'The Living Dog and the Dead Lion':

> Nay, fed as he was (and this makes a *dark* case)
> With sops every day from the Lion's own pan,
> He lifts up a leg at the noble beast's carcass,
> And does all a dog so diminutive can.

Without
stopping to settle this point, I had concluded that Lord Byron had
naturally as much regard for his title as any other nobleman; perhaps
more, because he had professed not to care about it. Besides, he had
a poetical imagination. Mr. Shelley, who, though he had not known
him longer, had known him more intimately, was punctilious in giving
him his title, and told me very plainly that he thought it best for
all parties. His oldest acquaintances, it is true, behaved in this respect,
as it is the custom to behave in great familiarity of intercourse. Mr.
Shelley did not choose to be so familiar; and he thought, that although
I had acted differently in former times, a long suspension of intercourse would give farther warrant to a change, desirable on many
accounts, quite unaffected, and intended to be acceptable. I took
care, accordingly, not to accompany my new punctilio with any air
of study or gravity. In every other respect, things appeared the same
as before. We laughed, and chatted, and rode out, and were as
familiar as need be; and I thought he regarded the matter just as
I wished. However, he did not like it.

This may require some explanation. Lord Byron was very proud
of his rank. M. Beyle (" Count Stendhal"), when he saw him at the
opera in Venice, made this discovery at a glance; and it was a discovery no less subtle than true. He would appear sometimes as jealous
of his title, as if he had usurped it. A friend told me, that an Italian
apothecary having sent him one day a packet of medicines, addressed to
" Mons. Byron," this mock-heroic mistake aroused his indignation, and
he sent back the physic to learn better manners. His coat of arms
was fixed up in front of his bed. I have heard that it was a joke
with him to mystify the sense of the motto to his fair friend, who

wished particularly to know what " Crede Byron" meant. The motto, it must be acknowledged, was awkward. The version, to which her Italian helped her, was too provocative of comment to be allowed. There are mottoes, as well as scutcheons, of pretence, which must often occasion the bearers much taunt and sarcasm, especially from indignant ladies. Custom, indeed, and the interested acquiescence of society, enable us to be proud of imputed merits, though we contradict them every day of our life: otherwise it would be wonderful how people could adorn their equipages, and be continually sealing their letters with maxims and stately moralities, ludicrously inapplicable. It would be like wearing ironical papers in their hats.

But Lord Byron, besides being a lord, was a man of letters, and he was extremely desirous of the approbation of men of letters. He loved to enjoy the privileges of his rank, and at the same time to be thought above them. It is true, if he thought you not above them yourself, he was the better pleased. On this account among others, no man was calculated to delight him in a higher degree than Thomas Moore; who with every charm he wished for in a companion, and a reputation for independence and liberal opinion, admired both genius and title for their own sakes. But his Lordship did not always feel quite secure of the bon-mots of his brother wit. His conscience had taught him suspicion; and it was a fault with him and his *cóterie*, as it is with most, that they all talked too much of one another behind their backs. But " admiration at all events" was his real motto. If he thought you an admirer of titles, he was well pleased that you should add that homage to the other, without investigating it too nicely. If not, he was anxious that you should not suppose him anxious about the matter. When he beheld me, therefore, in the first instance, taking such pains to show my philosophy, he knew very well that he was secure, address him as I might; but now that he found me grown older, and suspected from my general opinions and way of life, that my experience, though it adopted the style of the world when mixing with it, partook less of it than ever in some respects, he was chagrined at this change in my appellatives. He did not feel so at once; but the more we associated, and the greater insight he obtained into the tranquil and unaffected conclusions I had come to on a great many points, upon which he was desirous of being thought as indifferent as myself, the less satisfied he became with it. At last, thinking I had ceased to esteem him, he petulantly bantered me on the subject. I knew, in fact, that, under all the circumstances, neither of us could afford a change back again to the old entire familiarity : he, because he would have regarded it as a triumph warranting very peculiar consequences, and such as would by no means have saved me from the penalties of the previous offence; and I, because I was under certain disadvantages, that would not allow me to indulge him. With any other man, I would not have stood it out. It would have ill become the very sincerity of my feelings. But even the genius of Lord Byron did not enable him to afford being conceded to. He was so annoyed one day at Genoa at not succeeding in bantering me out of my epistolary proprieties, that he addressed me a letter beginning, " Dear Lord Hunt." This sally made me laugh heartily. I told him so; and my unequivocal relish of the joke pacified him; so that I heard no more on the subject.

The familiarities of my noble acquaintance, which I had taken at first for a compliment and a cordiality, were dealt out in equal portions to all who came near him. They proceeded upon that royal instinct of an immeasurable distance between the parties, the safety of which, it is thought, can be compromised by no appearance of encouragement. The farther you are off, the more securely the personage may indulge your good opinion of him. The greater his merits, and the more transporting his condescension, the less can you be so immodest as to have pretensions of your own. You may be intoxicated into familiarity. That is excusable, though not desirable. But not to be intoxicated any how,—not to show any levity, and yet not to be possessed with a seriousness of the pleasure, is an offence. When I agreed to go to Italy and join in setting up the proposed work, Shelley, who was fond of giving his friends appellations, happened to be talking one day with Lord Byron of the mystification which the name of " Leigh Hunt " would cause the Italians ; and passing from one fancy to another, he proposed that they should translate it into Leontius. Lord Byron approved of this conceit, and at Pisa was in the habit of calling me so. I liked it ; especially as it seemed a kind of new link with my beloved friend, then, alas ! no more. I was pleased to be called in Italy, what he would have called me there had he been alive : and the familiarity was welcome to me from Lord Byron's mouth, partly because it pleased himself, partly because it was not of a worldly fashion, and the link with my friend was thus rendered compatible. In fact, had Lord Byron been what I used to think him, he might have called me what he chose ; and I should have been as proud to be at his call, as I endeavoured to be pleased. As it was, there was something not unso-cial nor even unenjoying in our intercourse, nor was there any appear-ance of constraint ; but, upon the whole, it was not pleasant : it was not cordial. There was a sense of mistake on both sides. However, this came by degrees. At first there was hope, which I tried hard to in-dulge ; and there was always some joking going forward ; some melan-choly mirth, which a spectator might have taken for pleasure.

Our manner of life was this. Lord Byron, who used to sit up at

night, writing Don Juan (which he did under the influence of gin
and water), rose late in the morning. He breakfasted; read; lounged
about, singing an air, generally out of Rossini, and in a swaggering
style, though in a voice at once small and veiled ; then took a bath, and
was dressed; and coming down-stairs, was heard, still singing, in the
court-yard, out of which the garden ascended at the back of the house.
The servants at the same time brought out two or three chairs. My
study, a little room in a corner, with an orange-tree peeping in at the
window, looked upon this court-yard. I was generally at my writing
when he came down, and either acknowledged his presence by getting
up and saying something from the window, or he called out " Leontius!"
and came halting up to the window with some joke, or other challenge
to conversation. (Readers of good sense will do me the justice of discerning where any thing is spoken of in a tone of objection, and where it
is only brought in as requisite to the truth of the picture.) His dress, as
at Monte-Nero, was a nankin jacket, with white waistcoat and trowsers,
and a cap, either velvet or linen, with a shade to it. In his hand was a
tobacco-box, from which he helped himself like unto a shipman, but for
a different purpose; his object being to restrain the pinguifying impulses of hunger. Perhaps also he thought it good for the teeth.
We then lounged about, or sat and talked, Madame Guiccioli with her
sleek tresses descending after her toilet to join us. The garden was
small and square, but plentifully stocked with oranges and other shrubs ;
and, being well watered, looked very green and refreshing under the
Italian sky. The lady generally attracted us up into it, if we had not
been there before. Her appearance might have reminded an English
spectator of Chaucer's heroine—

> " Yclothed was she, fresh for to devise.
>
> Her yellow hair was braided in a tress
>
> Behind her back, a yardè long, I guess:
>
> And in the garden (as the sun uprist)
>
> She walketh up and down, where as her list :"

And then, as Dryden has it :

> " At every turn she made a little stand,
>
> And thrust among the thorns her lily hand."

Madame Guiccioli, who was at that time about twenty, was hand-some and lady-like, with an agreeable manner, and a voice not partaking too much of the Italian fervour to be gentle. She had just enough of it to give her speaking a grace. None of her graces appeared entirely free from art ; nor, on the other hand, did they betray enough of it to give you an ill opinion of her sincerity and good-humour. I was told, that her Romagnese dialect was observable ; but to me, at that time, all Italian in a lady's mouth was Tuscan pearl ; and she trolled it over her lip, pure or not, with that sort of conscious grace, which seems to belong to the Italian language as a matter of right. I amused her with speaking bad Italian out of Ariosto, and saying *speme* for *speranza ;* in which she goodnaturedly found something pleasant and *pellegrino ;* keeping all the while that considerate countenance, for which a foreigner has so much reason to be grateful. Her hair was what the poet has described, or rather *blond,* with an inclination to yellow ; a very fair and delicate yellow at all events, and within the limits of the poetical. She had regular features, of the order properly called handsome, in distinction to pretti-ness or to piquancy ; being well proportioned to one another, large rather than otherwise, but without coarseness, and more harmonious than interesting. Her nose was the handsomest of the kind I ever saw ; and I have known her both smile very sweetly, and look intelligently, when Lord Byron has said something kind to her. I should not say, however, that she was a very intelligent person. Both her wisdom and her want of wisdom were on the side of her feelings, in which there was doubt-less mingled a good deal of the self-love natural to a flattered beauty. She wrote letters in the style of the " Academy of Compliments ;" and made plentiful use, at all times, of those substitutes for address and dis-course, which flourished in England at the era of that polite compilation, and are still in full bloom in Italy.

> " And evermore
> She strewed a *mi rallegro* after and before."

In a word, Madame Guiccioli was a kind of buxom parlour-boarder, com-pressing herself artificially into dignity and elegance, and fancying she walked, in the eyes of the whole world, a heroine by the side of a poet. When I saw her at Monte-Nero, she was in a state of excitement and exaltation, and had really something of this look. At that time also she looked no older than she was; in which respect a rapid and very singular change took place, to the surprise of every body. In the course of a few months she seemed to have lived as many years. It was most likely in that interval that she discovered she had no real hold on the affections of her companion. The portrait of her by Mr. West,

> " In Magdalen's loose hair and lifted eye,"

is flattering upon the whole; has a look of greater delicacy than she possessed ; but it is also very like, and the studied pretension of the atti-tude has a moral resemblance. Being a half-length, it shows her to ad-vantage; for the fault of her person was, that her head and bust were hardly sustained by limbs of sufficient length. I take her to have been a good-hearted zealous person, capable of being very natural if she had been thrown into natural circumstances, and able to show a companion, whom she was proud of, that good-humoured and grateful attachment, which the most brilliant men, if they were wise enough, would be as happy to secure, as a corner in Elysium. But the greater and more selfish the vanity, the less will it tolerate the smallest portion of it in another. Lord Byron saw, in the attachment of any female, nothing but what the whole sex were prepared to entertain for him ; and instead of allowing himself to love and be beloved for the qualities which can only be realized upon intimacy, and which are the only securers at last of all attachment, whether for the illustrious or the obscure, he gave up his comfort, out of a wretched compliment to his self-love. He enabled this adoring sex to discover, that a great man might be a very small one. It must be owned, however, as the reader will see presently, that Madame Guiccioli did not in the least know how to manage him, when he was wrong.

The effect of these and the other faults in his Lordship's character was similar, in its proportion, upon all who chanced to come within his sphere. Let the reader present to his imagination the noble poet and any intimate acquaintance (not a mere man of the world) living together. He must fancy them, by very speedy degrees, doubting and differing with one another, how quietly soever, and producing such a painful sense of something not to be esteemed on one side, and something tormented between the wish not to show it and the impossibility of not feeling it on the other, that separation becomes inevitable. It has been said in a magazine, that I was always arguing with Lord Byron. Nothing can be more untrue. I was indeed almost always differing, and to such a degree, that I was fain to keep the difference to myself. I differed so much, that I argued as little as possible. His Lordship was so poor a

logician, that he did not even provoke argument. When you openly differed with him, in any thing like a zealous manner, the provocation was
caused by something foreign to reasoning, and not pretending to it. He
did not care for argument, and what is worse, was too easily convinced at
the moment, or appeared to be so, to give any zest to disputation. He gravely asked me one day, " What it was that convinced me in argument ?"   I
said, I thought I was convinced by the strongest reasoning. " For my
part," said he, " it is the last speaker that convinces me."   And I believe he
spoke truly ; but then he was only convinced, till it was agreeable to him
to be moved otherwise. He did not care for the truth. He admired
only the convenient and the ornamental. He was moved to and fro, not
because there was any ultimate purpose which he would give up, but
solely because it was most troublesome to him to sit still and resist.
" Mobility," he has said, in one of his notes to " Don Juan," was his
weakness ; and he calls it " a very painful attribute." It is an attribute
certainly not very godlike ; but it still left him as self-centered and
unsympathising with his movers, as if he had been a statue or a ball. In
this respect he was as *totus teres atque rotundus*, as Mr. Hazlitt could
desire ; and thus it was, that he was rolled out of Mr. Hazlitt's own company and the Liberal.

I shall come to that matter presently. Meanwhile, to return to our
mode of life. In the course of an hour or two, being an early riser,
I used to go in to dinner. Lord Byron either stayed a little longer, or
went up stairs to his books and his couch. When the heat of the day
declined, we rode out, either on horseback or in a barouche, generally
towards the forest. He was a good rider, graceful, and kept a firm seat.
He loved to be told of it ; and being true, it was a pleasure to tell him.
Good God ! what homage might not that man have received, and what

love and pleasure reciprocated, if he could have been content with the truth, and had truth enough of his own to think a little better of his fellow-creatures! But he was always seeking for uneasy sources of satisfaction. The first day we were going out on horseback together, he was joking upon the bad riding of this and that acquaintance of his. He evidently hoped to have the pleasure of adding me to the list; and finding, when we pushed forward, that there was nothing particular in the spectacle of my horsemanship, he said in a tone of disappointment, "Why, Hunt, you ride very well!" Trelawney sometimes went with us, on a great horse, smoking a cigar. We had blue frock-coats, white waistcoats and trowsers, and velvet caps, *à la Raphael*; and cut a gallant figure. Sometimes we went as far as a vineyard, where he had been accustomed to shoot at a mark, and where the brunette lived, who came into his drawing-room with the basket of flowers. The father was an honest-looking man, who was in trouble with his landlord, and heaved great sighs; the mother a loud swarthy woman, with hard lines in her face. There was a little sister, delicate-looking and melancholy, very different from the confident though not unpleasing countenance of the elder, who was more handsome. They all, however, seemed good-humoured. We sat under an arbour, and had figs served up to us, the mother being loud in our faces, and cutting some extraordinary jokes, which made me anything but merry. Upon the whole, I was glad to come away.

Madame Guiccioli was very curious on these occasions, but could get no information. Unfortunately, she could not see beyond a common-place of any sort, nor put up with a distressing one in the hope of doing it away. The worst thing she did (and which showed to every body else, though not to herself, that she entertained no real love for Lord Byron) was to indulge in vehement complaints of him to his acquaintances. The first time she did so to me, I shocked her so excessively with endeavouring to pay a compliment to her understanding, and leading her into a more generous policy, that she never made me her confidant again. " No wonder," she said, "that my Lord was so bad, when he had friends who could talk so shockingly." " Oh, Shelley !" thought I, " see what your friend has come to with the sentimental Italian whom he was to assist in reforming our Don Juan !" When Lord Byron talked freely to her before others, she was not affected by what would have startled a delicate Englishwoman, (a common Italian defect), but when he alluded to any thing more pardonable, she would get angry, and remonstrate, and " wonder at him ;" he all the while looking as if he enjoyed her vehemence, and did not believe a word of it. A delicate lover would have spared her this, and at the same time have elevated her notions of the behaviour suitable for such occasions ; but her own understanding did not inform her any better ; and in this respect I doubt whether Lord Byron's could have supplied it ; what is called sentiment having been so completely taken out of him by ill company and the world.

Of an evening I seldom saw him. He recreated himself in the balcony, or with a book ; and at night, when I went to bed, he was just thinking of setting to work with Don Juan. His favourite reading was history and travels. I think I am correct in saying that his favourite authors were Bayle and Gibbon. Gibbon was altogether a writer calculated to please him. There was a show in him, and at the same time a tone of the world, a self-complacency and a sarcasm, a love of things aristocratical, with a tendency to be liberal on other points of opinion

and to crown all, a splendid success in authorship, and a high and pi-
quant character with the fashionable world, which found a strong sympathy in the bosom of his noble reader. Then, in his private life,
Gibbon was a voluptuous recluse ; he had given celebrity to a foreign residence, possessed a due sense of the merits of wealth as
well as rank, and last, perhaps not least, was no speaker in Parliament. I may add, that the elaborate style of his writing pleased
the lover of the artificial in poetry, while the cynical turn of his satire amused the genius of Don Juan. And finally, his learning and
research supplied the indolent man of letters with the information which
he had left at school.

Lord Byron's collection of books was poor, and consisted chiefly
of new ones. I remember little among them but the English works
published at Basle, (Kames, Robertson, Watson's History of Philip
II. &c.) and new ones occasionally sent him from England. He was
anxious to show you that he possessed no Shakspeare and Milton ;
" because," he said, " he had been accused of borrowing from them !"
He affected to doubt whether Shakspeare was so great a genius as
he has been taken for, and whether fashion had not a great deal to
do with it ; an extravagance, of which none but a patrician author
could have been guilty. However, there was a greater committal
of himself at the bottom of this notion than he supposed ; and, perhaps, circumstances had really disenabled him from having the *proper*
idea of Shakspeare, though it could not have fallen so short of the
truth as he pretended. Spenser he could not read ; at least he said
so. All the gusto of that most poetical of the poets went with
him for nothing. I lent him a volume of the " Fairy Queen," and
he said he would try to like it. Next day he brought it to my

study-window, and said, "Here, Hunt, here is your Spenser. I cannot see any thing in him:" and he seemed anxious that I should take it out of his hands, as if he was afraid of being accused of copying so poor a writer. That he saw nothing in Spenser is not very likely ; but I really do not think that he saw much. Spenser was too much out of the world, and he too much in it. It would have been impossible to persuade him, that Sandys's Ovid was better than Addison's and Croxall's. He wanted faith in the interior of poetry, to relish it, unpruned and unpopular. Besides, he himself was to be mixed up somehow with every thing, whether to approve it or dis- approve. When he found Sandys's "Ovid" among my books, he said, " God! what an unpleasant recollection I have of this book ! I met with it on my wedding-day ; I read it while I was waiting to go to church." Sandys, who is any thing but an anti-bridal poet, was thenceforward to be nobody but an old fellow who had given him an unpleasant sensation. The only great writer of past times, whom he read with avowed satisfaction, was Montaigne, as the reader may see by an article in the " New Monthly Magazine." In the same article may be seen the reasons why, and the passages that he marked in that author. Franklin he liked. He respected him for his acquisition of wealth and power; and would have stood in awe, had he known him, of the refined worldliness of his character, and the influence it gave him. Franklin's Works, and Walter Scott's, were among his favourite reading. His liking for such of the modern authors as he preferred in general, was not founded in a compliment to them ; but Walter Scott, with his novels, his fashionable repute, and his ill opinion of the world whom he fell in with, enabled him to enter heartily into his merits; and he read him over and over again with unaffected delight. Sir Walter was his correspondent, and appears to have returned the regard ; though, if I remember, the dedication of "The Mystery" frightened him.   They did not hold each other in the less estimation, the one for being a lord, and the other a lover of lords : neither did Sir Walter's connexion with the calumniating press of Edinburgh at all shock his noble friend.   It added rather " a fearful joy" to his esteem ; carrying with it a look of something " bloody, bold, and resolute :" at the same time, more resolute than bold, and more death-dealing than either ;—a sort of available other-man's weapon, which increased the sum of his power, and was a set-off against his character for virtue.

The first number of the Liberal was now on the anvil, and Mr. Shelley's death had given me a new uneasiness.   The reader will see in Mr. Shelley's Letters, that Lord Byron had originally proposed a work of the kind to Mr. Moore ; at least, a periodical work of some sort, which they were jointly to write.   Mr. Moore doubted the beatitude of such divided light, and declined it.   His Lordship then proposed it through Mr. Shelley to me.   I wrote to both of them to say, that I should be happy to take such an opportunity of restoring the fortunes of a battered race of patriots ; and as soon as we met in Pisa, it was agreed that the work should be political, and assist in carrying on the good cause.   The title of Liberal was given it by Lord Byron.   We were to share equally the profits, the work being printed and published by my brother ; and it was confidently anticipated that money would pour in upon all of us.

Enemies however, had been already at work.   Lord Byron was alarmed for his credit with his fashionable friends ; among whom, although on the liberal side, patriotism was less in favour, than the talk about it.   This man wrote to him, and that wrote, and another came.   Mr. Hobhouse rushed over the Alps, not knowing which was the more awful, the mountains, or the Magazine.   Mr. Murray wondered, Mr. Gifford smiled, (a lofty symptom!) and Mr. Moore (tu quoque, Horati!) said that the Liberal had "a taint" in it!   This however was afterwards.   But Lord Byron, who was as fond as a footman of communicating unpleasant intelligence, told us from the first, that his "friends" had all been at him; friends, whom he afterwards told me he had "libelled all round," and whom (to judge of what he did by some of them) he continued to treat in the same impartial manner.   He surprised my friend, Mr. Brown, at Pisa, by volunteering a gossip on this matter, in the course of which he drew a comparison between me and one of his "friends," to whom, he said, he had been accused of preferring me; "and," added he, with an air of warmth, "so I do."   The meaning of this was, that the person in question was out of favour at the moment, and I was in.   Next day the tables may have been turned.   I met Mr. Hobhouse soon after in the Casa Lanfranchi.   He was very polite and complimentary; and then, if his noble friend was to be believed, did all he could to destroy the connexion between us. One of the arguments used by the remonstrants with his Lordship was, that the connexion was not "gentlemanly;" a representation which he professed to treat with great scorn, whether birth or manners were concerned; and I will add, that he had reason to do so.   It was a ridiculous assumption, which, like all things of that sort, was to tell upon the mere strength of its being one.   The manners of such of his Lordship's friends as I ever happened to meet with, were, in fact, with one exception, nothing superior to their birth, if two such unequal things may be put on a level.   It is remarkable (and, indeed, may account for the cry about gentility, which none are so given to as the vulgar,) that they were almost all persons of humble origin; one of a race of booksellers; another the son of a grocer; another, of a glazier; and a fourth, though the son of a baronet, the grandson of a linen-draper. Readers who know any thing of me, or such as I care to be known by, will not suspect me of undervaluing tradesmen or the sons of tradesmen, who may be, and very often are, both as gentlemanly and accomplished as any men in England. It did not require the Frenchman's discovery, (that, at a certain remove, every body is related to every body else,) to make a man think sensibly on this point now-a-days. Pope was a linen-draper's son, and Cowley a grocer's. Who would be coxcomb enough to venture to think the worse on that account of either of those illustrious men, whether for wit or gentility; and both were gentlemen as well as wits. But when persons bring a charge upon things indifferent, which, if it attaches at all, attaches to none but themselves who make it, the thing indifferent becomes a thing ridiculous. Mr. Shelley, a baronet's son, was also of an old family: and, as to his manners, though they were in general those of a recluse, and of an invalid occupied with his thoughts, they were any thing but vulgar. They could be, if he pleased, in the most received style of his rank. He was not incapable, when pestered with moral vulgarity, of assuming even an air of aristocratic pride and remoteness. Some of Lord Byron's friends would have given him occasion for this twenty times in a day. They did wisely to keep out of his way. As to my birth, the reader may see what it was in another part of the volume; and my manners I leave him to construe kindly or otherwise, according to his own.

There is nothing on the part of others, from which I have suffered so much in the course of my life, as reserve and disingenuousness. Had Lord Byron, incontinent in every thing else, told me at once, that in case it did not bring him an influx of wealth, he could not find it in his heart to persist in what was objected to by a *côterie* on the town,—or had his friends, whom he "libelled all round," and some of whom returned him the compliment, been capable of paying me or themselves the compliment of being a little sincere with me, and showing me any reasons for supposing that the work would be injurious to Lord Byron (for I will imagine, for the sake of argument, that such might have been the case), I should have put an end to the design at once. As it was, though his Lordship gave in before long, and had undoubtedly made up his mind to do so long before he announced it, yet not only did the immediate influence prevail at first over the remoter one, but it is a mistake to suppose that he was not mainly influenced by the expectation of profit. He expected very large returns from " The Liberal." Readers in these days need not be told that periodical works, which have a large sale, are a mine of wealth. Lord Byron had calculated that matter well; and when it is added, that he loved money, adored notoriety, and naturally entertained a high opinion of the effect of any new kind of writing which he should take in hand, nobody will believe it probable (nobody who knew him will believe it possible) that he should voluntarily contemplate the rejection of profits which he had agreed to receive. He would have beheld in them the most delightful of all proofs, that his reputation was not on the wane. For here, after all, lay the great secret, both of what he did and what he did not do. He was subject, it is true, to a number of weak impulses; would agree to this thing and propose another, purely out of incontinence of will ; and offer to do one day what he would bite his fingers off to get rid of the next. But this plan of a periodical publication was no sudden business; he had proposed it more than once, and to different persons ; and his reasons for it were, that he thought he should get both money and fame. A pique with " The

Quarterly Review," and his Tory admirers, roused his regard for the opposite side of the question. He thought to do himself good, and chagrin his critics, by assisting an enemy. The natural Toryism of some pretended lovers of liberty first alarmed him by a hint, that he might possibly not succeed. He supported his resolution by the hopes I have just mentioned, and even tried to encourage himself into a pique with his friends; but the failure of the large profits — the non-appearance of the golden visions he had looked for,—of the Edinburgh and Quarterly returns,—of the solid and splendid proofs of this new country which he should conquer in the regions of notoriety, to the dazzling of all men's eyes and his own,—this it was, this was the bitter disappointment which made him determine to give way, and which ultimately assisted in carrying him as far as Greece, in the hope of another redemption of his honours. From the moment he saw the moderate profits of " The Liberal," (quite enough to encourage perseverance, if he had had it, but not in the midst of a hundred wounded vanities and inordinate hopes,) he resolved to have nothing farther to do with it in the way of real assistance. He made use of it only for the publication of some things which his Tory bookseller was afraid to put forth. Indeed, he began with a contribution of that sort; but then he thought it would carry every thing before it. It also enabled him to make a pretence, with his friends, of doing as little as possible ; while he secretly indulged himself in opposition both to them and his enemies. It failed ; and he then made an instrument of the magazine, in such a manner as to indulge his own spleen, and maintain an appearance of co-operation, while in reality he did nothing for it but hasten its downfal.

There were undoubtedly other causes which conspired to this end; but they were of minor importance, and would gradually have been done away, had he possessed spirit and independence enough to persevere. It was thought that Mr. Shelley's co-operation would have hurt the magazine; and so it might in a degree; till the public became too much interested to object to it; but Mr. Shelley was dead, and people were already beginning to hear good of him and to like him. *Extinctus amabitur.* I myself, however, who was expected to write a good deal, and probably to be inspired beyond myself by the delight and grandeur of my position, was in very bad health, and as little conscious of delight and grandeur as possible. I had been used to write under trying circumstances; but latterly I had been scarcely able to write at all; and at the time I never felt more oppressed in my life with a sense of what was to be done. Then the publisher was a much better patriot than man of business: he was also new to his work as a bookseller; and the trade (who can do more in these matters than people are aware of) set their faces against him; particularly Lord Byron's old publisher, who was jealous and in a frenzy. To crown all, an article (the " Vision of Judgment") was sent my brother for insertion, which would have frightened any other publisher, or at least set him upon garbling and making stars. My brother saw nothing in it but Lord Byron, and a prodigious hit at the Tories; and he prepared his machine accordingly for sending forward the blow unmitigated. Unfortunately it recoiled, and played the devil with all of us. I confess, for my part, having been let a little more into the interior in these matters, that had I seen the article, before it was published, I should have advised against the appearance of certain passages; but Lord Byron had no copy in Italy. It was sent, by his direction, straight from Mr. Murray to the publisher's; and the first time I beheld it, was in the work that I edited.

That first number of " The Liberal" got us a great number of enemies, some of a nature which we would rather have had on our side ; a great many because they felt their self-love wounded as authors, and more out of a national prejudice.   The prejudice is not so strong as it was upon the particular subject alluded to ; but it is the least likely to wear out, because the national vanity is concerned in it, and it can only be conquered by an admission of defects.   What renders the case more inveterate is, that none partake of it more strongly than the most violent of its opponents.   In addition to the scandal excited by the " Vision of Judgment," there was the untimely seasonableness of the epigrams upon poor Lord Castlereagh,   Lord Byron wrote them.   They arose from the impulse of the moment; were intended for a newspaper, and in that more fugitive medium, would have made a comparatively fugitive impression. Arrested in a magazine, they were kept longer before the eyes of the public, and what might have been pardoned as an impulse, was regarded with horror as a thing deliberate.   Politicians in earnest, and politicians not in earnest, were mortified by the preface ; all the real or pretended orthodox, who can admire a startling poem from a state-minister (Goethe), were vexed to see that Mr. Shelley could translate it ; and all the pretenders in literature were vexed by the attack upon Hoole, and the article headed " Rhyme and Reason ;" in which latter, I fear, even a wit, whom I could name, was capable of finding an ill intention.   I began to think so when I heard of his criticisms, and saw his next poem. But the " Vision of Judgment," with which none of the articles were to be compared, and which, in truth, is the best piece of satire Lord Byron ever put forth, was grudged us the more, and roused greater hostility on that account.   Envy of the silliest kind, and from the silliest people, such as it is really degrading to be the object of, pursued us at every turn ; and when Mr. Hazlitt joined us, alarm as well as envy was at its height.

After all, perhaps, there was nothing that vexed these people, more than their inability to discover which were Lord Byron's articles, and which not. It betrayed a secret in the shallows of criticism, even to themselves, and was not to be forgiven.   The work struggled on for a time, and then, owing partly to private circumstances, which I had explained in my first writing of these pages, but which it has become unnecessary to record, was quietly dropped.   I shall only mention, that Lord Byron, after the failure of the "great profits," had declared his intention of receiving nothing from the work till it produced a certain sum ; and that I unexpectedly turned out to be in the receipt of the whole profits of the proprietorship, which I regarded, but too truly, as one of a very ominous description.   All which publickly concerns the origin and downfal of the Magazine the readers are acquainted with, excepting perhaps the political pique which Mr. Hobhouse may have felt against us, and the critical one which has been attributed to Mr. Moore.   Mr. Hazlitt is supposed to have had his share in the offence ; and certainly, as far as writing in the work was concerned, he gave stronger reasons for it than I could do. But he shall speak for himself in a note, at the hazard of blowing up my less gunpowder text.*   Mr. Hobhouse was once called upon by the

* "At the time," says Mr. Hazlitt, "that Lord Byron thought proper to join with Mr. Leigh Hunt and Mr. Shelley in the publication called The Liberal, Blackwood's Magazine overflowed, as might be expected, with tenfold gall and bitterness; the John Bull was outrageous, and Mr. ———— black in the face, at this unheard-of and disgraceful union. But who would have supposed that Mr. Thomas Moore and Mr. Hobhouse, those staunch friends and partisans of the people, should also be thrown into almost hysterical agonies of well-bred horror at the coalition between their noble and ignoble acquaintance—between the patrician and ' the newspaper-man ?'   Mr. Moore darted backwards and forwards from Cold-Bath-Fields Prison to the Examiner office, from Mr. Longman's to Mr. Murray's shop in a state of ridiculous trepidation, to see what was to be done to prevent this degradation of the aristocracy of letters, this indecent encroachment of plebeian pretensions, this undue

electors of Westminster for an explicit statement of his opinions on the
subject of reform. He gave a statement which was thought not to be

extension of patronage and compromise of privilege. The Tories were shocked that Lord
Byron should grace the popular side by his direct countenance and assistance; the Whigs
were shocked that he should share his confidence and counsels with any one who did not
unite the double recommendations of birth and genius—but themselves ! Mr. Moore had
lived so long among the great, that he fancied himself one of them, and regarded the indig-
nity as done to himself. Mr. Hobhouse had lately been blackballed by the Clubs, and
must feel particularly sore and tenacious on the score of public opinion. Mr. Shelley's
father, however, was an elder baronet than Mr. Hobhouse's; Mr. Leigh Hunt was ' to the
full as genteel a man' as Mr. Moore, in birth, appearance, and education ; the pursuits of all
four were the same—the Muse, the public favour, and the public good. Mr. Moore was
himself invited to assist in the undertaking, but he professed an utter aversion to, and warned
Lord Byron against, having any concern with *joint publications*, as of a very neutralizing and
levelling description. He might speak from experience. He had tried his hand in that
Ulysses' bow of critics and politicians, the Edinburgh Review, though his secret had never
transpired. Mr. Hobhouse, too, had written Illustrations of Childe Harold (a sort of partnership concern)—yet, to quash the publication of The Liberal, he seriously proposed that
his noble friend should write once a-week, *in his own name*, in the Examiner. The Liberal
scheme, he was afraid, might succeed ; the newspaper one he knew could not. I have been
whispered, that the member for Westminster (for whom I once gave an ineffectual vote)
has also conceived some distaste for me—I do not know why, except that I was at one time
named as the writer of the famous Trecenti Juravimus Letter to Mr. Canning, which appeared
in the Examiner, and was afterwards suppressed. He might feel the disgrace of such a
supposition : I confess I did not feel the honour. The cabal, the bustle, the significant hints,
the confidential rumours were at the height, when, after Mr. Shelley's death, I was invited
to take a part in this obnoxious publication (obnoxious alike to friend and foe) ; and when
the Essay on the *Spirit of Monarchy* appeared, (which must indeed have operated like a
bomb-shell thrown into the coteries that Mr. Moore frequented, as well as those that he had
left,) this gentleman wrote off to Lord Byron, to say that, ' there was a taint in The Liberal,
and that he should lose no time in getting out of it.' And this, from Mr. Moore to Lord
Byron—the last of whom had just involved the publication, against which he was cautioned
as having a taint in it, in a prosecution for libel by his *Vision of Judgment*, and the first of
whom had scarcely written any thing all his life that had not a taint in it. It is true, the
Holland-house party might be somewhat staggered by a *jeu-d'esprit* that set their Blackstone
and De Lolme theories at defiance, and that they could as little write as answer. But it was

explicit, or even intelligible ; and I had the misfortune, in " The Examiner," to be compelled to say that I was among the number of the dull

not that. Mr. Moore also complained that ' I had spoken against Lalla Rookh,' though he had just before sent me his ' Fudge Family.' Still it was not that. But at the time he sent me that very delightful and spirited publication, my little bark was seen ' hulling on the flood,' in a kind of dubious twilight, and it was not known whether I might not prove a vessel of gallant trim. Mr. Blackwood had not then directed his Grub-street battery against me : but as soon as this was the case, Mr. Moore was willing to " whistle me down the wind and let me prey at fortune ;" not that I " proved haggard," but the contrary. It is sheer cowardice and want of heart. The sole object of the rest is not to stem the tide of prejudice and falsehood, but to get out of the way themselves. The instant another is assailed (however unjustly,) instead of standing manfully by him, they *cut* the connection as fast as possible, and sanction by their silence and reserve the accusations they ought to repel. *Sauve qui peut*—every one has enough to do to look after his own reputation or safety without rescuing a friend or propping up a falling cause. It is only by keeping in the background on such occasions (like Gil Blas, when his friend Ambrose Lamela was led by in triumph to the *auto-da fe*) that they can escape the like honours and a summary punishment. A shower of mud, a flight of nicknames (glancing a little out of their original direction) might obscure the last glimpse of royal favour, or stop the last gasp of popularity. Nor could they answer it to their noble friends and more elegant pursuits, to be received in such company, or to have their names coupled with similar outrages. Their sleek, glossy, aspiring pretensions should not be exposed to vulgar contamination, or to be trodden under foot of a swinish multitude. Their birthday suits (unused) should not be dragged through the kennel, nor their "tricksy" laurel wreaths stuck in the pillory. This would make them equally unfit to be taken into the palaces or the carriages of peers. If excluded from both, what would become of them ? The only way, therefore, to avoid being implicated in the abuse poured upon others, is to pretend that is just—the way not to be made the object of the *hue* and *cry* raised against a friend, is to aid it by underhand whispers. It is pleasant neither to participate in disgrace nor to have honours divided. The more Lord Byron confined his intimacy and friendship to a few persons of middling rank, but of extraordinary merit, the more it must redound to his and their credit. The lines of Pope,

> " To view with scornful, yet with jealous eyes,
> And hate for arts which caused himself to rise,"—

might still find a copy in the breast of more than one scribbler of politics and fashion. Mr. Moore might not think without a pang of the author of " Rimini," sitting at his ease with the author of " Childe Harold ; " Mr. Hobhouse might be averse to see my dogged prose bound up perceptions. A few days afterwards, meeting him in St. James's-street, he said he wondered at my coming to that conclusion, and asked me how it could happen. I did not enter into the origin of the phenomenon, but said that I could not help it, and that the statement did appear to me singularly obscure. Since that time, I believe, I never saw him till we met in the Casa Lanfranchi. As to Mr. Moore, he did not relish, I know, the objection which I had made to the style of " Lalla Rookh ;" but then he had told me so ; he encouraged me to speak freely ; he had spoken freely himself ; and I felt all the admiration of him, if not of his poem, which candour, in addition to wit, can excite. I never suspected that he would make this a ground of quarrel with me in after-times ; nor do I now wish to give more strength to Lord Byron's way of representing things on this point than on any other. There may be as little foundation for his reporting that Mr. Moore would never forgive Hazlitt for saying that he " ought not to have written ' Lalla Rookh,' even for three thousand guineas ;" a condemnation which, especially with the context that follows it, involves a compliment in its very excess.* But Mr. Moore was not candid, when he wrote secretly to

in the same volume with his Lordship's splendid verse; and assuredly it would not facilitate his admission to the Clubs, that his friend Lord Byron had taken the Editor of " The Examiner" by the hand, and that their common friend, Mr. Moore, had taken no active steps to prevent it !"—*Plain Speaker*, vol. ii. p. 437.

" * Mr. Moore ought not to have written " Lalla Rookh," even for three thousand guineas. His fame is worth more than that. He should have minded the advice of Fadladeen. It is not, however, a failure, so much as an evasion and a consequent disappointment of public expectation. He should have left it to others to break conventions with nations, and faith with the world. He should, at any rate, have kept his with the public. " Lalla Rookh " is not what people wanted to see whether Mr. Moore could do ; namely, whether he could write a long epic poem. It is four short tales. The interest, however, is often high-wrought and tragic, but the execution still turns to the effeminate and voluptuous side. Fortitude of mind

Lord Byron, to induce him to give up the Magazine; and to tell him, there was " a taint" in it. He says he ought to have recollected, that Lord Byron always showed the letters that were written to him. This regret he has expressed to a mutual friend; but I do not see how it mends the matter. And what did he mean by " a taint?" Was it a taint of love—(very loth am I to put two such words together, but it is for him to explain the inconsistency)—Was it a taint of love, or of libel? or of infidelity? or of independence ? And was the taint the greater, because the independence was true? Yes: Mr. Hazlitt has explained that matter but too well.

Towards the end of September, Lord Byron and myself, in different parties, left Pisa for Genoa. He was restless, as he had always been; Tuscany was uncomfortable to him; and at Genoa he would hover on the borders of his inclination for Greece. Perhaps he had already made arrangements for going there. We met at Lerici on our way. He had an illness at that place; and all my melancholy was put to its height by seeing the spot my departed friend had lived in, and his solitary mansion on the sea-shore. The place is wild and retired, with a bay and rocky eminences; the people suited to it, something between inhabitants of sea and land. In the summer-time they will be up all night, dabbling in the water, and making wild noises. Here Mr. Trelawney joined us. He took me to the Villa Magni (the house just alluded to); and we paced over its empty rooms, and neglected garden. The sea fawned upon the shore, as though it could do no harm.

is the first requisite of a tragic or epic writer. Happiness of nature and felicity of genius are the pre-eminent characteristics of the bard of Erin. If he is not perfectly contented with what he is, all the world beside is. He had no temptation to risk any thing in adding to the love and admiration of his age, and more than one country."—*Lectures on the English Poets*, p. 301.

At Lerici we had an earthquake. It was the strongest we experienced in Italy. At Pisa there had been a dull intimation of one, such as happens in that city about once in three years. In the neighbourhood of Florence we had another, pretty smart of its kind, but lasting only for an instant. It was exactly as if somebody with a strong hand had jerked a pole up against the ceiling of the lower room, right under one's feet. This was at Maiano, among the Fiesolan hills. People came out of their rooms, and inquired of one another what was the matter; so that it was no delusion. At Lerici nobody could have mistaken. I was awakened at dawn with an extraordinary sensation, and directly afterwards the earthquake took place. It was strong enough to shake the pictures on the wall; and it lasted a sufficient time to resemble the rolling of a waggon under an archway, which it did both in noise and movement. I got up, and went to the window. The people were already collecting in the open place beneath it; and I heard, in the clear morning air, the word *Terremoto* repeated from one to another. The sensation for the next ten minutes or quarter of an hour, was very great. You expected the shock to come again, and to be worse. However, we had no more of it. We congratulated ourselves the more, because there was a tower on a rock just over our heads, which would have stood upon no ceremony with our inn. They told us, if I remember, that they had an earthquake on this part of the coast of Italy, about once every five years. Italy is a land of volcanoes, more or less subdued. It is a great grapery, built over a flue.

From Lerici, we proceeded part of our way by water, as far as Sestri. Lord Byron and Madame Guiccioli went in a private boat; Mr. Trelawney in another; and myself and family in a felucca. It was pretty to see the boats with their white sails, gliding by the rocks, over that blue sea. A little breeze coming on, our gallant seamen were afraid, and put into Porto Venere, a deserted town a short distance from Lerici. I asked them if they really meant to put in, upon which they looked very determined on that point, and said, that " Englishmen had no sense of danger." I smiled internally to think of the British Channel. I thought also of the thunder and lightning in this very sea, where they might have seen British tars themselves astonished with fear. In Italy, Englishmen are called " the mad English," from the hazards they run. They like to astonish the natives by a little superfluous peril. If you see a man coming furiously down the street on horseback, you may be pretty certain he is an Englishman. An English mail-coach, with that cauliflower of human beings a-top of it, lumping from side to side, would make the hearts of a Tuscan city die within them.

Porto Venere is like a petrified town in a story-book. The classical name took us, and we roamed over it. It was curious to pass the houses one after the other, and meet not a soul. Such inhabitants as there are, confine themselves to the sea-shore. After resting a few hours, we put forth again, and had a lazy, sunny passage to Sestri, where a crowd of people assailed us, like savages at an island, for our patronage and portmanteaus. They were robust, clamorous, fishy fellows, like so many children of the Tritons in Raphael's pictures ; as if those plebeian gods of the sea had been making love to Italian chambermaids. Italian goddesses have shown a taste not unsimilar, and more condescending ; and English ones too in Italy, if scandal is to be believed. But Naples is the head-quarters of this overgrowth of wild luxury. Marini, a Neapolitan, may have had it in his eye, when he wrote that fine sonnet of his, full of aboriginal gusto, brawny and bearded, about Proteus pursuing Cymothoe. (See *Parnaso Italiano*, *tom.* 41, *p.* 10.)   Liking every thing real in poetry, I should be tempted to give a specimen ; but am afraid of Mr. Moore.

From Sestri, we proceeded over the maritime part of the Apennines to Genoa. Their character is of the least interesting sort of any mountains, being neither distinct nor wooded ; but barren, savage, and coarse ; without any grandeur but what arises from an excess of that appearance.   They lie in a succession of great doughy billows, like so much enormous pudding, or petrified mud.

Genoa again ! With what different feelings we beheld it the first time ! Mrs. Shelley, who preceded us to the city, had found houses both for Lord Byron's family and my own at Albaro, a neighbouring village on a hill. We were to live in the same house with her; and in the Casa Negroto we accordingly found an English welcome. There were forty rooms in it, some of them such as would be considered splendid in England, and all neat and new, with borders and arabesques. The balcony and staircase were of marble ; and there was a little flower-garden.   The rent of this house was twenty pounds a-year. Lord Byron paid four-and-twenty for his, which was older and more imposing, with rooms in still greater plenty, and a good piece of ground. It was called the Casa Saluzzi.*   Mr. Landor and his family had occupied a house in the same village—the Casa Pallavicini. He has recorded an interesting dialogue that took place in it.† Of Albaro I have given an account in another work.

---

* Any relation to "Saluces," whose "Markis" married the patient Griselda ? Saluces was in the maritime Apennines, by Piedmont, and might have originated a family of Genoese nobles.   Classical and romantic associations abound so at every turn in Italy, that upon the least hint a book speaketh.

† Imaginary Conversations, Vol. i. p. 179, Second Edition.

The Genoese post brought us the first number of " The Liberal," accompanied both with hopes and fears, the latter of which were too speedily realized.   Living now in a separate house from Lord Byron, I saw less of him than before ; and under all the circumstances, it was as well.   It was during our residence in this part of Italy, that the remaining numbers of " The Liberal" were published.   I did what I could to make him persevere ; and have to take shame to myself, that in my anxiety on that point, I persuaded him to send over " The Blues" for insertion, rather than contribute nothing.   It is the only thing connected with " The Liberal" that I gave myself occasion to regret.   I cannot indeed boast of my communications to it.   Illness and unhappiness must be my excuse.   They are things under which a man does not always write his worst.   They may even supply him with a sort of fevered inspiration ; but this was not my case at the time.   The only pieces I would save, if I could, from oblivion, out of that work, are the " Rhyme and Reason," the " Lines to a Spider," and the copy of verses entitled " Mahmoud."   The little gibe on his native place, out of " Al Hamadani," might accompany them.   I must not omit, that Lord Byron would have put his " Island" in it, and I believe another poem, if I had thought it of use.   It would all have been so much dead weight ; especially as the readers, not being certain it was contributed by his Lordship, would not have known whether they were to be enraptured or indifferent.   By and by he would have taken them out, published them by themselves, and then complained that they would have sold before, if it had not been for " The Liberal."   What he should have done for the work was to stand by it openly and manfully, to make it the obvious channel of his junction with the cause of freedom, to contribute to it not his least popular or his least clever productions, but such as the nature of the work should have inspired and recommended, or in default of being able to do this (for perhaps he was not fitted to write for a periodical work) he should have gained all the friends for it he could, not among those whom he " libelled all round," but among thousands of readers all prepared to admire, and love him, and think it an honour to fight under his banner.   But he had no real heart in the business, nor for any thing else but a feverish notoriety.   It was by this he was to shake at once the great world and the small ; the mountain and the mouse ; the imagina-tions of the public, and the approving nod of the " men of wit and fashion about town."   Mr. Hazlitt, habitually paradoxical, sometimes pastoral, and never without the self-love which he is so fond of discern-ing in others, believed at the moment that a lord had a liking for him, and that a lord and a sophisticate poet would put up with his sincerities about the aristocratical and the primitive.   It begat in him a love for the noble Bard ; and I am not sure that he has got rid, to this day, of the notion that it was returned.   He was taken in, as others had been, and as all the world chose and delighted to be, as long as the flattering self-reflec-tion was allowed a remnant to act upon.   The mirror was pieced at Mis-solonghi, and then they could expatiate at large on the noble lord's image and their own !   Sorry cozenage !   Poor and melancholy conclusion to come to respecting great as well as little ; and such as would be frightful to think of, if human nature, after all, were not better than they pretend. Lord Byron in truth was afraid of Mr. Hazlitt ; he admitted him like a courtier, for fear he should be treated by him as an enemy ; but when he beheld such articles as the " Spirit of Monarchy," where the "taint" of polite corruption was to be exposed, and the First Acquaintance with Poets, where Mr. Wordsworth was to be exalted above depreciation,

"In spite of pride, in erring reason's spite—"

(for such was Mr. Hazlitt's innocent quotation) his Lordship could only wish him out again, and take pains to show his polite friends that he had nothing in common with so inconsiderate a plebeian. Mr. Hazlitt is a little too angry with Mr. Moore. He ought to include himself, who undertook to be still more independent of high life, and who can afford better to be mistaken. A person who knew Mr. Moore well, told me, that asking him one day how he should feel, if the King were to offer to make him a baronet, the author of the " Irish Melodies" replied, " Good God! how those people can annihilate us!" I told this answer to Mr. Hazlitt, who justly admired the candour of it. It would have been more admirable, however, if the poet were to omit those innocent scoffs at the admirers of lords and titles, with which he sometimes thinks fit to mystify himself: and the philosopher's admiration of candour would be better, if he were always candid himself, and now and then a little philosophic.

I passed a melancholy time at Albaro, walking about the stony alleys, and thinking of Mr. Shelley. My intercourse with Lord Byron, though less than before, was considerable ; and we were always, as the phrase is, " on good terms." He knew what I felt, for I said it. I also knew what he thought, for he said that, " in a manner ;" and he was in the habit of giving you a good deal to understand, in what he did not say. In the midst of all his strange conduct, he professed a great personal regard. He would do the most humiliating things, insinuate the bitterest, both of me and my friends, and then affect to do all away with a soft word, protesting that nothing he ever said was meant to apply to myself.

I will take this opportunity of recording some more anecdotes as they occur to me. We used to walk in the grounds of the Casa Saluzzi, talking for the most part of indifferent matters, and endeavouring to joke away the consciousness of our position. We joked even upon our differences of opinion. It was a jest between us, that the only book that was unequivocally a favourite on both sides, was Boswell's "Life of Johnson." I used to talk of Johnson when I saw him out of temper, or wished to avoid other subjects. He asked me one day, how I should have felt in Johnson's company. I said it was difficult to judge; because, living in other times, and one's character being modified by them, I could not help thinking of myself as I was now, and Johnson as he was in times previous: so that it appeared to me that I should have been somewhat Jacobinical in his company, and not disposed to put up with his *ipse dixits*. He said, that "Johnson would have awed him, he treated lords with so much respect." This was better said than it was meant to be, and I have no doubt was very true. Johnson would have made him a bow like a churchwarden; and Lord Byron would have been in a flutter of worshipped acquiescence. He liked to imitate Johnson, and say, "Why, Sir," in a high mouthing way, rising, and looking about him. Yet he hardly seemed to relish Peter Pindar's imitations, excellent as they were. I used to repeat to him those laughable passages out of "Bozzy and Piozzy."

> Dear Dr. Johnson,——
>
> (It is Mrs. Thrale who speaks)——
>
> "*Dear* Dr. Johnson was in size an ox,
> And of his uncle Andrew learnt to box,

LORD BYRON.

> A man to wrestlers and to bruisers dear,
> Who kept the ring in Smithfield a whole year.
> The Doctor had an uncle too, ador'd
> By jumping gentry, called Cornelius Ford;
> Who jump'd in boots, which jumpers never choose,
> Far as a famous jumper jump'd in shoes."

See also the next passage in the book—

> " At supper rose a dialogue on witches,"

which I would quote also, only I am afraid Mr. Moore would think I was trespassing on the privileges of high life. Again; Madame Piozzi says,

> " Once at our house, amidst our Attic feast,
> We liken'd our acquaintances to beasts :
> As for example—some to calves and hogs,
> And some to bears and monkeys, cats, and dogs.
>
> We said, (which charm'd the Doctor much, no doubt,)
> His mind was like, of elephants the snout ;
> That could pick pins up, yet possess'd the vigour
> Of trimming well the jacket of a tiger."

> *Bozzy.* When Johnson was in Edinburgh, my wife
> To please his palate, studied for her life :
> With ev'ry rarity she fill'd her house,
> And gave the Doctor, for his dinner, *grouse.*

> *Piozzi.* Dear Doctor Johnson left off drinks fermented,
> With quarts of chocolate and cream contented ;
> Yet often down his throat's prodigious gutter,
> Poor man! he pour'd whole floods of melted butter."

At these passages, which make me laugh so for the thousandth time, that I can hardly write them, Lord Byron had too invincible a relish of a good thing not to laugh also, but he did it uneasily. The cause is left to the reader's speculation.

With the commiseration about the melted butter, we agreed heartily. When Lord Castlereagh killed himself, it was mentioned in the papers that he had taken his usual tea and buttered toast for breakfast. I said there was no knowing how far even so little a thing as buttered toast might not have fatally assisted in exasperating that ill state of stomach, which is found to accompany melancholy. As " the last feather breaks the horse's back," so the last injury done to the organs of digestion may make a man kill himself. He agreed with me entirely in this; and said, the world were as much in the wrong, in nine cases out of ten, respecting the immediate causes of suicide, as they were in their notions about the harmlessness of this and that food, and the quantity of it.

Like many other wise theorists on this subject, he had wilfully shut his eyes to the practice, though I do not mean to say he was excessive in eating and drinking. He had only been in the habit, latterly, of taking too much for his particular temperament; a fault, in one respect, the most pardonable in those who are most aware of it, the uneasiness of a sedentary stomach tempting them to the very indulgence that is hurtful. I know what it is; and beg, in this, as on other occasions, not to be supposed to imply any thing to my own advantage, when I am upon points that may be construed to the disadvantage of others. But he had got fat, and then went to the other extreme. He came to me one day out of another room, and said, with great glee, " Look here ! what do you say to this?" at the same time doubling the lapells of his coat one over the other : —" three months ago," added he, " I could not button it." Sometimes, though rarely, with a desperate payment of his virtue, he would make an outrageous dinner; eating all sorts of things that were unfit for him, and suffering accordingly next day. He once sent to Paris for one of the travelling pies they make there—things that distribute indigestion by return of post, and cost three or four guineas. Twenty crowns, I think, he gave for it. He tasted, and dined. The next day he was fain to make a present of six-eighths of it to an envoy :—" Lord Byron's compliments, and he sends his Excellency a pasty that has seen the world." He did not write this; but this was implied in his compliment. It is to be hoped his Excellency had met the pasty before.

It is a credit to my noble acquaintance, that he was by far the pleasantest when he had got wine in his head. The only time I invited myself to dine with him, I told him I did it on that account, and that I meant to push the bottle so, that he should intoxicate me with his good company. He said he would have a set-to; but he never did it. I believe he was afraid. It was a little before he left Italy ; and there was a point in contest between us (not regarding myself) which he thought perhaps I should persuade him to give up. When in his cups, which was not often, nor immoderately, he was inclined to be tender ; but not weakly so, nor lachrymose. I know not how it might have been with every body, but he paid me the compliment of being excited to his very best feelings ; and when I rose late to go away, he would hold me down, and say with a look of intreaty, " Not yet." Then it was that I seemed to talk with the proper natural Byron as he ought to have been ; and there was not a sacrifice I could not have made to keep him in that temper; and see his friends love him, as much as the world admired. Next morning it was all gone. His intimacy with the worst part of mankind had got him again in its chilling crust ; and nothing remained but to despair and joke.

In his wine he would volunteer an imitation of somebody, generally of Incledon. He was not a good mimic in the detail ; but he could give a lively broad sketch ; and over his cups his imitations were goodnatured, which was seldom the case at other times. His Incledon was vocal. I made pretensions to the oratorical part; and between us, we boasted that we made up the entire phenomenon. Mr. Mathews would have found it defective; or rather, he would not; for had he been there, we should judiciously have secreted our pretensions, and had the true likeness. We just knew enough of the matter, to make proper admirers.

Good God! The mention of this imitation makes me recollect under what frightful circumstances of gaiety we returned from performing an office more than usually melancholy on the sea-shore. I dare allow myself only to allude to it. But we dined and drank after it,—dined little, and drank much. Lord Byron had not shone that day, even in his cups. For myself, I had bordered upon emotions which I have never suffered myself to indulge, and which foolishly as well as impatiently render calamity, as somebody termed it, "an affront, and not a misfortune." The barouche drove rapidly through the forest of Pisa. We sang, we laughed, we shouted. I even felt a gaiety the more shocking, because it was real and a relief. What the coachman thought of us, God knows; but he helped to make up a ghastly trio. He was a good-tempered fellow, and an affectionate husband and father; yet he had the reputation of having offered his master to knock a man on the head. I wish to have no such waking dream again. It was worthy of a German ballad.

This servant his Lordship had exalted into something wonderfully attached to him, though he used to fight hard with the man on some points. But alive as he was to the mock-heroic in others, he would commit it with a strange unconscious gravity, where his own importance was concerned. Another servant of his, a great baby of a fellow, with a florid face and huge whiskers, who, with very equivocal symptoms of valour, talked highly about Greece and fighting, and who went strutting about in a hussar dress, and a sword by his side, gave himself, all on a sudden, such ludicrous airs at the door, as his Lordship's porter, that notice was taken of it.   " Poor fellow!" said Lord Byron, " he is too full of his attachment to me. He is a sort of *Dolabella !*" Thus likening a great simpleton of a footman to the follower of Antony !

   " Have you seen my three helmets?" he inquired one day, with an air between hesitation and hurry.   Upon being answered in the negative, he said he would show them me, and began to enter a room for that purpose, but stopped short, and put it off to another time. The mock-heroic was a little too strong for him. These three helmets he had got up in honour of his going to war, and as harbingers of achievement. They were of the proper classical shape, gilt, and had his motto, " Crede Byron," upon them.   One was for himself, and the two others were destined to illustrate the heads of the Count Pietro and Mr. Trelawney, who, I believe, declined the honour.   I saw a specimen afterwards—I never heard any more of them.

   It is a problem with the uninitiated, whether lords think much of their titles or not; whether the fair sound is often present to their minds. Some of them will treat the notion with contempt, and call the speculation vulgar. You may set these down in particular for thinking of them often.   The chance is, that most of them do, or what is a title worth? They think of them, as beauties think of their cheeks. Lord Byron, as M. Beyle guessed so well, certainly thought a great deal of his.   I have touched upon this point before ; but I may add, that this was one of the reasons why he was so fond of the Americans, and thought of paying them a visit. He concluded, that having no titles, they had the higher sense of them; otherwise they were not a people to his taste. He thought them shrewd, inasmuch as they were money-getters ; but vulgar, and to seek on all other points, and " stubborn dogs." All their patriotism, in his mind, was nothing but stubbornness. He laughed at them, sometimes to their faces : which they were grateful enough to take for companionship and a want of pretence. The homage of one or two of them, however, he had reason to doubt, whether he did or not. I could mention one who knew him thoroughly, and who could never sufficiently express his astonishment at having met with so unpoetical a poet, and so unmajestic a lord. Those who only paid him a short visit, or communicated with him from a distance, seemed as if they could not sufficiently express their flattered sense of his greatness ; and he laughed at this, while he delighted in it. Receiving one day a letter from an American, who treated him with a gravity of respect, at once stately and deferential : " Now," said he, " this man thinks he has hit the point to a nicety, and that he has just as proper a notion of a lord as is becoming on both sides ; whereas he is intoxicated with his new correspondent." I will not mention what he said of some others, not Americans, who thought themselves at a great advantage with the uninformed. But so minute was his criticism in these matters, that the most accomplished dedicators would have had reason to dread him, had they known all the niceties of knowledge, human and patrician, which he expected, before he could allow the approach to him to be perfect.

You were not to suppose, however, on your part, that he was more in earnest than he ought to be upon these matters, even when he was most so. He was to think and say what he pleased ; but his hearers were to give him credit, in spite of himself, only for what squared with their notions of the graceful. Thus he would make confessions of vanity, or some other fault, or of inaptitude for a particular species of writing, partly to sound what you thought of it, partly that while you gave him credit for the humility, you were to protest against the concession. All the perversity of his spoiled nature would then come into play ; and it was in these, and similar perplexities, that the main difficulty of living with him consisted. If you made every thing tell in his favour, as most people did, he was pleased with you for not differing with him, but then nothing was gained. The reverse would have been an affront. He lumped you with the rest ; and was prepared to think as little of you in the particular, as he did of any one else.* If you contested a claim, or allowed him to be in the right in a concession, he could neither argue the point nor really concede it. He was only mortified, and would take his revenge. Lastly, if you behaved neither like his admirers in general, nor in a sulky or disputatious manner, but naturally, and as if you had a right to your jest and your independence, whether to differ with or admire, and apart from an eternal consideration of himself, he thought it an assumption, and would perplex you with all the airs and humours of

* The following is an extract from a letter of Lord Byron's to Mr. Shelley. It will puzzle the adorers of his early narrative writing ; and furnish a subject of pleasing doubt to the public, whether to admire such cavalier treatment of them or not :—

" The only literary news that I have heard of the plays (contrary to your friendly augury), is that the Edinburgh R. has attacked them all three—as well as it could :—I have not seen the article.—Murray writes discouragingly, and says that nothing published this year has made the least impression, including, I presume, what he has published on my account also. —You see what it is to throw pearls to swine.—As long as I wrote the exaggerated nonsense which has corrupted the public taste, they applauded to the very echo ; and now that I have composed within these three or four years some things which should 'not willingly be let die,' —the whole herd snort and grumble, and return to wallow in their mire.—However, it is fit I should pay the penalty of spoiling them, as no man has contributed more than me in my earlier compositions to produce that exaggerated and false style.—It is a fit retribution that any really classical production should be received as these plays have been treated."

an insulted beauty. Thus nobody could rely, for a comfortable intercourse with him, either upon admissions, or non-admissions, or even upon
flattery itself. An immeasurable vanity kept even his adorers at a distance ; like Xerxes enthroned, with his millions a mile off. And if, in a
fit of desperation, he condescended to come closer and be fond, he laughed
at you for thinking yourself of consequence to him, if you were taken
in ; and hated you if you stood out, which was to think yourself of
greater consequence. Neither would a knowledge of all this, if you had
made him conscious, have lowered his self-admiration a jot. He would
have thought it the mark of a great man,—a noble capriciousness,—an
evidence of power, which none but the Alexanders and Napoleons of the
intellectual world could venture upon. Mr. Hazlitt had some reason to
call him " a sublime coxcomb." Who but he (or Rochester perhaps,
whom he resembled) would have thought of avoiding Shakspeare, lest he
should be thought to owe him any thing ? And talking of Napoleon,—
he delighted, when he took the additional name of Noel, in consequence
of his marriage with an heiress, to sign himself N.B.; " because," said he,
" Bonaparte and I are the only public persons whose initials are the same."

I have reason to think, that the opinions I entertained of breeding
and refinement puzzled him extremely. At one time he would pay me
compliments on the score of manners and appearance ; at another, my
Jacobinical friends had hurt me, and I had lived too much out of the
world. He was not a good judge in either case. His notion of what
was gentlemanly in appearance was a purely conventional one, and could
include nothing higher. And what was essentially unvulgar, he would
take for the reverse, because the polite vulgar did not practise it. I have
no doubt he had a poorer opinion of me, from the day that he met me
carrying an old painting, which I had picked up. He had beguiled me

formerly by bringing parcels of books under his arm; but I now concluded that he had not ventured them in the public eye. His footman
must have brought them to the door. For my part, having got rid of
some fopperies which I had at that time, I was not going to commence
others which I had never been guilty of. I had seen too much of the
world for that; not omitting the one that he chose for his arbiter.

Lord Byron knew nothing of the Fine Arts, and did not affect to
care for them. He pronounced Rubens a dauber. The only pictures I
remember to have seen in his rooms (with the exception of the Italian
family pictures, that remained in the houses which he occupied) were a
print of Jupiter and Antiope, and another of his little daughter, whom
he always mentioned with pride. Pope, before he spoke of Handel,
applied to Arbuthnot to know whether the composer really deserved
what was said of him. It was after making a similar inquiry, respecting
Mozart, that Lord Byron wrote the passage in his notes to Don Juan,
giving him the preference to Rossini. Rossini was his real favourite.
He liked his dash and animal spirits. All the best music, he said, was
lively:—an opinion, in which few lovers of it will agree with him. Mr.
Hazlitt, who is a connoisseur in the spirit of contradiction, may think that
he said this out of spleen against some remark to the contrary; but in
this, as in other instances, the critic is misled by his own practice. It
was not difficult to discern the occasions on which Lord Byron spoke out
of perversity; nor when it was that he was merely hasty and inconse-
quential; nor at what times he gave vent to an habitual persuasion; that
is to say, translated his own practice and instinct into some sudden opinion.
Such was the case in the present instance. I never knew him attempt any
air but a lively one; and he was fondest of such as were the most blus-
tering. You associated with it the idea of a stage-tyrant, or captain of

banditti. One day he was splenetic enough on the subject of music. He said that all lovers of music were effeminate. He was not in good humour, and had heard me, that morning, dabbling on a piano-forte. This was to provoke me to be out of humour myself; but I was provoked enough not to oblige him. I was ill, with an internal fever preying upon me, and full of cares of all sorts. He, the objector to effeminacy, was sitting in health and wealth, with rings on his fingers, and baby-work to his shirt; and he had just issued, like a sultan, out of his bath. I was nevertheless really more tranquil than he, ill and provoked as I was. I said that the love of music might be carried to a pitch of effeminacy, like any other pleasure but that he would find it difficult to persuade the world, that Alfred, and Epaminondas, and Martin Luther, and Frederick the Second, all eminent lovers of music, were effeminate men. He made no answer. I had spoilt a stanza in " Don Juan."

Speaking of " Don Juan," I will here observe that he had no plan with regard to that poem; that he did not know how long he should make it, nor what to do with his hero. He had a great mind to make him die a Methodist—a catastrophe which he sometimes anticipated for himself. I said I thought there was no reason for treating either his hero or himself so ill. That as to his own case, he would find himself mustering up his intellectual faculties in good style, as the hour came on, and there was something to do,—barring drugs and a bit of delirium; and with regard to Don Juan, he was a good, careless, well-intentioned fellow, (though he might not have liked to be told so in the hearing of every body); and that he deserved at least to be made a retired country gentleman, very speculative and tolerant, and fond of his grandchildren. He lent an ear to this, and seemed to like it; but after all, as he had not himself died or retired, and wanted experience to draw upon, the termination of the poem would have depended on what he thought the fashionable world expected of it. His hero in this work was a picture of the better part of his own nature. When the author speaks in his own person, he is endeavouring to bully himself into a satisfaction with the worse, and courting the eulogies of the " knowing."

This reminds me of the cunning way in which he has spoken of that passion for money in which he latterly indulged. He says, in one of his most agreeable, off-hand couplets in " Don Juan," after telling us what a poor inanimate thing life has become for him—

> " So for a good old gentlemanly vice,
> I think I shall take up with avarice."

This the public were not to believe. It is a specimen of the artifice noticed in another place. They were to regard it only as a pleasantry, issuing from a generous mouth. However, it was very true. He had already taken up with the vice, as his friends were too well aware ; and this couplet was at once to baffle them with a sort of confession, and to secure the public against a suspicion of it. It was curious to see what mastery he suffered the weakest passions to have over him ; as if his public fame and abstract superiority were to bear him out privately, in every thing. He confessed that he felt jealous of the smallest accomplishments. The meaning of this was, that supposing every one else, in all probability, to feel so, you were to give him credit for being candid on a point which others concealed ; or if they were not, the confession was to strike you as a piece of extraordinary acknowledgment on the part of a great man. The whole truth of the matter was to be found in the indiscriminate admiration he received. Those who knew him, took him at his word. They thought him so little above the weakness, that they did not care to exhibit any such accomplishment before him. We have been told of authors who were jealous even of beautiful women, because they divided attention. I do not think Lord Byron would have entertained a jealousy of this sort. He would have thought the women too much occupied with himself. But he would infallibly have been jealous, had the beautiful woman been a wit, or drawn a circle round her pianoforte. With men I have seen him hold the most childish contests for superiority ; so childish, that had it been possible for him to divest himself of a sense of his pretensions and public character, they would have exhibited something of the conciliating simplicity of Goldsmith. He would then lay imaginary wagers ; and in a style which you would not have looked for in high life, thrust out his chin, and give knowing, self-estimating nods of the head, half nod and half shake, such as boys playing at chuck-farthing give, when they say, " Come ; I tell you what now." A fat dandy who came upon us at Genoa, and pretended to be younger than he was, and to wear his own hair, discomposed him for the day. He declaimed against him in so deploring a tone, and uttered the word " wig" so often, that my two eldest boys, who were in the next room, were obliged to stifle their laughter.

His jealousy of Wordsworth and others, who were not town-poets, was more creditable to him, though he did not indulge it in the most becoming manner. He pretended to think worse of them than he did. He had the modesty one day to bring me a stanza, intended for " Don Juan," in which he had sneered at them all, adding, with respect to one of them, that nobody but myself thought highly of him. He fancied I should put up with this, for the sake of being mentioned in the poem, let the mention be what it might : an absurdity, which nothing but his own vanity had suggested. I told him, that I should be unable to consider the introduction of such a stanza as any thing but an affront, and that he had better not put it in. He said he would not, and kept his word. I am now sorry I did not let it go; for it would have done me honour with posterity, far from what he intended. He did not equally keep his word, when he promised me to alter what he had said respecting the cause of Mr. Keats's death. But I speak more of this circumstance hereafter. For Southey he had as much contempt as any man can well have for another, especially for one who can do him an injury. He thought him a washy writer, and a canting politician; half a mercenary, and half a moral coxcomb. He was sadly out, however, when he compared his generosities with those of the Lake poet, and gave himself the preference. Mr. Southey, from all that I have heard, is a truly generous man, and says nothing about it. Lord Byron was not a generous man; and, in what he did, he contrived either to blow a trumpet before it himself, or to see that others blew one for him. I speak of his conduct latterly. What he might have done, before he thought fit to put an end to his doubts respecting the superiority of being generous, I cannot say; but if you were to believe himself, he had a propensity to avarice from a child. At Harrow, he told me, he would save up his money, not as other boys did, for the pleasure of some great purchase or jovial expense, but in order to look at it and count it. I was to believe as much of this, or in such a manner, as to do him honour for the confession; but, unluckily, it had become too much like the practice of his middle age, not to be believed entirely. It was too obvious a part of the predominant feature in his character,— which was an indulgence of his self-will and self-love united, denying himself no pleasure that could add to the intensity of his consciousness, and the means of his being powerful and effective, with a particular satisfaction in contributing as little as possible to the same end in others.

His love of notoriety was superior even to his love of money; which is giving the highest idea that can be entertained of it. But he was extremely anxious to make them go hand in hand. At one time he dashed away in England and got into debt, because he thought expense became him; but he looked to retrieving all this, and more, by marrying a fortune. When Shelley lived near him in Switzerland, he appeared to be really generous, because he had a generous man for his admirer, and one whose influence he felt extremely. Besides, Mr. Shelley had money himself, or the expectation of it; and he respected him the more, and was anxious to look well in his eyes on that account. In Italy, where a different mode of life, and the success of Beppo and Don Juan, had made him conclude that the romantic character was not necessary to fame, he shocked his companion one day, on renewing their intimacy, by asking him, whether he did not feel a real respect for a wealthy man, or, at least, a greater respect for the rich man of the company, than for any other? Mr. Shelley gave him what Napoleon would have called "a superb no." It is true, the same question might have been put at random to a hundred Englishmen; and all, if they were honest, might have answered "Yes;" but these would have come from the middling ranks, where the possession of wealth is associated with the idea of cleverness and industry. Among the privileged orders, where riches are inherited, the estimation is much more equivocal, the richest man there being often the idlest and stupidest. But Mr. Shelley had as little respect for the possession or accumulation of wealth under any circumstances, as Lord Byron had the reverse; and he would give away hundreds with as much zeal for another man's comfort, as the noble Lord would willingly save a guinea even in securing his pleasures. Perhaps, at one period of his residence there, no man in Italy, certainly no Englishman, ever contrived to practise more rakery and economy at one and the same time. Italian women are not averse to accepting presents, or any other mark of kindness; but they can do without them, and his Lordship put them to the test. Presents, by way of showing his gratitude, or as another mode of interchanging delight and kindness between friends, he had long ceased to make. I doubt whether his fair friend, Madame Guiccioli, ever received so much as a ring or a shawl from him. It is true, she did not require it. She was happy to show her disinterestedness in all points unconnected with the pride of her attachment; and I have as little doubt, that he would assign this as a reason for his conduct, and say he was as happy to let her prove it. But to be a poet and a wit, and to have had a liberal education, and write about love and lavishment, and not to find it in his heart, after all, to be able to put a friend and a woman upon a footing of graceful comfort with him in so poor a thing as a money-matter,—these were the sides of his character, in which love, as well as greatness, found him wanting, and in which it could discern no relief to its wounded self-respect, but at the risk of a greater mortification. The love of money, the pleasure of receiving it, even the gratitude he evinced when it was saved him, had not taught him the only virtue upon which lovers of money usually found their claims to a good construction :—he did not like paying a debt, and would undergo pestering and pursuit to avoid it. " But what," cries the reader, " becomes then of the stories of his making presents of money and manuscripts, and his not caring for the profits of his writings, and his giving 10,000*l.* to the Greeks?" He did care for the profits of what he wrote. and he reaped a great deal : but, as I have observed before, he cared for celebrity still more ; and his presents, such as they were, were judiciously made to that end. " Good heavens !" said a fair friend to me the other day, who knew him well,—" if he had but foreseen that you would have given the world an account of him ! What would he not have done to cut a figure in your eyes !" As to the Greeks, the *present* of 10,000*l.* was first of all well trumpeted to the world : it then became a *loan* of 10,000*l.*; then a loan of 6000*l.*; and he told me, in one of his incontinent fits of communication and knowingness, that he did not think he should " *get off* under 4000*l.*" I know not how much was lent after all ; but I have been told, that good security was taken for it ; and I was informed the other day, that the whole money had been repaid. He was so jealous of your being easy upon the remotest points connected with property, that if he saw you ungrudging even upon so small a tax on your liberality as the lending of books, he would not the less fidget and worry you in lending his own. He contrived to let you feel that you had got them, and would insinuate that you had treated them carelessly, though he did not scruple to make marks and dogs'-ears in your's. O Truth ! what scrapes of portraiture have you not got me into !

I believe there did exist one person to whom he would have been generous, if she pleased ; perhaps was so. At all events, he left her the bulk of his property, and always spoke of her with the greatest esteem. This was his sister, Mrs. Leigh. He told me she used to call him " baby Byron !" It was easy to see, that of the two persons, she had by far the greater judgment : I will add, without meaning to impeach her womanhood, the more masculine sense. She has recorded him on his tomb as the author of " Childe Harold," which was not so judicious ; but this may have been owing to a fit of affectionate spleen at " Don Juan," which she could not bear, and (I was told) would never speak of. She thought he had committed his dignity in it. I believe she was the only woman for whom he ever entertained a real respect; a feeling, which was mixed up perhaps with something of family self-love. The only man he professed to entertain a real friendship for, was Lord Clare. I conclude that his Lordship may be excepted from the number of friends whom he " libelled all round."

His temper was not good. Reading one day in Montaigne the confession of that philosopher and " Seigneur," that a saddle not well fastened, or the flapping of a leather against his boot, would put him out of sorts for the day, he said it was his own case; and he seemed to think it that of every body else of any importance, if people would but confess it; otherwise they were dull or wanted vigour. For he was always mistaking the subtlety of that matter, and confounding patience with weakness, because there was a weak patience as well as a strong one. But it was not only in small things that he was " put out." I have seen the expression of his countenance on greater occasions, absolutely festered with ill-temper,—all the beauty of it corrugated and made sore,— his voice at the same time being soft, and struggling to keep itself in, as if on the very edge of endurance. On such occasions, having no address, he did not know how to let himself be extricated from his position; and if I found him in this state, I contrived to make a few remarks, as serious as possible, on indifferent subjects, and so come away. An endeavour to talk him out of it, as a weakness, he might have had reason to resent:—sympathy would probably have drawn upon you a discussion of matters too petty for your respect; and gaiety would have been treated as an assumption, necessary to be put down by sarcasms, which it would have been necessary to put down in their turn. There was no living with these eternal assumptions and inequalities. When he knew me in England, independent and able to do him service, he never ventured upon a raillery.   In Italy, he soon began to treat me with it; and I was obliged, for both our sakes, to tell him I did not like it, and that he was too much in earnest.   Raillery, indeed, unless it is managed with great delicacy, and borne as well by him that uses it as it is expected to be borne by its object, is unfit for grown understandings.   It is a desperate substitute for animal spirits; and no more resembles them, than a jostle resembles a dance.   Like boys fighting in sport, some real blow is given, and the rest is fighting in earnest.   A passing, delicate raillery is another matter, and may do us both a good and a pleasure; but it requires exquisite handling.   You can imagine it is Sir Richard Steele, or Garth, or any other good-natured wit, who is not in the habit of objecting.   My friend Charles Lamb has rallied me, and made me love him the more.   So has Mr. Shelley.   But in a man of more doubtful candour or benevolence, in Addison for instance, with his natural reserve and his born *parsonism*, you would begin to suspect the motive to it; and in the case of Swift or Johnson, it no doubt much oftener produced awkward retaliations, than biographers have thought fit to record.

If Lord Byron had been a man of address, he would have been a kinder man.   He never heartily forgave either you or himself for his deficiency on this point; and hence a good deal of his ill-temper, and his carelessness of your feelings.   By any means, fair or foul, he was to make up for the disadvantage; and with all his exaction of conventional propriety from others, he could set it at nought in his own conduct in the most remarkable manner.   He had an incontinence, I believe unique, in talking of his affairs, and showing you other people's letters.   He would even make you presents of them; and I have accepted one or two that they might go no farther.   But I have mentioned this before.   If his five-hundred confidants, by a retinence as remarkable as his laxity, had not kept his secrets better than he did himself, the very devil might have been played with I know not how many people. But there was always this saving reflection to be made, that the man who could be guilty of such extravagances for the sake of making an impression, might be guilty of exaggerating or inventing what astonished you ; and indeed, though he was a speaker of the truth on ordinary occasions,—that is to say, he did not tell you he had seen a dozen horses, when he had seen only two,—yet, as he professed not to value the truth when in the way of his advantage, (and there was nothing he thought more to his advantage than making you stare at him,) the persons who were liable to suffer from his incontinence, had all the right in the world to the benefit of this consideration.

His superstition was remarkable. I do not mean in the ordinary sense, because it was superstition, but because it was petty and old-womanish. He believed in the ill-luck of Fridays, and was seriously disconcerted if any thing was to be done on that frightful day of the week. Had he been a Roman, he would have startled at crows, while he made a jest of augurs. He used to tell a story of somebody's meeting him, while in Italy, in St. James's-street. The least and most childish of superstitions may, it is true, find subtle corners of warrant in the greatest minds; but as the highest pictures in Lord Byron's poetry were imitations, so in the smallest of his personal superstitions he was maintained by something not his own. His turn of mind was material egotism, and some remarkable experiences, had given it a compulsory twist the other way; but it never grew kindly or loftily in that quarter. Hence his taking refuge from uneasy thoughts, in sarcasm, and trifling, and notoriety. What there is of a good-natured philosophy in " Don Juan" was not foreign to his wishes; but it was the commonplace of the age, repeated with an air of discovery by the noble Lord, and as ready to be thrown in the teeth of those from whom he took it, provided any body laughed at them. His soul might well have been met in St. James's-street, for in the remotest of his poetical solitudes it was there. As to those who attribute the superstition of men of letters to infidelity, and then object to it for being inconsistent, because it is credulous, there is no greater inconsistency than their own ; for as it is the very essence of infidelity to doubt, so according to the nature it inhabits, it may as well doubt whether such and such things do not exist, as whether they do : whereas, on the other hand, belief in particular dogmas, by the very nature of its tie, is precluded from this uncertainty, perhaps at the expense of being more foolishly certain.

It has been thought by some, that there was madness in his composition. He himself talked sometimes as if he feared it would come upon him. It was difficult in his most serious moments, to separate what he spoke out of conviction, and what he said for effect. In moments of ill-health, especially when jaded and overwrought by the united effects of composition, and drinking, and sitting up, he might have had nervous misgivings to that effect ; as more people perhaps are accustomed to have, than choose to talk about it. But I never saw any thing more mad in his conduct, than what I have just been speaking of ; and there was enough in the nature of his position to account for extravagances in him, that would not have attained to that head under other circumstances. If every extravagance of which men are guilty, were to be pronounced madness, the world would be nothing but the Bedlam which some have called it ; and then the greatest madness of all would be the greatest rationality ; which, according to others, it is. There is no end to these desperate modes of settling and unsettling every thing at a jerk. There was great perversity and self-will in Lord Byron's composition. It arose from causes which it would do honour to the world's rationality to consider a little closer, and of which I shall speak presently. This it was, together with extravagant homage paid him, that pampered into so regal a size every inclination which he chose to give way to. But he did not take a hawk for a handsaw ; nor will the world think him deficient in brain. Perhaps he may be said to have had something, in little, of the madness which was brought upon the Roman emperors in great. His real pretensions were mixed up with imaginary ones, and circumstances contributed to give the whole a power, or at least a presence in the eyes of men, which his temperament was too feeble to manage properly. But it is not in the light of a madman that the world will ever seriously consider a man whose productions delight them, and whom they place in the rank of contributors to the stock of wit. It is not as the madman witty, but as the wit, injured by circumstances considered to be rational, that Lord Byron is to be regarded. If his wit indeed would not have existed without these circumstances, then it would only show us that the perversest things have a tendency to right themselves, or produce their ultimate downfal : and so far, I would as little deny that his Lordship had a spice of madness in him, as I deny that he had not every excuse for what was unpleasant in his composition ; which was none of his own making. So far, also, I would admit that a great part of the world are as mad as some have declared all the rest to be ; that is to say, that although they are rational enough to perform the common offices of life, and even to persuade the rest of mankind that their pursuits and passions are what they should be, they are in reality but half rational beings, contradicted in the very outset of existence, and dimly struggling through life with the perplexity sown within them.

To explain myself very freely. I look upon Lord Byron as an

excessive instance of what we see in hundreds of cases every day; namely, of the unhappy consequences of a parentage that ought never to have existed,—of the perverse and discordant humours of those who were the authors of his being. His father was a rake of the wildest description ; his mother a violent woman, very unfit to improve the offspring of such a person. She would vent her spleen by loading her child with reproaches ; and add, by way of securing their bad effect, that he would be as great a reprobate as his father. Thus did his parents embitter his nature : thus they embittered his memory of them, contradicted his beauty with deformity, and completed the mischances of his existence. Perhaps both of them had a goodness at heart, which had been equally perplexed. It is not that individuals are to blame, or that human nature is bad ; but that experience has not yet made it wise enough. Animal beauty they had at least a sense of. In this our poet was conceived ; but contradiction of all sorts was superadded, and he was born handsome, wilful, and lame. A happy childhood might have corrected his evil tendencies ; but he had it not ; and the upshot was, that he spent an uneasy over-excited life, and that society have got an amusing book or two by his misfortunes. The books may even help to counteract the spreading of such a misfortune ; and so far it may be better for society that he lived. But this is a rare case. Thousands of such mistakes are round about us, with nothing to show for them but complaint and unhappiness.

Lord Byron's face was handsome; eminently so in some respects. He had a mouth and chin fit for Apollo; and when I first knew him, there were both lightness and energy all over his aspect. But his countenance did not improve with age, and there were always some defects in it. The jaw was too big for the upper part. It had all the wilfulness of a despot in it. The animal predominated over the intellectual part of his head, inasmuch as the face altogether was large in proportion to the skull. The eyes also were set too near one another; and the nose, though handsome in itself, had the appearance when you saw it closely in front, of being grafted on the face, rather than growing properly out of it. His person was very handsome, though terminating in lameness, and tending to fat and effeminacy; which makes me remember what a hostile fair one objected to him, namely, that he had little beard; a fault which, on the other hand, was thought by another lady, not hostile, to add to the divinity of his aspect,—*imberbis Apollo.* His lameness was only in one foot, the left; and it was so little visible to casual notice, that as he lounged about a room (which he did in such a manner as to screen it) it was hardly perceivable. But it was a real and even a sore lameness. Much walking upon it fevered and hurt it. It was a shrunken foot, a little twisted. This defect unquestionably mortified him exceedingly, and helped to put sarcasm and misanthropy into his taste of life. Unfortunately, the usual thoughtlessness of schoolboys made him feel it bitterly at Harrow. He would wake, and find his leg in a tub of water. The reader will see in the correspondence at the end of this memoir, how he felt it, whenever it was libelled; and in Italy, the only time I ever knew it mentioned, he did not like the subject, and hastened to change it. His handsome person so far rendered the misfortune greater, as it pictured to him all the occasions on which he might have figured in the eyes of company; and doubtless this was a great reason, why he had no better address. On the other hand, instead of losing him any real regard or admiration, his lameness gave a touching character to both. Certainly no reader would have liked him, or woman loved him, the less, for the thought of this single contrast to his superiority.   But the very defect had taught him to be im-patient with deficiency.   Good God! when I think of these things, and of the common weaknesses of society, as at present constituted, I feel as if I could shed tears over the most willing of my resentments, much more over the most unwilling, and such as I never intended to speak of; nor could any thing have induced me to give a portrait of Lord Byron and his infirmities, if I had not been able to say at the end of it, that his faults were not his own, and that we must seek the causes of them in mistakes common to us all.   What is delightful to us in his writings will still remain so, if we are wise; and what ought not to be, will not only cease to be perilous, but be useful.   Faults which arise from an exuberant sociality, like those of Burns, may safely be left to them-selves.   They at once explain themselves by their natural candour, and carry an advantage with them; because any thing is advantageous in the long run to society, which tends to break up their selfishness.   But doc-trines, or half-doctrines, or whatever else they may be, which tend to throw individuals upon themselves, and overcast them at the same time with scorn and alienation, it is as well to see traced to their sources.   In comparing notes, humanity gets wise; and certainly the wiser it gets, it will not be the less modest or humane, whether it has to find fault, or to criticise the fault-finder.

I believe if any body could have done good to Lord Byron, it was Goethe and his correspondence.   It was a pity he did not live to have more of it.   Goethe might possibly have enabled him, as he wished he could, " to know himself," and do justice to the yearnings after the good and beautiful inseparable from the nature of genius.   But the danger was, that he would have been influenced as much by the rank and reputation of that great man, as by the reconciling nobleness of his philosophy; and personal intercourse with him would have spoilt all. Lord Byron's nature was mixed up with too many sophistications to receive a proper impression from any man: and he would have been jealous, if he once took it in his head that the other was thought to be his superior.

Lord Byron had no conversation, properly speaking. He could not interchange ideas or information with you, as a man of letters is expected to do. His thoughts required the concentration of silence and study to bring them to a head; and they deposited the amount in the shape of a stanza. His acquaintance with books was very circumscribed. The same personal experience, however, upon which he very properly drew for his authorship, might have rendered him a companion more interesting by far than men who could talk better; and the great reason why his conversation disappointed you was, not that he had not any thing to talk about, but that he was haunted with a perpetual affectation, and could not talk sincerely. It was by fits only that he spoke with any gravity, or made his extraordinary disclosures; and at no time did you well know what to believe. The rest was all quip and crank, not of the pleasantest kind, and equally distant from simplicity or wit. The best thing to say of it was, that he knew playfulness to be consistent with greatness; and the worst, that he thought every thing in him was great, even to his vulgarities.

Mr. Shelley said of him, that he never made you laugh to your own content. This, however, was said latterly, after my friend had been disappointed by a close intimacy. Mr. Shelley's opinion of his natural powers in every respect was great; and there is reason to believe, that Lord Byron never talked with any man to so much purpose as he did with him. He looked upon him as his most admiring listener; and probably was never less under the influence of affectation. If he could have got rid of this and his title, he would have talked like a man; not like a mere man of the town, or a great spoilt schoolboy. It is not to be concluded, that his jokes were not now and then very happy, or that admirers of his Lordship, who paid him visits, did not often go away more admiring. I am speaking of his conversation in general, and of the impression it made upon you, compared with what was to be expected from a man of wit and experience.

He had a delicate white hand, of which he was proud; and he attracted attention to it by rings. He thought a hand of this description almost the only mark remaining now-a-days of a gentleman; of which it certainly is not, nor of a lady either; though a coarse one implies handiwork. He often appeared holding a handkerchief, upon which his jewelled fingers lay imbedded, as in a picture. He was as fond of fine linen, as a quaker; and had the remnant of his hair oiled and trimmed with all the anxiety of a Sardanapalus.

The visible character to which this effeminacy gave rise appears to have indicated itself as early as his travels in the Levant, where the Grand Signior is said to have taken him for a woman in disguise. But he had tastes of a more masculine description. He was fond of swimming to the last, and used to push out to a good distance in the Gulf of Genoa. He was also, as I have before mentioned, a good horseman; and he liked to have a great dog or two about him, which is not a habit observable in timid men. Yet I doubt greatly whether he was a man of courage. I suspect, that personal anxiety, coming upon a constitution unwisely treated, had no small hand in hastening his death in Greece.

The story of his bold behaviour at sea in a voyage to Sicily, and of

Mr. Shelley's timidity, is just reversing what I conceive would have been the real state of the matter, had the voyage taken place. The account is an impudent fiction. Nevertheless, he volunteered voyages by sea, when he might have eschewed them: and yet the same man never got into a coach without being afraid. In short, he was the contradiction his father and mother had made him. To lump together some more of his personal habits, in the style of old Aubrey, he spelt affectedly, swore somewhat, had the Northumbrian burr in his speech, did not like to see women eat, and would merrily say that he had another reason for not liking to dine with them; which was, that they always had the wings of the chicken.

For the rest,

> " Ask you why *Byron* broke through every rule?
> 'Twas all for fear the knaves should call him fool."

He has added another to the list of the Whartons and Buckinghams, though his vices were in one respect more prudent, his genius greater, and his end a great deal more lucky. Perverse from his birth, educated under personal disadvantages, debauched by ill companions, and perplexed between real and false pretensions, the injuries done to his nature were completed by a success, too great even for the genius he possessed; and as his life was never so unfortunate as when it appeared to be most otherwise, so nothing could happen more seasonably for him, or give him what he would most have desired under any other circumstances, than his death.

NOTES

p. 167, l. 20: Marie-Henri Beyle (1783–1842) who wrote under the pseudonym Stendhal He met Byron in Switzerland, and left a jaundiced account of the poet.

p. 177, l. 25: Pierre Bayle (1647–1706) the famous French author of the *Dictionnaire Historique et Critique* (1695–7) – an enormously influential statement of philosophical and religious scepticism

Edward Gibbon (1737–94), the celebrated author of the *History of the Decline and Fall of the Roman Empire* (1776–88). Like Bayle, he was a sceptic who was no friend of the Church.

p. 181, l. 3: John Murray (1778–1843) was probably the most important publisher in the Romantic period. An enthusiastic and extremely intelligent Tory, his keen business sense exerted a tremendous but as yet uncharted influence on the course of British Romanticism. He remained Byron's publisher until the increasingly radical tone of *Don Juan* prompted the dissolution of the partnership.

p. 211, l. 11: Robert Southey (1774–1843) was one of the pre-eminent poets of his day. After his early radicalism had given way to a vehement Toryism he was made Poet Laureate in 1813, Walter Scott having declined the honour. His epic poems were read by most of the writers now regarded as the major romantics, and his work was a central constituent of Romanticism during the Regency period.

Thomas Medwin, *Journal of the Conversations of Lord Byron* (London, 1824)

Thomas Medwin, the second cousin of Percy Shelley, was born in Horsham in March 1788. He was educated at the same school as his cousin, and the two were friends as boys. Medwin was intended by his father for a career in law, but after an affair and a bout of reckless spending he decided instead for a military career, and signed up with the 24th Dragoon Guards. Between 1812 and 1819 he served in India, rising to the rank of Lieutenant but favouring the title of Captain as more decorous. On returning he retired on half pay and spent some time in Geneva, where he published his mediocre orientalist fantasy *Oswald and Edwin*, before moving to join Shelley in Pisa in October 1820. Having met both Trelawny and Edward Williams in India he played a key role in the creation of the so-called Pisan Circle, but his conversational talents were a poor match for the prevailing intellectual climate at Pisa, and he returned to Geneva, touring Italy on his way. In late 1821, however, a letter from Shelley to announce the arrival of Byron in Pisa brought Medwin dashing back. Within a few days the two men became friends, and Medwin spent some time riding and dining with Byron. He was quite bowled over by the great poet, and almost instantly appears to have conceived the idea of 'Boswellizing' Byron – although unfortunately for posterity he did not think it necessary to take immediate notes of his conversations, and on occasions failed to record what had been said for days or weeks. After the death of Byron Medwin married a rich Swiss Countess and ran rapidly through her fortune by adopting an extravagant lifestyle in Florence and speculating in a number of largely fake Italian paintings. When the money came to an end he abandoned his wife in Italy, moved back to England, and supported himself until his death by writing for the reviews. Besides the *Journal* his most notable work was *Ahasuerus, the Wanderer*, which he published in 1823 – a fantastic and unjustly neglected concoction of orientalist mythology which clearly shows the influence of both Byron and Shelley.

Like Trelawny, Medwin thought of himself during the time he knew Byron as a man of action rather than letters, and it was this side of him that appears to have appealed to the poet. Reading between the lines of the *Journal*, however, suggests him to have been the most accomplished sycophant that Byron met – Dallas in comparison was clumsy and obvious – and this seems to have compensated Byron in part for what even Shelley regarded as the dullness of Medwin's character. His accounts of Byron's conversations have traditionally been greeted with a great deal of scepticism. The appearance of the *Journal of the Conversations of Lord Byron* prompted Hobhouse to publish a pamphlet contradicting much of what Medwin claimed he had overheard Byron say, while the London papers castigated him for his representation of Byron's comments on his estranged wife. In this latter case, however, the fault may have been more readily attributable to his lack of discretion than to any fault of his memory. More seriously, however, Thomas Moore claimed 'I know more than half of the conversations to be downright forgeries'. And Byron's lifelong servant Fletcher told the poet's half-sister Augusta Leigh that the *Conversations* were 'a Mass of falsehoods Gleaned from one or a Nother, And no Conversation's of my Lord's.' Others, however, including Lady Caroline Lamb and Robert Southey (neither of whom should be treated as amongst the most reliable of character witnesses) thought Medwin was close to the mark in his portrayal of Byron. In fact Medwin's account may well be the most successful at recapturing the tone and the rhythms of Byron's speech. Medwin was a man of action – a man after Byron's own heart – and one who did not rely on the poet for charity; and he seems as a result to have approached Byron with a more open mind than many who – like Hunt or Dallas – had difficulty seeing far beyond their own sense of obligation to the poet. That said, there is no denying that Medwin was as caught up in the cult of Byronic hero-worship as anyone. He wrote in 1834 that poetry 'died with Byron, and is not likely to have a second resuscitation', and this is the point of view from which the *Journal* is written (see Marchand, XI, p. 236). His aim in writing the *Journal* is quite clear; it is to represent the character of Byron as he knew it (his own character, unusually for a memoirist of Byron, is kept firmly in the background) and to repair the damage done to history by the 'manifest injustice' of Thomas Moore's destruction of Byron's own memoirs (see the short 'Preface' to *The Journal of the Conversations of Lord Byron*, p. iii).

The *Journal of the Conversations of Lord Byron* was widely and instantly successful in its day, going through fifteen editions in six countries by 1842. Perhaps more than any other account of Byron's life it was responsible for creating the nineteenth-century view in Europe of the character of Byron, and on that basis alone it deserves its place here. Clearly the *Conversations* differ from the other memoirs in that they are not strictly speaking a memoir at all, but an account of Byron's conversations. In view of their importance, however, and also bearing in mind that they are not really a record but an imaginative reconstruction of Byron's character, they are well worth their place.

CONVERSATIONS,

&c.

I WENT to Italy late in the autumn of 1821, for the benefit of my health. Lord Byron, accompanied by Mr. Rogers as far as Florence, had passed on a few days before me, and was already at Pisa when I arrived.

His travelling equipage was rather a singular one, and afforded a strange catalogue for the *Dogana:* seven servants, five carriages, nine horses, a monkey, a bull-dog and a mastiff, two cats, three pea-fowls and some hens, (I do not know whether I have classed them in order of rank,) formed part of his live stock; these, and all his books, consisting of a very large library of modern

works, (for he bought all the best that came out,) together with a vast quantity of furniture, might well be
termed, with Cæsar, " impediments."

I had long formed a wish to see and be acquainted
with Lord Byron; but his known refusal at that time to
receive the visits of strangers, even of some who had
brought him letters of introduction from the most intimate friend he had, and a prejudice excited against his
own countrymen by a late insult, would have deterred
me from seeking an interview with him, had not the proposal come from himself, in consequence of his hearing
Shelley speak of me.

20th NOVEMBER.—" This is the Lung' Arno: he has
hired the Lanfranchi palace for a year.   It is one of those
marble piles that seem built for eternity, whilst the family
whose name it bears no longer exists," said Shelley, as
we entered a hall that seemed built for giants.   " I remember the lines in the Inferno," said I: " a Lanfranchi
was one of the persecutors of Ugolino."   " The same,"
answered Shelley; " you will see a picture of Ugolino
and his sons in his room.   Fletcher, his valet, is as
superstitious as his master, and says the house is haunted,

so that he cannot sleep for rumbling noises overhead, which he compares to the rolling of bowls. No wonder; old Lanfranchi's ghost is unquiet, and walks at night."

The palace was of such size, that Lord Byron only occupied the first floor; and at the top of the staircase leading to it was the English bull-dog, whose chain was long enough to guard the door, and prevent the entrance of strangers; he, however, knew Shelley, growled, and let us pass. In the anti-room we found several servants in livery, and Fletcher, (whom Shelley mentioned, and of whom I shall have occasion to speak,) who had been in his service from the time he left Harrow. " Like many old servants, he is a privileged person," whispered Shelley. " Don Juan had not a better Leporello, for imitating his master. He says that he is a Laurel struck by a *Metre*, and when in Greece remarked upon one of the bas-reliefs of the Parthenon, ' La! what mantel-pieces these would make, my Lord!' " When we were announced, we found his Lordship writing. His reception was frank and kind; he took me cordially by the hand, and said:

" You are a relation and schoolfellow of Shelley's—we " do not meet as strangers—you must allow me to con-

" tinue my letter on account of the post. Here's some-
" thing for you to read, Shelley, (giving him part of
" his MS. of 'Heaven and Earth;') tell me what you
" think of it."

During the few minutes that Lord Byron was finishing
his letter, I took an opportunity of narrowly observing
him, and drawing his portrait in my mind.* Thorwaldsen's bust is too thin-necked and young for Lord Byron.
None of the engravings gave me the least idea of him.

---

* Being with him, day after day, some time afterwards, whilst he
was sitting to Bertolini, the Florentine sculptor, for his bust, I had
an opportunity of analyzing his features more critically, but found
nothing to alter in my portrait. Bertolini's is an admirable likeness,
at least was so in the clay model. I have not seen it since it was
copied in marble, nor have I got a cast; he promised Bertolini should
send me one. Lord Byron prided himself on his neck; and it must
be confessed that his head was worthy of being placed on it. Bertolini destroyed his *ébauches* more than once before he could please
himself. When he had finished, Lord Byron said,

" It is the last time I sit to sculptor or painter."

This was on the 4th of January, 1822.

I saw a man of about five feet seven or eight, apparently forty years of age: as was said of Milton, he barely escaped being short and thick. His face was fine, and the lower part symmetrically moulded; for the lips and chin had that curved and definite outline that distinguishes Grecian beauty. His forehead was high, and his temples broad; and he had a paleness in his complexion, almost to wanness. His hair, thin and fine, had almost become grey, and waved in natural and graceful curls over his head, that was assimilating itself fast to the "bald first Cæsar's." He allowed it to grow longer behind than it is accustomed to be worn, and at that time had mustachios, which were not sufficiently dark to be becoming. In criticising his features it might, perhaps, be said that his eyes were placed too near his nose, and that one was rather smaller than the other; they were of a greyish brown, but of a peculiar clearness, and when animated possessed a fire which seemed to look through and penetrate the thoughts of others, while they marked the inspirations of his own. His teeth were small, regular, and white; these, I afterwards found, he took great pains to preserve.*

---

* For this purpose he used tobacco when he first went into the open air; and he told me he was in the habit of grinding his teeth in

I expected to discover that he had a club, perhaps a *cloven* foot; but it would have been difficult to have distinguished one from the other, either in size or in form.

On the whole, his figure was manly, and his countenance handsome and prepossessing, and very expressive; and the familiar ease of his conversation soon made me perfectly at home in his society. Our first interview was marked with a cordiality and confidence that flattered while it delighted me; and I felt anxious for the next day, in order that I might repeat my visit.

When I called on his Lordship at two o'clock, he had just left his bed-room, and was at breakfast, if it can be called one. It consisted of a cup of strong green tea, without milk or sugar, and an egg, of which he ate the yolk raw. I observed the abstemiousness of his meal.

" My digestion is weak; I am too bilious," said he, " to " eat more than once a-day, and generally live on vegeta-

_____

his sleep, to prevent which he was forced to put a napkin between them.

" bles.   To be sure, I drink two bottles of wine at dinner,
" but they form only a vegetable diet.   Just now I live on
" claret and soda-water.   You are just come from Geneva,
" Shelley tells me.   I passed the best part of the summer
" of 1816 at the Campagna Diodati, and was very nearly
" passing this last there.   I went so far as to write to
" Hentsh the banker; but Shelley, when he came to visit
" me at Ravenna, gave me such a flattering account of
" Pisa that I changed my mind.   Then it is troublesome
" to travel so far with so much live and dead stock as I do ;
" and I don't like to leave behind me any of my pets that
" have been accumulating since I came on the Continent.*
" One cannot trust to strangers to take care of them.   You
" will see at the farmer's some of my pea-fowls *en pension*.
" Fletcher tells me that they are almost as bad fellow-tra-
" vellers as the monkey †, which I will shew you."

---

* He says afterwards in " Don Juan," canto X, stanza 50 :

> ———" He had a kind of inclination, or
> Weakness, for what most people deem mere vermin,
> Live animals."

† He afterwards bought another monkey in Pisa, in the street,
because he saw it ill-used.

Here he led the way to a room, where, after playing with and caressing the creature for some time, he proposed a game of billiards.

I brought the conversation back on Switzerland and his travels, and asked him if he had been in Germany?

" No," said he, " not even at Trieste. I hate despot-
" ism and the Goths too much. I have travelled little
" on the Continent, at least never gone out of my way.
" This is partly owing to the indolence of my disposition,
" partly owing to my incumbrances. I had some idea, when
" at Rome, of visiting Naples, but was at that time anxious
" to get back to Venice. But Pæstum cannot surpass the
" ruins of Agrigentum, which I saw by moonlight ; nor
" Naples, Constantinople. You have no conception of
" the beauty of the twelve islands where the Turks have
" their country-houses, or of the blue Symplegades
" against which the Bosphorus beats with such resistless
" violence.

" Switzerland is a country I have been satisfied with
" seeing once ; Turkey I could live in for ever. I never
" forget my predilections. I was in a wretched state of

" health, and worse spirits, when I was at Geneva; but
" quiet and the lake, physicians better than Polidori, soon
" set me up. I never led so moral a life as during my
" residence in that country; but I gained no credit by
" it. Where there is a mortification, there ought to be
" reward. On the contrary, there is no story so absurd
" that they did not invent at my cost. I was watched by
" glasses on the opposite side of the Lake, and by glasses
" too that must have had very distorted optics. I was
" waylaid in my evening drives—I was accused of cor-
" rupting all the *grisettes* in the Rue Basse. I believe
" that they looked upon me as a man-monster, worse
" than the *piqueur.*

" Somebody possessed Madame de Staël with an opinion
" of my immorality. I used occasionally to visit her at
" Coppet; and once she invited me to a family-dinner,
" and I found the room full of strangers, who had come
" to stare at me as at some outlandish beast in a raree-
" show. One of the ladies fainted, and the rest looked
" as if his Satanic Majesty had been among them. Ma-
" dame de Staël took the liberty to read me a lecture
" before this crowd; to which I only made her a low
" bow.

" I knew very few of the Genevese. Hentsh was very
" civil to me; and I have a great respect for Sismondi.
" I was forced to return the civilities of one of their Pro-
" fessors by asking him, and an old gentleman, a friend
" of Gray's, to dine with me. I had gone out to sail
" early in the morning, and the wind prevented me from
" returning in time for dinner. I understand that I offend-
" ed them mortally. Polidori did the honours.

" Among our countrymen I made no new acquaintances;
" Shelley, Monk Lewis, and Hobhouse were almost the
" only English people I saw. No wonder; I shewed a
" distaste for society at that time, and went little among
" the Genevese; besides, I could not speak French.
" What is become of my boatman and boat? I suppose
" she is rotten; she was never worth much. When I
" went the tour of the Lake in her with Shelley and
" Hobhouse, she was nearly wrecked near the very spot
" where St. Preux and Julia were in danger of being
" drowned. It would have been classical to have been
" lost there, but not so agreeable. Shelley was on the
" Lake much oftener than I, at all hours of the night and
" day: he almost lived on it; his great rage is a boat.
" We are both building now at Genoa, I a yacht, and
" he an open boat."

We played at billiards till the carriage was announced, and I accompanied him in his drive. Soon after we got off the stones, we mounted our horses, which were waiting for us. Lord Byron is an admirable horseman, combining grace with the security of his seat. He prides himself much on this exercise. He conducted us for some miles till we came to a farm-house, where he practises pistol-firing every evening. This is his favourite amusement, and may indeed be called almost a pursuit. He always has pistols in his holster, and eight or ten pair by the first makers in London carried by his courier. We had each twelve rounds of ammunition, and in a diameter of four inches he put eleven out of twelve shots. I observed his hand shook exceedingly. He said that when he first began at Manton's he was the worst shot in the world, and Manton was perhaps the best. The subject turned upon duelling, and he contended for its necessity, and quoted some strong arguments in favour of it.

" I have been concerned," said he, " in many duels as " second, but only in two as principal; one was with " Hobhouse before I became intimate with him. The " best marksmen at a target are not the surest in the " field. Cecil's and Stackpoole's affair proved this. They

" fought after a quarrel of three years, during which they
" were practising daily. Stackpoole was so good a shot
" that he used to cut off the heads of the fowls for dinner
" as they drank out of the coops about. He had every
" wish to kill his antagonist, but he received his death-
" blow from Cecil, who fired rather fine, or rather was the
" quickest shot of the two. All he said when falling was,
" ' D——n it, have I missed him ?' Shelley is a much
" better shot than I am, but he is thinking of metaphysics
" rather than of firing."

I understand that Lord Byron is always in better spirits
after having *culped* (as he calls it) the targe often, or hit a
five-franc piece, the counterpart of which is always given
to the farmer, who is making a little fortune. All the
pieces struck, Lord Byron keeps to put, as he says, in his
museum.

We now continued our ride, and returned to Pisa by the
Lucca gate.

" Pisa with its hanging tower and Sophia-like dome re-
" minds me," said Lord Byron, " of an eastern place."

He then remarked the heavy smoke that rolled away from the city, spreading in the distance a vale of mist, through which the golden clouds of evening appeared.

" It is fine," said Lord Byron, " but no sunsets are to be " compared with those of Venice. They are too gorgeous " for any painter, and defy any poet. My rides, indeed, " would have been nothing without the Venetian sunsets. " Ask Shelley."

" Stand on the marble bridge," said Shelley, " cast your eye, if you are not dazzled, on its river glowing as with fire, then follow the graceful curve of the palaces on the Lung' Arno till the arch is naved by the massy dungeon-tower (erroneously called Ugolino's), forming in dark relief, and tell me if any thing can surpass a sunset at Pisa."

The history of one, is that of almost every day. It is impossible to conceive a more unvaried life than Lord Byron led at this period. I continued to visit him at the same hour daily. Billiards, conversation, or reading, filled up the intervals till it was time to take our evening drive, ride, and pistol-practice. On our return, which was always in the same direction, we frequently met the Countess Guiccioli, with whom he stopped to converse a few minutes.

He dined at half an hour after sunset, (at twenty-four o'clock); then drove to Count Gamba's, the Countess Guiccioli's father, passed several hours in her society, returned to his palace, and either read or wrote till two or three in the morning; occasionally drinking spirits diluted with water as a medicine, from a dread of a nephritic complaint, to which he was, or fancied himself, subject. Such was his life at Pisa.

The Countess Guiccioli is twenty-three years of age, though she appears no more than seventeen or eighteen. Unlike most of the Italian women, her complexion is delicately fair. Her eyes, large, dark, and languishing, are shaded by the longest eyelashes in the world; and her hair, which is ungathered on her head, plays over her falling shoulders in a profusion of natural ringlets of the darkest auburn. Her figure is, perhaps, too much *embonpoint* for her height, but her bust is perfect; her features want little of possessing a Grecian regularity of outline; and she has the most beautiful mouth and teeth imaginable. It is impossible to see without admiring—to hear the Guiccioli speak without being fascinated. Her amiability and gentleness shew themselves in every intonation of her voice, which, and the music of her perfect Italian, give a peculiar charm to every thing she utters. Grace and elegance seem component parts of her nature. Notwithstanding that she adores Lord Byron, it is evident that the exile and poverty of her aged father sometimes affect her spirits, and throw a shade of melancholy on her countenance, which adds to the deep interest this lovely girl creates.

" Extraordinary pains," said Lord Byron one day, " were " taken with the education of Teresa. Her conversation is " lively, without being frivolous ; without being learned, she " has read all the best authors of her own and the French " language. She often conceals what she knows, from the " fear of being thought to know too much; possibly because " she knows I am not fond of blues. To use an expression " of Jeffrey's, ' If she has blue stockings, she contrives that " her petticoat shall hide them.' "

☆ ★ ☆

" Harrow," said he, " has been the nursery of almost
" all the politicians of the day."

" I wonder," said I, " that you have never had the ambition of being one too."

" I take little interest," replied he, " in the politics at
" home.   I am not made for what you call a politician,
" and should never have adhered to any party.*   I should
" have taken no part in the petty intrigues of cabinets,
" or the pettier factions and contests for power among
" parliamentary men.   Among our statesmen, Castlereagh

---

* " The consequence of being of no party,
  I shall offend all parties.   Never mind ! "

     Don Juan, Canto IX. Stanza 26.

" is almost the only one whom I have attacked; the only
" public character whom I thoroughly detest, and against
" whom I will never cease to level the shafts of my political
" hate.

" I only addressed the House twice, and made little
" impression. They told me that my manner of speak-
" ing was not dignified enough for the Lords, but was
" more calculated for the Commons. I believe it was a
" Don Juan kind of speech. The two occasions were,
" the Catholic Question,* and (I think he said) some Man-
" chester affair.

" Perhaps, if I had never travelled,—never left my own
" country young,—my views would have been more limited.
" They extend to the good of mankind in general—of the
" world at large. Perhaps the prostrate situation of Por-
" tugal and Spain—the tyranny of the Turks in Greece—

---

* A gentleman who was present at his maiden speech, on the
Catholic question, says, that the Lords left their seats and gathered
round him in a circle; a proof, at least, of the interest which he excited: and that the same style was attempted in the Commons the
next day, but failed.

" the oppressions of the Austrian Government at Venice—
" the mental debasement of the Papal States, (not to men-
" tion Ireland,)—tended to inspire me with a love of liberty.
" No Italian could have rejoiced more than I, to have seen
" a Constitution established on this side the Alps. I felt
" for Romagna as if she had been my own country, and
" would have risked my life and fortune for her, as I may
" yet for the Greeks.* I am become a citizen of the world.
" There is no man I envy so much as Lord Cochrane.
" His entrance into Lima, which I see announced in to-
" day's paper, is one of the great events of the day. Mauro-
" cordato, too, (whom you know so well,) is also worthy of

---

*   " And I will war, at least in words, (and—should
         My chance so happen,—deeds) with all who war
         With Thought. And of thought's foes by far most rude
         Tyrants and Sycophants have been and are.
         I know not who may conquer: if I could
         Have such a prescience, it should be no bar
         To this my plain, sworn, downright detestation
         Of every despotism in every nation !"

                              Don Juan, Canto IX. Stanza 24.

" the best times of Greece. Patriotism and virtue are not
" quite extinct."

I told him that I thought the finest lines he had ever
written were his " Address to Greece," beginning—

" Land of the unforgotten brave !"

" I should be glad," said he, " to think that I have added
" a spark to the flame.* I love Greece, and take the
" strongest interest in her struggle."

" I did not like," said I, " the spirit of Lambrino's ode ;
it was too desponding."

" That song," replied he, " was written many years ago,
" though published only yesterday. Times are much
" changed since then. I have learned to think very diffe-
" rently of the cause,—at least of its success. I look upon
" the Morea as secure. There is more to be apprehended

---

* " But words are things ;—and a small drop of ink,
" Falling, like dew, upon a thought, produces
" That which makes thousands, perhaps millions, think."

Don Juan, Canto III. Stanza 88.

" from friends than foes. Only keep the Vandals out of it;
" they would be like the Goths here."

" What do you think of the Turkish power," I asked,
" and of their mode of fighting?"

" The Turks are not so despicable an enemy as people
" suppose. They have been carrying on a war with Rus-
" sia, or rather Russia with them, since Peter the Great's
" time;—and what have they lost, till lately, of any import-
" ance? In 1788 they gained a victory over the Austrians,
" and were very nearly making the Emperor of Austria
" prisoner, though his army consisted of 80,000 men.

" They beat us in Egypt, and took one of our Generals.
" Their mode of fighting is not unformidable. Their ca-
" valry falls very little short of ours, and is better mounted
" —their horses better managed. Look, for instance,
" at the Arab the Turkish Prince here rides!— They
" are divided into parties of sixty, with a flag or stand-
" ard to each. They come down, discharge their pieces,
" and are supplied by another party; and so on in suc-
" cession. When they charge, it is by troops, like our
" successive squadrons."

" I reminded you," said I, " the other day of having said, in ' Childe Harold,' that the Greeks would have to fight their own battles,—work out their own emancipation. That was your prophetic age; Voltaire and Alfieri had theirs, and even Goldsmith."

Shelley, who was present, observed :—" Poets are sometimes the echoes of words of which they know not the power,—the trumpet that sounds to battle, and feels not what it inspires."

" In what year was it," I asked, " that you wrote that line,

" ' Will Frank or Muscovite assist you ?—No !' "

" Some time in 1811. The ode was written about the " same time. I expressed the same sentiments in one of " its stanzas.*

---

* The lines to which he alluded were—

" Trust not for freedom to the Franks ;
They have a King who buys and sells :

" I will tell you a plan I have in embryo. I have formed
" a strong wish to join the Greeks. Gamba is anxious to
" be of the party. I shall not, however, leave Italy with-
" out proper authority and full power from the Patriot
" Government. I mean to write to them, and that will
" take time ;—besides, the Guiccioli !*"

" In native swords and native ranks,
The only hope of freedom dwells !"

Don Juan, Canto III. page 51.

* I have heard Lord Byron reproached for leaving the Guiccioli.
Her brother's accompanying him to Greece, and his remains to England, prove at least that the family acquitted him of any blame. The
disturbed state of the country rendered her embarking with him out
of the question ; and the confiscation of her father's property made
her jointure, and his advanced age her care, necessary to him.—It
required all Lord Byron's interest with the British Envoy, as well
as his own guarantee, to protect the Gambas at Genoa. But his own
house at length ceased to be an asylum for them, and they were
banished the Sardinian States a month before he sailed for Leghorn ;
whence, after laying in the supplies for his voyage, he directed his
fatal course to the Morea.

" I have received," said he, " from my sister, a lock of
" Napoleon's hair, which is of a beautiful black. If Hunt
" were here, we should have half-a-dozen sonnets on it. It
" is a valuable present; but, according to my Lord Carlisle,
" I ought not to accept it. I observe, in the newspapers of
" the day, some lines of his Lordship's, advising Lady
" Holland not to have any thing to do with the snuff-box
" left her by Napoleon, for fear that horror and murder
" should jump out of the lid every time it is opened! It is
" a most ingenious idea—I give him great credit for it."

He then read me the first stanza, laughing in his usual
suppressed way,—

" Lady, reject the gift," &c.

and produced in a few minutes the following parody on it:

" Lady, accept the box a hero wore,
    In spite of all this elegiac stuff:
Let not seven stanzas written by a bore,
    Prevent your Ladyship from taking snuff!"

" When will my wise relation leave off verse-inditing?"
said he. "I believe, of all manias, authorship is the most

" inveterate.   He might have learned by this time, indeed
" many years ago, (but people never learn any thing by ex-
" perience,) that he had mistaken his *forte*.   There was
" an epigram, which had some logic in it, composed on the
" occasion of his Lordship's doing two things in one day,—
" subscribing 1000*l*. and publishing a sixpenny pamphlet!
" It was on the state of the theatre, and dear enough at
" the money.   The epigram I think I can remember :

> ' Carlisle subscribes a thousand pound
>
>   Out of his rich domains ;
>
>   And for a sixpence circles round
>
>   The produce of his brains.
>
>   'Tis thus the difference you may hit
>
>   Between his fortune and his wit.'

" A man who means to be a poet should do, and should
" have done all his life, nothing else but make verses.
" There 's Shelley has more poetry in him than any man
" living ; and if he were not so mystical, and would not write
" Utopias and set himself up as a Reformer, his right to
" rank as a poet, and very highly too, could not fail of being
" acknowledged.   I said what I thought of him the other
" day ; and all who are not blinded by bigotry must think

" the same. The works he wrote at seventeen are much
" more extraordinary than Chatterton's at the same age."

A question was started, as to which he considered the
easiest of all metres in our language.

" Or rather," replied he, " you mean, which is the least
" difficult? I have spoken of the fatal facility of the octo-
" syllabic metre. The Spenser stanza is difficult, because
" it is like a sonnet, and the finishing line must be good.
" The couplet is more difficult still, because the last line,
" or one out of two, must be good. But blank verse is the
" most difficult of all, because every line must be good."

" You might well say then," I observed, " that no man
can be a poet who does any thing else."

During our evening ride the conversation happened to
turn upon the rival Reviews.

" I know no two men," said he, " who have been so infa-
" mously treated, as Shelley and Keats. If I had known

" that Milman had been the author of that article on ' The
" Revolt of Islam,' I would never have mentioned ' Fazio'
" among the plays of the day,—and scarcely know why
" I paid him the compliment. In consequence of the
" shameless personality of that and another number of
" ' The Quarterly,' every one abuses Shelley,—his name is
" coupled with every thing that is opprobrious: but he is
" one of the most moral as well as amiable men I know.
" I have now been intimate with him for years, and every
" year has added to my regard for him.—Judging from
" Milman, Christianity would appear a bad religion for a
" poet, and not a very good one for a man. His ' Siege of
" Jerusalem' is one *cento* from Milton; and in style and
" language he is evidently an imitator of the very man
" whom he most abuses. No one has been puffed like
" Milman: he owes his extravagant praise to Heber.
" These Quarterly Reviewers scratch one another's backs
" at a prodigious rate. Then as to Keats, though I am
" no admirer of his poetry, I do not envy the man, who-
" ever he was, that attacked and killed him. Except a
" couplet of Dryden's,

' On his own bed of torture let him lie,
Fit garbage for the hell-hound infamy,'

" I know no lines more cutting than those in ' Adonais,' *
" or more feeling than the whole elegy.

" As Keats is now gone, we may speak of him. I am
" always battling with *the Snake* about Keats, and wonder
" what he finds to make a god of, in that idol of the
" Cockneys : besides, I always ask Shelley why he does
" not follow his style, and make himself one of the school,
" if he think it so divine. He will, like me, return some
" day to admire Pope, and think ' The Rape of the Lock'
" and its sylphs worth fifty ' Endymions,' with their faun
" and satyr machinery.   I remember Keats somewhere
" says that ' flowers would not blow, leaves bud,' &c. if
" man and woman did not kiss.   How sentimental !

---

* The lines to which he referred were these:—

" Expect no heavier chastisement from me,
  But ever at thy season be thou free
  To spill their venom when thy fangs o'erflow.
  Remorse and self-contempt shall cling to thee ;
  Hot shame shall burn upon thy Cain-like brow,
  And like a beaten hound tremble thou shalt as now."

Adonais.

I remarked that ' Hyperion' was a fine fragment, and a proof of his poetical genius.

" ' Hyperion!'" said he : " why, a man might as well pre-
" tend to be rich who had one diamond. ' Hyperion' indeed!
" ' Hyperion ' to a satyr! Why, there is a fine line in Lord
" Thurlow (looking to the West that was gloriously golden
" with the sunset) which I mean to borrow some day :
          ' And all that gorgeous company of clouds ' —
" Do you think they will suspect me of taking from Lord
" Thurlow ? "

Speaking to him of ' Lalla Rookh,' he said :

" Moore did not like my saying that I could never
" attempt to describe the manners or scenery of a country
" that I had not visited. Without this it is almost im-
" possible to adhere closely to costume. Captain Ellis once
" asked him if he had ever been in Persia. If he had, he
" would not have made his Parsee guilty of such a profanity.
" It was an Irishism to make a Gheber die by fire."

" I have been reading," said I, "' The Lusiad,' and some
of Camoens' smaller poems. Why did Lord Strangford call
his beautiful Sonnets, &c. translations? "

" Because he wrote," said Lord Byron, " in order to get
" the situation at the Brazils, and did not know a word of
" Portuguese when he commenced."

" Moore was suspected of assisting his Lordship," said I.
" Was that so ? "

" I am told not," said Lord Byron. " They are great
" friends ; and when Moore was in difficulty about the
" Bermuda affair, in which he was so hardly used, Lord
" Strangford offered to give him 500*l*. ; but Moore had too
" much independence to lay himself under an obligation.
" I know no man I would go further to serve than Moore.

" ' The Fudge Family' pleases me as much as any of his
" works. The letter which he versified at the end was
" given him by Douglas Kinnaird and myself, and was
" addressed by the Life-guardsman, after the battle of
" Waterloo, to Big Ben. Witty as Moore's epistle is, it
" falls short of the original. 'Doubling up the *Mounseers*
" in brass,' is not so energetic an expression as was used by
" our hero,—all the alliteration is lost.

" Moore is one of the few writers who will survive the

" age in which he so deservedly flourishes. He will live in
" his ' Irish Melodies ; ' they will go down to posterity with
" the music ; both will last as long as Ireland, or as music
" and poetry."

———————————

I took leave of Lord Byron on the 15th of March, to
visit Rome for a few weeks. Shortly after my departure
an affray happened at Pisa, the particulars of which were
variously stated. The *Courier François* gave the following account of it:—

" A superior officer went to Lord Byron a few days ago.
A very warm altercation, the reason of which was unknown,
occurred between this officer and the English poet. The
threats of the officer became so violent, that Lord Byron's
servant ran to protect his master. A struggle ensued, in
which the officer was struck with a poniard by the servant,
and died instantly. The servant fled."

This was one among many reports that were circulated at
Rome, to which I was forced one day to give a somewhat
flat contradiction. But the real truth of the story cannot
be better explained than by the depositions before the

Governor of Pisa, the copies of which were sent me, and are in my possession.*   They state that

"Lord Byron, in company with Count Gamba, Captain Hay, Mr. Trelawney, and Mr. Shelley, was returning from his usual ride, on the 21st March, 1822, and was perhaps a quarter of a mile from the Piaggia gate, when a man on horseback, in a hussar uniform, dashed at full speed through the midst of the party, violently jostling (*urtando*) one of them.   Shocked at such ill-breeding, Lord Byron pushed forward, and all the rest followed him, and pulled up their horses on overtaking the hussar.   His Lordship then asked him what he meant by the insult?   The hussar, for first and only answer, began to abuse him in the grossest manner; on which Lord Byron and one of his companions drew out a card with their names and address, and passed on.   The hussar followed, vociferating and threatening, with his hand on his sabre, that he would draw it, as he had often done, effectually.   They were now about ten paces from the Piaggia gate.   Whilst this altercation was going on, a common soldier of the artillery interfered, and called out to the hussar, ' Why don't you arrest them?   Com-

---

* See the Appendix for the original depositions.

mand us to arrest them!' Upon which the hussar gave the word to the guard at the gate, ' Arrest—arrest them!' still continuing the same threatening gestures, and using language, if possible, more offensive and insulting.

" His Lordship, hearing the order given for their arrest, spurred on his horse, and one of the party did the same; and they succeeded in forcing their way through the soldiers, who flew to their muskets and bayonets, whilst the gate was closed on the rest, together with the courier, who was foremost.

" Mr. Trelawney now found his horse seized by the bridle by two soldiers, with their swords drawn, and himself furiously assaulted by the hussar, who made several cuts at him with his sabre, whilst the soldiers struck him about the thighs. He and his companions were all unarmed, and asked this madman the reason of his conduct; but his only reply was blows.

" Mr. Shelley received a sabre-stroke on the head, which threw him off his horse. Captain Hay, endeavouring to parry a blow with a stick that he used as a whip, the edge of the weapon cut it in two, and he received a wound on his nose. The courier also suffered severely from several thrusts he received from the hussar and the rest of the soldiers. After all this, the hussar spurred on his horse, and took the road to the Lung' Arno.

" When his Lordship reached the palace, he gave directions to his secretary to give immediate information to the police of what was going on; and, not seeing his companions come up, turned back towards the gate. On the way he met the hussar, who rode up to him, saying, ' Are you satisfied ?' His Lordship, who knew nothing or hardly any thing of the affray that had taken place at the gate, answered, 'No, I am not! Tell me your name!'—' Serjeant-Major Masi,' said he. One of his Lordship's servants came up at the moment, and laid hold of the bridle of the Serjeant's horse. His Lordship commanded him to let it go; when the Serjeant spurred his horse, and rushed through an immense crowd collected before the Lanfranchi palace, where, as he deposes, he was wounded and his *chaco* found, but how or by whom they knew not, seeing that they were either in the rear or in their way home. They had further to depose that Captain Hay was confined to his house by reason of his wound; also that the courier had spit blood from the thrust he received in the breast, as might be proved by the evidence of the surgeons."

There was also another deposition from a Mr. James Crawford. It stated that " the dragoon would have drawn his sabre against Lord Byron, in the Lung' Arno, had it not been for the interposition of the servant; and that Signor Major Masi was knocked off his horse as he galloped past the Lanfranchi palace, Lord Byron and his servants being at a considerable distance therefrom at the time."

It appears that Signor Major Masi was wounded with a pitchfork, and his life was for some time in danger; but it was never known by whom the wound had been given. One of the Countess's servants, and two of Lord Byron's, were arrested and imprisoned. It was suspected by the police that, being Italians and much attached to their master,* they had revenged his quarrel; but no proof was adduced to justify the suspicion.

---

* Lord Byron was the best of masters, and was perfectly adored by his servants. His kindness was extended even to their children. He liked them to have their families with them : and I remember one day, as we were entering the hall after our ride, meeting a little boy, of three or four years old, of the coachman's, whom he took up in his arms and presented with a ten-Paul piece.

During the time that the examination was taking place before the police, Lord Byron's house was beset by the dragoons belonging to Signor Major Masi's troop, who were on the point of forcing open the doors, but they were too well guarded within to dread the attack. Lord Byron, however, took his ride as usual two days after.

" It is not the first time," said he, " that my house has " been a *bender,* and may not be the last."

All Lord Byron's servants were banished from Pisa, and with them the Counts Gamba, father and son.

Lord Byron was himself advised to leave it; and as the Countess accompanied her father, he soon after joined them at Leghorn, and passed six weeks at Monte Nero. His return to Pisa was occasioned by a new persecution of the Gambas. An order was issued for them to leave the Tuscan States in four days; and on their embarkation for Genoa, the Countess and himself took up their residence (for the first time together) at the Lanfranchi palace where Leigh Hunt and his family had already arrived.

———————————

☆ ★ ☆

" Since you left us," said Lord Byron, " I have seen
" Hobhouse for a few days. Hobhouse is the oldest and
" the best friend I have. What scenes we have witnessed
" together ! Our friendship began at Cambridge. We
" led the same sort of life in town, and travelled in com-
" pany a great part of the years 1809, 10, and 11. He
" was present at my marriage, and was with me in 1816,
" after my separation. We were at Venice, and visited
" Rome together, in 1817. The greater part of my
" ' Childe Harold' was composed when we were together,
" and I could do no less in gratitude than dedicate the

" complete poem to him. The First Canto was inscribed
" to one of the most beautiful little creatures I ever saw,
" then a mere child: Lady Charlotte Harleigh was my
" Ianthe.

" Hobhouse's Dissertation on Italian literature is much
" superior to his Notes on 'Childe Harold.' Perhaps he
" understood the antiquities better than Nibbi, or any of
" the Cicerones; but the knowledge is somewhat mis-
" placed where it is. Shelley went to the opposite ex-
" treme, and never made any notes.

" Hobhouse has an excellent heart: he fainted when he
" heard a false report of my death in Greece, and was
" wonderfully affected at that of Matthews—a much more
" able man than the *Invalid*. You have often heard me
" speak of him. The tribute I paid to his memory was a
" very inadequate one, and ill expressed what I felt at
" his loss."

It may be asked *when* Lord Byron writes. The same
question was put to Madame de Staël: " *Vous ne comptez
pas sur ma chaise-à-porteur,*" said she. I am often with him

from the time he gets up till two or three o'clock in the morning, and after sitting up so late he must require rest ; but he produces, the next morning, proofs that he has not been idle. Sometimes when I call, I find him at his desk ; but he either talks as he writes, or lays down his pen to play at billiards till it is time to take his airing. He seems to be able to resume the thread of his subject at all times, and to weave it of an equal texture. Such talent is that of an *improvisatore*. The fairness too of his manuscripts (I do not speak of the handwriting) astonishes no less than the perfection of every thing he writes. He hardly ever alters a word for whole pages, and never corrects a line in subsequent editions. I do not believe that he has ever read his works over since he examined the proof-sheets ; and yet he remembers every word of them, and every thing else worth remembering that he has ever known.

I never met with any man who shines so much in conversation. He shines the more, perhaps, for not seeking to shine. His ideas flow without effort, without his having occasion to think. As in his letters, he is not nice about expressions or words ; — there are no concealments in him, no injunctions to secresy. He tells every thing that he has thought or done without the least reserve, and as if he wished the whole world to know it; and does not throw the slightest gloss over his errors. Brief himself, he is impatient of diffuseness in others, hates long stories, and seldom repeats his own. If he has heard a story you are telling, he will say, " You told me that," and with good humour sometimes finish it for you himself.

He hates argument, and never argues for victory. He gives every one an opportunity of sharing in the conversation, and has the art of turning it to subjects that may bring out the person with whom he converses. He never shews the author, prides himself most on being a man of the world and of fashion, and his anecdotes of life and living characters are inexhaustible. In spirits, as in every thing else, he is ever in extremes.

Miserly in trifles—about to lavish his whole fortune on the Greeks; to-day diminishing his stud—to-morrow taking a large family under his roof, or giving 1000*l.* for a yacht;*

---

* He sold it for 300*l.* and refused to give the sailors their jackets; and offered once to bet Hay that he would live on 60*l.* a-year!

dining for a few Pauls when alone,—spending hundreds when he has friends. " *Nil fuit unquam sic impar sibi.*"

I am sorry to find that he has become more indolent. He has almost discontinued his rides on horseback, and has starved himself into an unnatural thinness; and his digestion is become weaker. In order to keep up the stamina that he requires, he indulges somewhat too freely in wine, and in his favourite beverage, Hollands, of which he now drinks a pint almost every night.

He said to me humorously enough—

" Why don't you drink, Medwin ? Gin-and-water is the " source of all my inspiration. If you were to drink as " much as I do, you would write as good verses: depend " on it, it is the true Hippocrene."

On the 28th of August I parted from Lord Byron with increased regret, and a sadness that looked like presentiment. He was preparing for his journey to Genoa, whither he went a few days after my departure. I shall,

I hope, be excused in presenting the public with the following sketch of his character, drawn and sent to a friend a few weeks after his death, and to which I adapted the following motto :*

Αστηρ πριν μεν ελαμπες ενι ζωοισιν Εωος,

Νυν δε θανων λαμπεις Εσπερος εν φθιμενοις.

" Born an aristocrat, I am naturally one by temper," said Lord Byron. Many of the lines in ' The Hours of Idleness,' particularly the Farewell to Newstead, shew that in early life he prided himself much on his ancestors : but it is their exploits that he celebrates ; and when he mentioned his having

---

* The following passage in an unpublished life of Alfieri, which I lately met with, might not inaptly be applied to Lord Byron :

" Dès son enfance tous les symptômes d'un caractère fier, indomtable et mélancolique se manifestèrent. Taciturne et tranquille à l' ordinaire, mais quelquefois très babillard, très vif, et presque toujours dans les extrêmes—obstiné et rebelle à la force, très soumis aux avis donnés par amitié ; contenu plutôt par la crainte d' être grondé, que par toute autre chose ; inflexible quand on voudroit le prendre à rebours ;—tel fut-il dans ses jeunes années."

had his pennant hauled down, he said they might have re-spected a descendant of the great navigator. Almost from infancy he shewed an independence of character, which a long minority and a maternal education contributed to en-courage. His temper was quick, but he never long re-tained anger. Impatient of control, he was too proud to justify himself when right, or if accused, to own himself wrong; yet no man was more unopiniated, more open to conviction, and more accessible to advice,* when he knew that it proceeded from friendship, or was motived by affec-tion or regard.

" Though opposed to the foreign policy of England, he was no revolutionist. The best proof of his prizing the

---

* " Perhaps of all his friends Sir Walter Scott had the most in-fluence over him. The sight of his hand-writing, he said, put him in spirits for the day. Shelley's disapprobation of a poem caused him to destroy it. In compliance with the wishes of the public, he relinquished the drama. Disown it as he may, he is ambitious of fame, and almost as sensitive as Voltaire or Rousseau : even the gossip of this little town annoys him."

Extract from a Letter to a Friend, written at Pisa.

constitution of his own country, was that he wished to see it transplanted on the Continent, and over the world : and his first and last aspirations were for Greece, her liberty and independence.

" Like Petrarch, disappointed love, perhaps, made him a poet. You know my enthusiasm about him. I consider him in poetry what Michael Angelo was in painting : he aimed at sublime and effect, rather than the finishing of his pictures ; he flatters the vanity of his admirers by leaving them something to fill up. If the eagle flights of his genius cannot always be followed by the eye, it is the fault of our weak vision and limited optics. It requires a mind particularly organized to dive into and sound the depths of his metaphysics. What I admire is the hardihood of his ideas—the sense of power that distinguishes his writings from all others. He told me that, when he wrote, he neither knew nor cared what was coming next.* This is the real inspiration of the poet.

---

* ————————" But, note or text,
I never know the word which will come next."

Don Juan, Canto IX. Stanza 41.

" Which is the finest of his works ?—It is a question I
have often heard discussed. I have been present when
' Childe Harold,' ' Manfred,' ' Cain,' ' The Corsair,' and
even ' Don Juan,' were named ;—a proof, at least, of the
versatility of his powers, and that he succeeded in many
styles of writing.   But I do not mean to canvass the merits
of these works,—a work on his poetical character and
writings is already before the public.*

" Lord Byron's has been called *the Satanic school of
poetry*.   It is a name that never has stuck, and never will
stick, but among a faction.

" To superficial or prejudiced readers he appeared to con-
found virtue and vice ; but if the shafts of his ridicule fell
on mankind in general, they were only *levelled* against the
hypocritical cant, the petty interests, and despicable cabals
and intrigues of the age.   No man respected more the
liberty from which the social virtues emanate.   No writings
ever tended more to exalt and ennoble the dignity of man
and of human nature.   A generous action, the memory of

---

* I alluded to Sir E. Brydges' Letters.

patriotism, self-sacrifice, or disinterestedness, inspired him with the sublimest emotions, and the most glowing thoughts and images to express them; and his indignation of tyranny, vice, or corruption, fell like a bolt from Heaven on the guilty.   We need look no further for the cause of the hate, private and political, with which he has been assailed.   But ' in defiance of politics,—in defiance of personality,—his strength rose with oppression; and, laughing his opponents to scorn, he forced the applause he disdained to solicit.'

" That he was not perfect, who can deny?   But how many men are better?—how few have done more good, less evil, in their day?

' Bright, brave, and glorious was his young career!'

And on his tomb may be inscribed, as is on that of Raleigh—

> ' Reader! should you reflect on his errors,
> Remember his many virtues,
> And that he was a mortal!' "

NOTES

p. 237, l. 14: Anne-Louise-Germaine Necker, Baronne de Staël-Holstein (1766–1817) met Byron in 1816 at Coppet on the banks of Lake Geneva. She was a celebrated conversationalist, liberal, author, battleaxe – and bluestocking, which made the friendship between her and Byron all the more surprising. She was a key figure in the Romantic period, and knew personally many of the leading European figures of the day.

p. 238, l. 2: Jean Charles Léonard Simonde de Sismondi (1773–1842) was one of the leading economists and historians of the period. His *History of the Italian Republics of the Middle Ages* (1809–18) was read and admired by Byron.

Matthew Gregory Lewis (1775–1818) was the author of the celebrated novel *The Monk*, perhaps the most infamous gothic work of the period. A Whig MP, he shared Byron's politics and many of his views, and by translating verbally parts of Goethe's *Faust* to Byron during their stay at Lake Geneva may have influenced Byron's later poetry, in particular *Manfred*.

p. 244, l. 10: Robert Stewart, Viscount Castlereagh, and later second Marquis of Londonderry (1769–1822) was one of the leading statesmen of his day. He was British Foreign Secretary from 1812 until his death, and his brilliant diplomatic skills played a key part in cementing the alliance against Napoleon. He was a major figure in the 1815 Congress of Vienna, and because of his Tory politics was one of the most loathed enemies of the British radicals.

p. 254, l. 1: Henry Milman (1791–1868) was a translator, divine and poet – though very far from being a divine poet. His play *Fazio,* however, published in 1815, enjoyed great success.

p. 257, l. 14: Douglas James William Kinnaird (1788–1830) was a banker and radical MP. A close friend of Byron's – especially in later life – he was on hand to help out when it was discovered that Byron's previous confidant in fincancial matters, Hanson, was dishonest and incompetent. Byron called him his 'banker... and sheet anchor'.

p. 265, l. 3: Lady Charlotte Harley (1801–80) was the youngest daughter of Lady Oxford, with whom Byron enjoyed an affair between 1812 and 1814. Byron greatly admired Charlotte, and in later life recorded his wish that she had been a few years older at the time he had met her mother.

Charles Skinner Matthews was one of Byron's closest friends while at Cambridge. He was known for his acerbic wit and atheistical views, and his drowning in the Cam in 1811 affected Byron deeply.

Teresa Guiccioli, *My Recollections of Lord Byron* (London, 1869)

To understand the importance of what is clearly one of the seminal documents in the corpus of contemporary accounts of Byron it is necessary to gain some understanding of the intense and peculiar relationship that arose between Teresa Guiccioli and Byron in 1819. The *Recollections* are the only account of Byron of any length written by one of his many lovers – at least the only account which claimed to be unreservedly factual – and their enormous impact in post-Byronic Europe was largely owing to the widespread recognition of the unique place Guiccioli held in Byron's affections during the years preceding his death. That and the fact that Guiccioli's account of Byron was virtually the only version published in the years after the poet's death which was not widely condemned for attempting to cash in on the lucrative fad for post-mortem Byronism. The disinterested sincerity this might suggest, however, falls a little wide of the mark.

The Contessa Guiccioli – she had been born Teresa Gamba Ghiselli – was nineteen when she first met Byron at a *conversazione* of the Contessa Benzoni in Venice. It was April 1819, and she had recently been married to the Count Alessandro Guiccioli, who was 58 and didn't look (or behave) a day younger. Within days Byron was boasting to his friends that he had found a new mistress – one who, he hinted broadly to his friends, had no more scruples than he himself about the proper consummation of their affair. Yet perhaps to call the remarkable relationship that sprung up between Byron and Guiccioli an 'affair' would be to miss its most salient feature. For this was no affair in the manner of Byron's other numerous liaisons during his time in Italy. This was easily the most enduring passion of his later years – and arguably of his entire life. It was what Byron himself would call, in a letter to Douglas Kinnaird on 26 September 1819, 'the strictest adultery'. In becoming Teresa Guiccioli's *cavalier servente* Byron acquired a semi-official status in Italian society; he was visibly recognisable as Guiccioli's lover – like other *cavaliers serventes* he had to carry around her fan and shawl if required – and was understood to be more than a passing fancy. In short, he was understood to have at least some degree of commitment to Guiccioli – a thought that would have been anathema to him only a year before he met her. Needless to say, a man with Byron's sexual appetite was unlikely to be enticed into such a relationship purely by Guiccioli's physical attractions (opinions vary as to her looks – though her face and shoulders at least are usually agreed to have been handsome). In the young countess Byron appears to have found the sympathetic feminine mind which had been so lacking in Annabella Milbanke. As such, Guiccioli was uniquely able to shed light on Byron's character during his time in Italy.

It has been the fate of Teresa Guiccioli more than any of Byron's acquaintances to have been discussed solely in terms of her relationship to the poet – a fate her intelligence and character hardly deserved. Even during the relatively short time that she knew Byron she could scarcely be described as the junior partner in the relationship; Mary Shelley could write to her friend Jane Williams in 1822 that Byron had been 'kept in excellent order, quarreled with & hen pecked to his heart's content' (see Marchand, p. 394) and even Byron himself wrote (on 29 September 1819) to Hoppner (who had written telling him of the lurid stories circulating in England about his alleged abduction of Guiccioli) 'I should like to know *who* has been carried off – except poor dear *me*. I have been more ravished myself than any body since the Trojan war'. Guiccioli's character was certainly formidable. Byron described her to his sister Augusta in September 1819 as 'pretty – a great Coquette – extremely vain – excessively affected – clever enough – without the smallest principle – with a good deal of imagination and some passion' but this does little justice to her tremendous stubbornness and strength of character. Throughout her relationship with Byron she quite literally had the former 'libertine' at her beck and call; she was able to drag him around Southern Italy when she and her husband were forced to move because of his alleged involvement in anti-Austrian politics, and she even successfully forbad him for several months to continue *Don Juan*, the masterpiece he had started in 1818. Byron repeatedly claimed in his correspondence that this domination was too much for him to bear: yet in the light of the sheer length of the relationship between the two – and of his former predilection for women of formidable character – it is tempting to believe that the opposite might have been true, and that this was in fact one of the most attractive aspects of Guiccioli.

After Byron's death Teresa Guiccioli embarked on a series of short-lived affairs, including one with the poet Lamartine. In 1832 she travelled to England on a pilgrimage to meet people who had known Byron, including his half sister Augusta Leigh and his publisher John Murray. After moving to Paris she married the Marquis de Boissy, and appears to have lived on memories of Byron and a new interest in spiritualism. Her husband is rather charmingly said to have been proud of having married the former mistress of Byron. Teresa Guiccioli died in 1879.

My Recollections of Lord Byron is one of the most infuriating records that remain of Byron's life. It appears to have been Byron's misfortune habitually to befriend people averse to telling the plain truth, and Guiccioli was no exception. The veracity of the *Recollections* was almost as seriously compromised by her vanity as it was by her late-discovered prudishness, and in most details of the affair it is notoriously fallible. Perhaps worse than this, however, is Guiccioli's idolization of her former lover. For her, Byron could do little wrong, and the *Recollections* in this respect offer an adequate balance to Leigh Hunt's twisted account of the poet. Various chapters of the *Recollections* are entitled 'His Constancy', 'His Generosity' etc, and were it the object of this selection to present a realistic portrait of Byron it would have been equally justifiable to have omitted the entire book. The aim of the exercise, however, is rather different, and the *Recollections* find a place because they faithfully represent the idealistic view of Byron that was to find surprisingly many supporters throughout the nineteenth and twentieth centuries – a view that even today remains unchanged for many 'Byronists' despite the recent wealth of biographical information now available. In defence of Teresa, it should be said that the side of Byron that she encountered every day appears to have been markedly different from the Byron many others knew; one only has to read his correspondence to her (in English as well as Italian) to be aware of how scrupulously he seems to have modified his personality in his encounters with the Italian countess. Yet this does not explain the inaccuracy of her account of the poet. She was not that bad a judge of character. Guiccioli found herself living in a century in which the media were increasingly dominated by a middle class which found it easy to condemn the lifestyle, and much of the work, of Byron. This was an attack on the memories she treasured more than anything else in her life, and *My Recollections of Lord Byron* was an attempt to protect them.

Byron's misfortune was to have been born in the England of those days.   Do you remember his beautiful lines in the ' Due Foscari '?—

> " He might have lived,
> So form'd for gentle privacy of life,
> So loving, so beloved; the native of
> Another land, and who so blest and blessing
> As my poor Foscari?   Nothing was wanting
> Unto his happiness and mine save not
> To be Venetian."

In writing these lines Byron must have thought of his own fate.   He was scarcely British by origin, and very little so by his turn of mind, or by his tastes or by the nature of his genius.   " My ancestors are not Saxon, they are Norman," he said; "and my blood is all meridian."

If, instead of being born in England then, he had come before the world when his star would have been hailed with the same love and regard that was granted to Dante in Italy, to Chateaubriand and Lamartine in France, or to Goethe in Germany, who would ever have blamed him for the slight errors which fell from his pen in ' Don Juan,'—a poem written hastily and with carelessness, but of which it can be said, as Montesquieu said of the prettiest women, " their part has more gravity and importance than is generally thought." If the sense of the ridiculous is ever stronger among people whose appreciation of the beautiful is keenest, who more than Byron could have possessed it to a higher degree?   Is it therefore to be marvelled at that, in order to make the truth he revealed accessible to all, and such whose minds had rusted in egotism

and routine, he should have given to them a new and
sarcastic form?

Had he been born anywhere but in the England
of those days, he never would have been accused of
mocking virtue because he claimed for it reality of
character, and not that superficial form which he saw
existed then in society.   He believed it right to
scorn the appearances of virtue put on only for the
purpose of reaping its advantages.   No one respected
more than he did all that was really holy, virtuous,
and respectable; but who could blame him for wishing
to denounce hypocrisy?   As for his supposed scepticism, and his expressions of despair, they may be
classed with the misgivings of Job, of Pascal, of
Lamartine, of Chateaubriand, and of other great
minds, for whom the unknown world is a source of
constant anxiety of thought, and whose cry of despair
is rather a supplication to the Almighty that He would
revealhimself more to their eyes.   It must be borne
in mind that the scepticism which some lines in his
poems denounce is one of which the desponding nature
calls more for our sympathy than our denunciations,
since " we discover in the midst of these doubts," says
Moore, " an innate piety which might have become
tepid but never quite cold."   His own words should
be remembered when he writes, as a note to the two
first cantos of ' Childe Harold,' that the spirit of the
stanzas reflects grief and illness, more than an obstinate and mocking scepticism; and so they do.   They
do not embody any conclusions, but are only the expression of a passionate appeal to the Almighty to
come to the rescue and proclaim the victory of faith.

Could anything but a very ordinary event be seen

in his separation from a wife who was in no way suited to him, and whose worth can be esteemed by the remark which she addressed to Byron some three weeks after her marriage : " When, my Lord, do you intend to give up your habit of versifying ? " And, alas ! could he possibly be happy, born as he was in a country where party prejudices ran so high ? where his first satire had created for him so many enemies ? where some of his poems had roused political anger against him, and where his truth, his honesty, could not patiently bear with the hypocrisy of those who surrounded him, and where, in fact, he had had the misfortune to marry Miss Milbank ?

The great minds whom God designs to be the apostles of truth on earth, make use for that purpose of the most efficacious means at their disposal. The universal genius of Byron allowed of his making use of every means to arrive at his end. He was able to be at once pathetic, comic, tragical, satirical, vehement, scoffing, bitter, and pleasant. This universality of talents, directed against Englishmen, was injurious to his peace of mind.

When Byron went to Italy his heart was broken down with real and not imaginary sorrows. These were not of that kind which create perfection, but were the result of an unheard-of persecution on account of a family difference in which he was much more the victim than the culprit.

He required to live in a milder climate, and a softer atmosphere to breathe in. He found both at Venice ; and under their influence his mind took a new turn, which had remained undeveloped whilst in his own clouded country.

In the study of Italian literature he met with the Bernesque poetry, which is so lightly and elegantly sarcastic. He made the acquaintance of Buratti, the clever and charming satirist. He began, himself, to perceive the baseness of men, and found in an æsthetical mockery of human failings the most copious of the poetical currents of his mind. The more his friends and his enemies told him of the calumnies which were uttered against him, so much the more did Byron's contempt swell into disdain; and to this circumstance did ‘Beppo’ and ‘Don Juan’ owe their appearance.

The social condition of his country and the prevalent cant opened to him a field for reflection at Venice, where customs were so different and manners so tolerant. Seeing new horizons before him, he was more than ever disgusted at the judgments of those who calumniated him, and ended by believing it to be best to laugh at their silly efforts to ruin him. He then wrote ‘Beppo’ and afterwards ‘Don Juan.’

He was mistaken, however, in believing that in England this new style of poetry would be liked. His jests and sarcasms were not understood by the greater portion of those against whom they were levelled. The nature of the Bernese poetry being essentially French, England could not, with its serious tendencies, like a production in which the moral purpose was artistically veiled. From that day forward a severance took place between Byron and his countrymen. What had enchanted the French displeased them, and Byron in vain translated the ‘Morgante’ of Pulci, to show them what a priest could say in that style of poetry in a Catholic country. In vain did he write to his friends that "'Don Juan' will be known by-and-bye for what it is intended,—a satire on the abuses of the present state of society, and not an eulogy of vice. It may be now and then voluptuous: I can't help it. Ariosto is worse; Smollett ten times worse; Fielding no better. No girl will ever be seduced by reading 'Don Juan,'" &c.

But he was blamed just because he jested. To his ultramontane tone they would have preferred him to blaspheme in coarse Saxon.

One of the best of Byron's biographers asserts that he was a French mind lost on the borders of the Thames. Lord Byron had every kind of mind, and that is why he was equally French. But in addressing his countrymen, as such, he heaped a mountain of abuse upon his head.

With the most moral portion of the English public a violent satire would have had better chance of success. With the higher classes the work was read with avidity and pleasure. It was not owned, because there were too many reasons for condemning it; but it found its way under many a pillow, to prove to the country how virtue and patriotism were endangered by this production.

Murray made himself the echo of all this wrath, and Lord Byron, not able at times to contain his, wrote to him much to the following purpose—

"I intend to write my best work in Italian, and I am working at it. As for the opinion of the English, which you mention, let them know how much it is worth before they come and insult me by their condescension.

"I have not written for their pleasure; if they find

theirs in the perusal of my works, it is because they wish it. I have never flattered their opinion or their pride, nor shall I ever do so. I have no intention either of writing books for women or to '*dilettar le femine e la plese.*' I have written merely from impulse and from passion, and not for their sweet voices. I know what their applause is worth; few writers have had more. They made of me a kind of popular idol without my ever wishing, and kicked me down from the pedestal upon which their caprice had raised me. But the idol did not break in the fall, and now they would like to raise it again, but they shall not." As soon as they saw that Byron was perfectly happy in Italy, and that their abuse did him but very little harm, they gave full vent to their rage.

They had shown how little they knew him when they identified him with his heroes; they found that they knew even less of him when he appeared to them in the reality of his character. Calumny followed upon calumny. Unable to find him at fault, they interpreted his words themselves, and gave them a different meaning. Everything was figurative of some wickedness, and to the simplest expressions some vile intention was attributed.

They depreciated his works, in which are to be found such admirable and varied types of women characters, that they even surpass in beauty those of Shakespeare (Angiolina, Myrrha, Annah): they said that Faliero wanted interest, that Sardanapalus was a voluptuary; that Satan in 'Cain' did not speak as a theologian (how could he?), that there were irreverent tendencies in his sacred dramas — and finally that his declaration—

"My altars are the mountains and the ocean,
Earth, air, stars,—all that springs from the great Whole,
Who hath produced, and will receive the soul,"

was hazardous, and almost that of an atheist.
Atheist! he! who considered atheists fools.

On leaving Venice for Ravenna,* where he had
spent a few months, only by way of distraction in the

* Galt says, "It was in the course of the passage to the island of Zea,
where he was put on shore, that one of the most emphatic incidents of
his life occurred; an incident which throws a remarkable gleam into the
springs and intricacies of his character, more perhaps than anything which
has yet been mentioned. One day, as he was walking the quarterdeck, he
lifted an attaghan (it might be one of the midshipmen's weapons), and
unsheathing it, said, contemplating the blade, '*I should like to know how
a person feels after committing murder.*' By those who have inquiringly
noticed the extraordinary cast of his metaphysical associations, this dagger
scene must be regarded as both impressive and solemn; the wish to know
how a man felt after committing murder does not imply any desire to
perpetrate the crime. The feeling might be appreciated by experiencing
any actual degree of guilt; for it is not the deed,—the sentiment which
follows it makes the horror. But it is doing injustice to suppose the
expression of such a wish dictated by desire. Lord Byron has been heard
to express, in the eccentricity of conversation, wishes for a more intense
knowledge of remorse than murder itself could give. There is, however,
a wide and wild difference between the curiosity that prompts the wish to
know the exactitude of any feeling or idea, and the direful passions that
instigate to guilty gratifications."—'Galt,' 152.

His curiosity was psychological and philosophical, that of a great artist
wishing to explore the heart of man in its darkest depths.

On the eve of his departure from Rome he assisted at the execution of
three assassins, remaining to the end, although this spectacle threw him
into a perfect fever, causing such thirst and trembling that he could hardly
hold up his opera-glass.

At Venice he preferred Madame Benzoni's conversation to that of
Madame Albrizzi, because she was more thoroughly Venetian, and as such
more fitted for the study he wished to make of national manners. He
used to say that *everything in the world ought to be seen once*, and it is to
this idea that we must specially attribute some of the oddities so exaggerated
and so much criticised during his short stay at Venice, for in reality he
had none of these tastes.

Parry says, "Lord Byron had an insatiable curiosity, he was for ever
making questions and researches. He wished me to relate to him all the
most trifling incidents of my life in America, Virginia, and Canada."—
'Parry,' 180.

midst of his sorrows and serious occupations, he was
accused of dissolute conduct; and the serious attachment which he had wished to avoid, but which had
mastered his whole heart, and induced him to live an
isolated life with the person he loved in a town of
Romagna, far from all that could flatter his vanity and
from all intercourse with his countrymen, was brought
against him to show that he lived the life of an Epicurean, and brought misery into the heart of families.

All this, no doubt, might have again called for his
contempt, but on his way from Ravenna to Pisa he
wrote the outpourings of his mind in a poem, the last
lines of which are :—

> "Oh Fame! if I e'er took delight in thy praises,
> 'Twas less for the sake of thy high-sounding phrases,
> Than to see the bright eyes of the dear one discover,
> The thought that I was not unworthy to love her.
>
> "*There* chiefly I sought thee, *there* only I found thee;
> Her glance was the best of the rays that surround thee;
> When it sparkled o'er aught that was bright in my story,
> I knew it was love, and I felt it was glory."

His heart was wounded by the persecutions to
which those he loved were subjected. His thoughts
were for his daughter, who was growing up in the
midst of her father's enemies, and for his beloved
sister who was praying for him. He contemplated
in the future the time when he could show the moral
and heroic power of his soul. He looked forward to
the great deeds by which he was going to astonish
them, and perhaps call for their admiration, instead
of his writings, which had never reaped for him anything but pain.

"If I live," he wrote to Moore, "you will see that
I shall do something better than rhyming."

Truth, however, when told by such men as Byron, and however ungraciously received, must guide in the end the steps of those who walk in its wake.

This has been the case with Byron's poetry. Its influence over the minds of Englishmen has been very salutary and great, and is one of the principal causes which brought on a reform of the rooted prejudices and opinions of the public in England, by the necessity under which it placed them of looking into the defects of the law and of the constitution, to which they had hitherto so crouchingly submitted. Since then the feeling of good-will towards other nations has materially increased in that great country.

Others have improved the way which Byron opened up for reform, and thanks to him England at his death began to lose her excessive susceptibility. She became accustomed to listen to the truth, and those who now proclaim it are not required to be exiled, or to suffer as Byron did up to the time of his death. His sufferings, no doubt, paved his way to everlasting glory, but his heroic death left him at the mercy of the enemies who survived him.

If ever a premature death was unfortunate, Byron's was; not only for him, because he was on the point of giving to the world the proof of those virtues which had been denied him, but also for humanity, by the loss of various treasures which will probably never be found again.

The epoch, however, of faint words and unbecoming silence has gone by even in England. Already one of the greatest men of England has claimed a monument in Westminster Abbey, which had been denied to his memory by the bigoted rancour of the man who was Dean at the time of Byron's death, denied to that poet whom another great English statesman has called "a great writer, but a still greater man."

There remains a still more imperious duty to be fulfilled by those who have been able to appreciate his great qualities.   That duty is to proclaim them and to prevent the further spread of falsehood and error as to his real character.

This is a very long letter, my dear Count, but you know how long all letters must be which are intended to refute opinions and to rectify judgments.   M. de Lamartine has the excellent habit of listening to your advice, and that is why I have had at heart to let you know the truth about Byron.   The present work will adduce the proofs of the appreciations contained in this letter.   I know that you do not require them, but also that the public does.

Pray accept, &c. ————.

CHAPTER II.

PORTRAIT OF LORD BYRON.

THE following letter was addressed to M. de Lamartine, who had asked the author of these pages to give him the " portrait physique" of Lord Byron.

MY DEAR MONSIEUR DE LAMARTINE,

Being on the point of departure, I nevertheless wish to send you a few explanations which must serve as my apology. You have asked me to draw the portrait of Lord Byron, and I have promised you that I would do so. I now see that my promise was presumptuous. Every time I have endeavoured to trace it, I have had to put down my pen, discouraged as I was by the fact of my always discovering too many obstacles between my reminiscences and the possibility of expressing them. My attempts appeared to me at times to be a profanation by the smallness of their character ; at others, they bore the mark of an extreme enthusiasm, which, however, seemed to me very weak in its results and very ridiculous in its want of power. Images which are preserved in thought to a degree which may almost be considered supernatural, are susceptible of too much change during the short transit of the mind to the pen.

The Almighty has created beings of such harmonious and ideal beauty that they defy description or

analysis. Such a one was Lord Byron. His wonderful beauty of expression has never been rendered
either by the brush of the painter or the sculptor's
chisel. It summed up in one magnificent type the
highest expression of every possible kind of beauty.
If his genius and his great heart could have chosen a
human form by which they could have been well represented, they could not have chosen another! Genius
shone in his very looks. All the effects and emotions
of a great soul were therein reflected as well as those
of an eminently good and generous heart, and indeed
contrasts were visible which are scarcely ever united
in one and the same person. His eyes seized and
betrayed the sentiments which animated him, with a
rapidity and transparency such as called forth from
Sir Walter Scott the remark, that the fine head of his
young rival " was like unto a beautiful alabaster
vase lightened up by an interior lamp." To see him,
was to understand thoroughly how really false were
the calumnies spread about as to his character. The
mass, by their obstinacy in identifying him with the
imaginary types of his poems, and in judging him by
a few eccentricities of early youth, as well as by
various bold thoughts and expressions, had represented to themselves a factitious Byron, totally at
variance with the real man. Calumnies, which unfortunately he passed over in disdainful silence,
have circulated as acknowledged facts. Time has destroyed many, but it would not be correct to say that
they have all entirely been destroyed. Lord Byron
was silent, because he depended upon time to silence
his calumniators. All those who saw him must have
experienced the charm which surrounded him as a

kind of sympathetic atmosphere, gaining all hearts to him. What can be said to those who never saw him? Tell them to look at the pictures of him which were painted by Saunders, by Phillips, by Holmes, or by Westall? All these, although the works of great artists, are full of faults. Saunders' picture represents him with thick lips, whereas his lips were harmoniously perfect: Holmes almost gives him a large instead of his well-proportioned and elegant head! In Phillips' picture the expression is one of haughtiness and affected dignity, never once visible to those who ever saw him.*

"These portraits," says Dallas, "will certainly present to the stranger and to posterity that which it is possible for the brush to reproduce so far as the features are concerned, but the charm of speech and the grace of movement must be left to the imagination of those who have had no opportunity to observe them. No brush can paint these."

The picture of Byron by Westall is superior to the others, but does not come up to the original. As for the copies and engravings which have been taken from these pictures, and circulated, they are all exaggerated, and deserve the appellation of caricatures.

Can his portrait be found in the descriptions given

---

* Among the bad portraits of Lord Byron spread over the world, there is one that surpasses all others in ugliness, which is often put up for sale, and which a mercantile spirit wishes to pass off for a good likeness; it was done by an American, Mr. West,—an excellent man, but a very bad painter. This portrait, which America requested to have taken, and which Lord Byron consented to sit for, was begun at Montenero, near Leghorn; but Lord Byron, being obliged to leave Montenero suddenly, could only give Mr. West two or three sittings. It was then finished from memory, and, far from being at all like Lord Byron, is a frightful caricature, which his family or friends ought to destroy.

by his biographers?   But biographers seek far more
to amuse and astonish, in order that their writings
may be read, than to adhere to the simple truth.

It cannot be denied, however, that in the portraits
which several, such as Moore, Dallas, Sir Walter Scott,
Disraeli, in London, the Countess Albrizzi at Venice,
Beyle (Stendhal) at Milan, Lady Blessington and Mrs.
Shelley in Italy, have drawn of Lord Byron there
is much truth, accompanied by certain qualifications
which it is well to explain.   I shall therefore give in
their own words (preferring them to my own impressions) the unanimous testimony of those who saw him,
be they friends or beings for whom he was indifferent.
Here are Moore's words :—" Of his face, the beauty
may be pronounced to have been of the highest
order, as combining at once regularity of features
with the most varied and interesting expression.

" His eyes, though of a light gray, were capable
of all extremes of expression, from the most joyous
hilarity to the deepest sadness, from the very sunshine
of benevolence to the most concentrated scorn or
rage. But it was in the mouth and chin that the great
beauty as well as expression of his fine countenance
lay.

" His head was remarkably small, so much so as to
be rather out of proportion with his face.   The forehead, though a little too narrow, was high, and appeared more so from his having his hair (to preserve
it, as he said) shaved over the temples.   Still the
glossy dark brown curls, clustering over his head,
gave the finish to its beauty.   When to this is added
that his nose, though handsomely was rather thickly
shaped, that his teeth were white and regular, and his

complexion colourless, as good an idea perhaps as it is in the power of mere words to convey may be conceived of his features.

" In height he was, as he himself has informed us, five feet eight inches and a half, and to the length of his limbs he attributed his being such a good swimmer. His hands were very white, and, according to his own notions of the size of hands as indicating birth, aristocratically small."

" What I chiefly remember to have remarked," adds Moore, " when I was first introduced to him, was the gentleness of his voice and manners, the nobleness of his air, his beauty, and his marked kindness to myself. Being in mourning for his mother, the colour as well of his dress, as of his glossy, curling and picturesque hair, gave more effect to the pure, spiritual paleness of his features, in the expression of which, when he spoke, there was a perpetual play of lively thought, though melancholy was their habitual character when in repose."

When Moore saw him again at Venice, some eight years after the first impressions which Byron's beauty had produced upon him in London (1812), he noted a change in the character of that beauty.

" He had grown fatter both in person and face, and the latter had most suffered by the change— having lost by the enlargement of the features some of that refined and spiritualised look that had in other times distinguished it. . . . . . He was still, however, eminently handsome, and in exchange for whatever his features might have lost of their high romantic character, they had become more fitted for the expression of that arch, waggish wisdom, that epicurean play of humour, which he had shown to be equally inherent in his various and prodigally gifted nature ; while by the somewhat increased roundness of the contours the resemblance of his finely-formed mouth and chin to those of the Belvedere Apollo had become still more striking." *

Here are now the words of Lady B———, who saw him a few weeks only before his last departure for Greece. This lady had conceived a totally different idea of Byron. According to her, Byron would have appeared affected, *triste*, in accordance with certain portraits and certain types in his poems. But, if in order not to cause any jealousy among the living, she dared not reveal all her admiration, she at least suffered it to appear from time to time.

" There are moments," she says, " when Lord Byron's face is shadowed over with the pale cast of thought, and then his head might serve as a model for a sculptor or a painter to represent the ideal of poesy. His head is particularly well formed : his forehead is high, and powerfully indicative of his intellect : his eyes are full of expression : his nose is beautiful in profile, though a little thickly shaped. His eyebrows are perfectly drawn, but his mouth is perfection. Many pictures have been painted of him, but the excessive beauty of his lips escaped every painter and sculptor. In their ceaseless play they represented every emotion, whether pale with anger, curled in disdain, smiling in triumph, or dimpled with archness and love."

This portrait cannot be suspected of partiality ;

* Moore, vol. ii., p. 248.

for, whether justly or not, she did not enjoy Lord Byron's sympathy, and knew it; she had also to forgive him various little circumstances which had wounded her "amour propre," and was obliged to measure her praise in order not to create any jealousy with certain people who surrounded him and who had some pretension to beauty.

Here is the portrait of him which another lady (the Comtesse Albrizzi of Venice) has drawn, notwithstanding her wounded pride at the refusal of Lord Byron to allow her to write a portrait of him and to continue her visits to him at Venice :—

" What serenity on his forehead! What beautiful auburn, silken, brilliant, and naturally curled hair! What variety of expression in his sky-blue eyes! His teeth were like pearls, his cheeks had the delicate tint of a pale rose ; his neck, which was always bare, was of the purest white. His hands were real works of art. His whole frame was faultless, and many found rather a particular grace of manner than a fault in the slight undulation of his person on entering a room. This bending of the body was, however, so slight that the cause of it was hardly ever inquired into."

As I have mentioned the deformity of his foot, even before quoting other testimonies to his beauty, I shall tarry awhile and speak of this defect, the only one in so pre-eminently favoured a being. What was this defect, since all becomes illustrious in an illustrious man? Was it visible? Was it true that Lord Byron felt this imperfection so keenly? Here is the truth.

No defect existed in the formation of his limbs; his

slight infirmity was nothing but the result of weakness of one of his ankles.

His habit of ever being on horseback had brought
on the emaciation of his legs, as evinced by the post-
mortem examination; besides which, the best proof
of this has been lately given in an English newspaper
much to the following effect :—

" Mrs. Wildman (the widow of the Colonel who
had bought Newstead) has lately given to the
Naturalist Society of Nottingham several objects
which had belonged to Lord Byron, and amongst
others his boot and shoe trees. These trees are
about nine inches long, narrow, and generally of a
symmetrical form. They were accompanied by the
following statement of Mr. Swift, bootmaker, who
worked for his Lordship from 1805 to 1807. Swift
is still alive, and continues to reside at Southwell.
His testimony as to the genuineness of the trees, and
to the nature of Lord Byron's deformity, of which
so many contradictory assertions have circulated, is
as follows :—

" ' William Swift, bootmaker at Southwell, Nottinghamshire, having had the honour of working for Lord
Byron when residing at Southwell from 1805 to 1807,
asserts that these were the trees upon which his
Lordship's boots and shoes were made, and that the
last pair delivered was on the 10th of May, 1807.
He, moreover, affirms that his Lordship had not a
club foot, as has been said, but that both his feet
were equally well formed, one, however, being an
inch and a half shorter than the other. The defect
was not in the foot but in the ankle, which, being
weak, caused the foot to turn out too much. To

remedy this his Lordship wore a very light and thin boot, which was tightly laced just under the sole, and, when a boy, he was made to wear a piece of iron with a joint at the ankle, which passed behind the leg and was tied behind the shoe. The calf of this leg was weaker than the other, and it was the left leg.

(Signed)   " ' WILLIAM SWIFT.' "

This, then, is the extent of the defect of which so much has been said, and which has been called a deformity. As to its being visible, all those who knew him assert that it was so little evident that it was even impossible to discover in which of the legs or feet the fault existed. To the testimonies already quoted I must add another :—

" His defect," says Mr. Galt, " was scarcely visible. He had a way of walking which made it appear almost imperceptible, and indeed entirely so. I spent several days on board a ship with him without discovering this defect; and, in truth, so little perceptible was it that a doubt always existed in my mind whether it might not be the effect of a temporary accident rather than a natural defect."

All those who knew him being therefore agreed in this opinion, that of people who were not acquainted with him is of no value. But if, in the material appreciation of a defect, they have not been able to err, several have erred in their moral appreciation of the fact by pretending that Lord Byron, for imaginary reasons, was exceedingly sensible of this defect. This excessive sensibility was a pure invention on the part of his biographers. When he did experience it (which was never but to a very moderate extent), it was only because, physically speaking, he suffered from it. Under the sole of the weak foot he at times experienced a painful sensation, especially after long walks.

"Once, at Genoa," says Mme. G., "he walked down the hill of Albaro to the seaside with me, by a rugged and rough path. When we had reached the shore he was very well and lively. But it was an exceedingly hot day, and the return home fatigued him greatly. When home I told him I thought he looked ill. 'Yes,' said he, 'I suffer greatly from my foot; it can hardly be conceived how much I suffer at times from that pain,' and he continued to speak to me about this defect with great simplicity and indifference."

He used often even to laugh at it, so superior was he to that weakness. "Beware," said Count Gamba to him on one occasion whilst riding with him, and on reaching some dangerous spot, "beware of falling and breaking your neck." "I should decidedly not like it," said Byron; "but if this leg of which I don't make much use were to break, it would be the same to me, and perhaps then I should be able to procure myself a more useful one."

The sensitiveness, therefore, which he was said to experience, and which would have been childish in him, was in reality only the occasional experience of a physical pain which did not, however, affect his strength, nor the grace of his movements, in all those physical exercises to which he was so much attached. It in no wise altered his good looks, and, as a proof of this, I shall again bring testimonies, giving first that of M. N., who was at Constantinople when Byron arrived there for the first time, and who thus describes him in a review which he wrote of him after Byron's death :—

" A stranger then entered the bazaar. He wore a scarlet cloak, richly embroidered with gold in the style of an English aide-de-camp's dress uniform. He was attended by a janissary attached to the English Embassy and by a cicerone : he appeared to be about twenty-two. His features were of so exquisite a delicacy, that one might almost have given him a feminine appearance, but for the manly expression of his fine blue eyes. On entering the inner shop he took off his hat, and showed a head of curly auburn hair, which improved in no small degree the uncommon beauty of his face. The impression his whole appearance made upon my mind, was such that it has ever remained most deeply engraven on it; and although fifteen years have since gone by, the lapse of time has not in the least impaired the freshness of the recollection." Then, speaking of his manner, he goes on to say :—" There was so irresistible an attraction in his manner, that only those who have been so fortunate as to be admitted to his intimacy can have felt its power."

Moore once asked Lady Holland whether she believed that Lady Byron had ever really loved Lord Byron. " Could it be otherwise ? " replied Lady Holland. " Was it possible not to love so loveable a creature ? I see him there now, surrounded as it were by that great light; oh, how handsome he was ! "

One of the most difficult things to define was the

colour of his eyes. It was a mixture of blue, grey, and violet, and these various colours were each uppermost according to the thought which occupied his mind or his heart. "Tell me, dear," said the little Eliza to her sister, whose enthusiasm for Byron she shared, "tell me what is the colour of his eyes?" "I cannot say; I believe them to be dark," answered Miss Eliza, "but all I know is that they have quite a supernatural splendour." And one day, having looked at them with greater attention in order to ascertain their colour, she said, "They are the finest eyes in the world, but not dark, as I had at first believed. Their hue is that of the eyes of Mary Stuart, and his long, black eye-lashes make them appear dark. Never did I before, nor ever again shall I, see such eyes! As for his hands, they are the most beautiful hands, for a man, I ever saw. His voice is a sweet melody." *

Sir Walter Scott was enchanted when he could dilate on the extraordinary beauty of Byron. One day, at Mr. Home Drummond's, he exclaimed:—"As for poets, I have seen the best that this country has produced, and although Burns had the finest eyes that can be imagined, I never thought that any man except Byron could give an artist the exact idea of a poet. His portraits do not do him the least justice; the varnish is there, but the ray of sunshine is wanting to light them up. The beauty of Byron," he added "is one which makes one dream."

Colonel Wildman, his colleague at Harrow, and his friend, was always wont to say, "Lord Byron is the only man among all those I have seen, who may be called, without restriction, a really handsome man."

* Miss E. Smith.

Disraeli, in his novel entitled 'Venetia,' speaks thus of the beauty of Hubert (who is Lord Byron) when Venetia finds his portrait :—

" That being of supernatural beauty is her father. Young as he was, command and genius, the pride of noble passions, all the glory of a creative mind, seemed stamped upon his brow. With all his marvellous beauty he seemed a being born for greatness. . . Its reality exceeded the wildest dreams of her romance, her brightest visions of grace and loveliness and genius seemed personified in this form. He was a man in the very spring of sunny youth and of radiant beauty. He was above the middle height, yet with a form that displayed exquisite grace. . . It was a countenance of singular loveliness and power. The lips and the moulding of the chin resembled the eager and impassioned tenderness of the shape of Antinous; but instead of the effeminate sullenness of the eye, and the narrow smoothness of the forehead, shone an expression of profound and piercing thought. On each side of the clear and open brow descended, even to the shoulders, the clustering locks of golden hair ; while the eyes, large and yet deep, beamed with a spiritual energy, and shone like two wells of crystalline water that reflect the all-beholding heavens."

M. Beyle (Stendhal) writes to Mr. Swanton Belloc :—" It was in the autumn of the year 1816 that I met Lord Byron at the theatre of the Scala, at Milan, in the box of the Bremen Minister. I was struck with Lord Byron's eyes at the time when he was listening to a sestetto in Mayer's opera of ' Elena. I never in my life saw anything more beautiful or more expressive. Even now, when I think of the expression which a great painter should give to genius, I always have before me that magnificent head. I had a moment of enthusiasm." And further, he adds that one day he saw him listening to Monti whilst the latter was singing his first couplet in the 'Mascheroniana.' "I shall never forget," said he, "the divine expression of his look; it was the serene look of genius and power."

I might multiply these testimonies of people who have seen him, and fill many pages; their particular character is their uniform resemblance. This proves the soundness of the ground on which their truth is based. I will add one more testimony to the others, that of Mrs. Shelley, which is even nearer the truth, and condenses all the others :—"Lord Byron," said this distinguished woman, "was the first genius of his age and the handsomest of men."

In all these portraits there is much truth, but they are not sufficiently complete to give those who never saw him any but a faint idea of his smile, or of his mouth, which seemed to be not suited to material purposes, and to be purely intellectual and divine; of his eyes, which changed from one colour to another according to the various emotions of his soul, but the habitual expression of which was that of an infinite and intense softness; of his sublime and noble brow; of his melodious voice, which attracted and captivated; and of that kind of supernatural light which seemed to surround him like a halo.

This inability on the part of artists and biographers to render exactly Byron's features and looks, is not to be wondered at, for although perfectly regular, his features derived their principal beauty from the life which his soul instilled into them.   The emotions of his heart, the changes of his thoughts, appeared so variously upon his countenance, and gave the latter so changeable a cast, that it sufficed not for the artist who had to portray him, to gaze at and study him, as one generally does less gifted or elevated organisations.   The reality was more likely to be well interpreted when it stood a prey to the various emotions of the soul; in his leisure hours, in the full enjoyment of life and love, he was satisfied with the knowledge that he was young, handsome, beloved, and admired.   Then it was that his beauty became, as it were, radiant and brilliant like a ray of sunshine.

The time to see him was when, under the influence of genius, his soul was tormented with the desire of pouring out the numberless ideas and thoughts which flooded his mind: at such moments one scarcely dared approach him, awed, as it were, by the feeling of one's own nothingness in comparison with his greatness.   Again, the time to see him was when, coming down from the high regions to which a moment before he had soared, he became once more the simple child adorned with goodness and every grace; taking an interest in all things, as if he were really a child.   It was impossible then to refrain from the contemplation of this placid beauty, which, without taking away in the least from the admiration which it inspired, drew one towards him, and made him more accessible to one, and more familiar by lessening a little the distance which separated one from him.   But, above all, he should have been seen during the last days of his stay in Italy, when his soul had to sustain the most cruel blows; when heroism got the better of his affections, of his worldly interests, and even of his love of ease and tranquillity; when his health, already shaken, appeared to fail him each day more and more, to the loss of his intellectual powers. Had one seen him then as we saw him, it would scarcely have been possible to paint him as he looked. Does not genius require genius to be its interpreter? Thorwaldsen alone has, in his marble bust of him, been able to blend the regular beauty of his features with the sublime expression of his countenance. Had the reader seen him, he would have exclaimed with Sir Walter Scott, " that no picture is like him."

Not only would he have observed in his handsome face the denial of all the absurd statements which had been made about him, but he would have noticed a soul greater even than the mind, and superior to the acts which he performed on this earth; he would have read in unmistakeable characters, not only what he was,—a good man,—but the promise of a moral and intellectual perfection ever increasing. If this progressive march towards perfection was at one time arrested by the trials of his life, and by the consequences of undeserved sorrow, it was well proved by his whole conduct towards the end of his life, and in the last poems which he wrote. His poems from year to year assumed a more perfect beauty, and increased constantly, not only in the splendour of their conception, but also in the force of their expressions, and their moral tendency, visible especially in his dramas. In them will be found types surpassing in purity, in delicacy, in grandeur, in heroism, without ever being untrue to nature, all that ever was conceived by the best poets of England. Shakespeare, in all his master creations, has not conceived a more noble soul than that of Angiolina, or a more tender one than Marina's, or even one more heroic than Myrra's. As his genius became developed, his soul became purified and more perfect. But the Almighty, who does not allow perfection to be of this world, did not permit him to remain on earth, when once he had reached that point. He allowed him, however,—and this perhaps as a compensation for all the injuries which he had suffered,—to die in the prime of life a death worthy of him; the death of a virtuous man, of a hero, of a philosopher.

Excuse this long letter, for if I have ventured to speak to you at such length of the moral, and—may I say the word?—"physical" beauty of the illustrious Englishman, it is because one genius can appreciate another, and that, in speaking of so great a man as Lord Byron, there is no fear of tiring the listeners.

CHAPTER III.

FRENCH PORTRAIT.

"I see that the greater part of the men of my time endeavour to blemish the glory of the generous and fine actions of olden days by giving to them some vile interpretation, or by finding some vain cause or occasion which produced them — very clever, indeed! I shall use a similar licence, and take the same trouble to endeavour to raise these great names."—MONTAIGNE, chap. "Glory."

THE portrait of Lord Byron, in a moral point of view, is still to be drawn. Many causes have conspired to make the task difficult, and the portrait unlike. Physically speaking, on account of his matchless beauty—mentally, owing to his genius—and morally, owing to the rare qualities of his soul, Lord Byron was certainly a phenomenon. The world agrees in this opinion; but is not yet agreed upon the nature and moral value of the phenomenon. But as all phenomena have, besides a primary and extraordinary cause, some secondary and accidental causes, which it is necessary to examine in order that they may be understood; so, to explain Byron's nature, we must not neglect to observe the causes which have contributed chiefly to the formation of his individuality.

His biographers have rather considered the results than the causes.

Even Moore, the best among them, if not, indeed, the only one who can claim the title of biographer, grants that the nature of Lord Byron and its opera-

tions were inexplicable, but does not give himself
the trouble to understand them.

Here are his own words:—" So various indeed, and
contradictory were his attributes, both moral and
intellectual, that he may be pronounced to have been
not one, but many : nor would it be any great exaggeration of the truth to say, that out of the mere
partition of the properties of his single mind, a
plurality of characters, all different and all vigorous,
might have been furnished. It was this multiform
aspect exhibited by him that led the world, during
his short, wondrous career, to compare him with
the medley host of personages, almost all differing
from each other, which he playfully enumerates in
one of his journals.

" The object of so many contradictory comparisons
must probably be like something different from them
all; but what *that* is, is more than I know, or anybody else."

But, while merely explaining the extraordinary
richness of this nature by the analysis of its
results, by his changeable character, by the frankness which ever made his heart speak that which
it felt, by his excessive sensitiveness, which made
him the slave of momentary impressions, by his
almost childlike delight and astonishment at things,
Moore does not arrive at the true causes of the phenomenon. He registers, it is true, certain effects
which become causes when they draw upon the head
of Lord Byron certain false judgments, and open the
door to every calumny.

Without adopting the system of the influence of
races on mankind,—which, if pushed to its extreme

consequences, must lead to the disastrous and deplorable doctrine of fatalism, and would make of man a
mere machine,—it is, however, impossible to deny
that races and their amalgamation do exercise a great
influence over our species.

It is to this very influence of race, which was so
evident in Lord Byron, that we attribute, in a measure,
the exceptional nature of the great English poet.

As the reader knows, Lord Byron was descended,
by his father, from the noble race of the Birons of
France. His ancestors accompanied William the
Conqueror to England, aided him in the conquest
of that country, and distinguished themselves in
the various fields of battle which ultimately led to the
total subjugation of the island.

In his family, the sympathies of the original race
always remained strong.

His father, a youthful and brilliant officer, was
never happy except in France. He was very intimate with the Maréchal de Biron, who looked upon
him as a connexion. He even settled in Paris with
his first wife, the Marchioness of Carmarthen. Soon
after his second marriage, he brought his wife
over to France, and it was in France that she conceived the future poet. When obliged to return to
England to be confined, she was so far advanced
in pregnancy that she could not reach London in
time, but gave birth to Lord Byron at Dover. It
was in France that Byron's father died at thirty-five
years of age. Through his mother—a Scotch lady
connected with the royal house of Stuart—he had
Scotch blood in his veins.

The powerful influence exercised by the Norman

Conquest, in the modification of all the old habits of
Great Britain, and in making the English that which
they now are, has descended as an heirloom to some
old aristocratic families of the kingdom, where it
discovers itself at different times in different individuals.   Nowhere, perhaps, did this influence show
itself more clearly than in the person of Lord
Byron.

His duplicate or triplicate origin was already
visible in the cast of his features.   Without any
analogy to the type of beauty belonging to the men
of his country (a beauty seldom found apart from a
kind of cold reserve), Lord Byron's beauty appeared
to unite the energy of the western with the splendour
and the mildness of the southern climes.

The influence of this mixture of races was equally
visible in his moral and intellectual character.

He belonged to the Gallic race (modified by the
Latin and Celtic elements) by his vivacity and
mobility of character, as well as by his wit and
his keen appreciation of the ridiculous, by those
smiles and sarcasms which hide or discover a profound philosophy, by his perception of humour
without malice, by all those amiable qualities which
in the daily intercourse of life made of him a being of
such irresistible attraction.   He belonged to that race
likewise by his great sensitiveness, by his expansive
good nature, by his politeness, by his tractableness,
by his universal character which rendered every
species of success easy to him; by his great generosity, by his love of glory, by his passion for honour,
his intuitive perception of great deeds, by a courage
which might have appeared rash, had it not been

heroic, and which, in presence of the greatest perils and even of death, ever preserved for him that serenity of mind which allowed him to laugh, even at such times; by his energy, and also by his numerous mental and bodily requirements; and by his defects,— which were, a slight tendency to indiscretion, a want of prudence injurious to his interests, impatience, and a kind of intermittent and apparent fickleness.

He belonged to the western race by his vast intellect, by his practical common sense, which formed the basis of his intellect, and which never allowed him to divorce sublime conceptions from sound sense and good reason,—two qualities, in fact, which so governed his imagination as to make people say he had not any; by the depth of his feelings, the extent of his learning, his passion for independence, his contempt of death, his thirst for the infinite, and by that kind of melancholy which seemed to follow him into the midst of every pleasure. All these various elements, which belonged separately to individuals in France, in England, and in various countries, being united in Lord Byron, produced a kind of anomaly which startled systematic critics, and even honest biographers. The apparent contradiction of all these qualities caused his critics to lose their psychological compass in their estimate of his charming nature, and justice, together with truth, suffered by the result. Thus a portrait, drawn over and over again, still remains to be painted.

The most imaginary portrait, however, of Lord Byron, and certainly the least like him, is that which has general currency in France : not only has that portrait not been drawn from nature, not only is it a

caricature, but it is also a calumny. Those who drew
it took romance for history. They charged or exaggerated incidents in his life and peculiarities of his
character ; thus the harmony of the *tout ensemble* was
lost. Ugliness and eccentricity, which amuse, succeeded beauty and truth, which are sometimes weari-
some.

Those who knew and loved Lord Byron even more
as a man than a genius (and, after all, these are those
who knew him personally) suffer by this injustice
done to him, and feel the absurdity of making so
privileged a being act so whimsical a part, and one
so contrary to his nature as well as to the reality of
his life.

If this imaginary portrait, however, were more
like those which his best biographers have drawn of
him, justice to his memory would become so difficult
a task as to be almost impossible. Happily it is not
so ; and those who would conscientiously consult
Moore, Parry, and Gamba, must at least, give up the
idea that this admirable genius was the eccentric
and unamiable being he has been represented. To
reach this point would, perhaps, require a greater
respect for truth.

Even in France there are many superior persons
who, struck by the force of facts, have at times
endeavoured to seize certain features which might
lead to the discovery of truth, and have attempted
to show that Lord Byron's noble character and
beauty of soul, as well as his genius, did honour
to humanity. But their efforts have been vain in
presence of the absurd and contradictory creation
of fancy which has been styled "Lord Byron," and

which, with few modifications, continues to be called so to this day.

How has this occurred? what gave rise to it? ignorance, or carelessness? Both causes in France, added to revenge in England, which found its expression in cant,—a species of scourge which is becoming quite the fashion.

The first of these French biographers (I mean of those who have written upon and wished to characterize Lord Byron), without knowing the man they were writing about, set to work with a ready-made Byron. This, no doubt, they found to be an easier method to follow, and one of which the results must prove at least original. But where had they found, and from whose hands did they receive this ready-made poet, whose features they reproduced and offered to the world? Probably from a few lines, not without merit, of Lamartine, who by the aid of his rich imagination had identified Byron with the types which he had conceived for his Oriental poems, mixing up the whole with a heap of calumnies which had just been circulated about him.

Perhaps also from certain critics who believed in the statements of various calumniators, and who themselves had probably not had any better authority than a few articles in badly informed papers, or in newspapers politically opposed to Lord Byron. We all know, by what we see daily in France, how little we can trust the moderation of these, and the justice they render to their adversaries; what must it not have been in England at that time, when passions ran so high?—Perhaps also from the jealousy of

dethroned rivals!—the echoes, perhaps, of the revenge
of a woman equally distinguished by her rank and
by her talent, but whose passion approached the
boundaries of madness, or of the implacable hatred
of a few fanatics who, substituting in the most shameless manner their worldly and sectarian interests for
the Gospel, denounced him as an atheist because
he himself had proclaimed them hypocrites. Finally,
perhaps, from a host of absurd rumours, equally
odious and vague, caused by his separation from his
wife, and by the articles published in newspapers
printed at Venice and at Milan.

For Byron's noble, simple, and sublime person was
therefore substituted an imaginary being, formed out
of these prejudices and these contradictory elements,
too outrageous even to be believed, and by dint of
sheer malice.

Thus enveloped in a dense atmosphere, which
became an obstacle to the disclosure of truth as the
clouds are to the rays of the sun, his image only
appeared in fantastical outlines borrowed from ' Conrad the Corsair,' or ' Childe Harold,' or ' Lara,' or
' Manfred,' or indeed ' Don Juan.' Analogies were
sought which do not exist, and to the poet were attributed the sentiments, and even the acts, of these
imaginary beings, albeit without any of the great
qualities which constituted his great and noble soul,
and which he has not imparted to any of his poetical
creations.

Upon him were heaped every possible and most contradictory accusation—of scepticism and pantheism,
of deism and atheism, of superstition and enthusiasm, of irony and passion, of sensuality and ideality,

of generosity and avarice. These went to form his portrait, presenting every contrast and every antagonism, which God Himself, the Father and Creator of all things, but also the Author of all harmony, could not have assembled in one and the same being unless He made of him a species of new Frankenstein, incapable of treading the ordinary paths of physical, moral, or intellectual, nay, of the most ordinary existence.

After thus producing such an eccentric character, —the more extraordinary that they entirely forgot to consult the true and most simple history of his life, where if some of the ordinary excusable faults of youth are to be found, "some remarkable qualities, however, must be noticed,"—these wonderful biographers exclaim, astonished as it were at their own conclusions:—" This is indeed a most singular, extraordinary, and not-to-be-defined being!"

I should think so : it is their own work, not the noble, amiable, and sublime mind, the work of God, and which he always exhibited in himself,

"Per far di colassà fede fra noi."—Petrarch.

Happily, if to paint the portrait of Byron has become impossible, now that

"Poca terra è rimasto il suo belviso,"

it is easy to describe his moral character. His invisible form is, it is true, above, but a conscientious examination of his whole life will give us an idea of it. He knew this so well himself, that a few days before his death he begged, as a favour, of his friend Lord Harrington, then Colonel Stan-

hope, at Missolonghi, to judge him only by his
deeds. "Judge me by my deeds."

All bombastic expressions, all systematic views
should be discarded, and attention paid only to
facts, in order to discover the fine intellectual figure
of Lord Byron so completely lost sight of by his detractors.

Since the imaginary creations of his pen in
moments of exalted passion should not be taken as
the real manifestation of his character, the latter
is to be found in his own deeds, and in the testimony of those who knew him personally. Herein
shall we seek truth by which we are to deal with
the fanciful statements which have too long been
received as facts. Let us consider the opinions of
those who by their authority have a right to portray
him, whilst we study the various causes which have
contributed to lead the public into errors which time
has nearly consecrated, but which shall be corrected in
France, and indeed in every country where passion
and animosity have no interest in maintaining
them.

"Public opinion," says M. Cousin, "has its errors,
but these cannot be of long duration." They lasted
a long time, however, as regards Lord Byron;
but, thanks to God, they will not be eternal. He
depended upon this himself, for he once at Ravenna
wrote these prophetic words in a memorandum :—

"Never mind the wicked, who have ever persecuted me with the help of Lady Byron: triumph-
ant justice will be done to me when the hand which
writes this is as cold as the hearts that have wounded
me."

In England, Lord Byron triumphed over many jealous enemies whom his first satire earned for him, no less than the rapid and wonderful rise of his genius, which, instead of appearing by degrees, burst forth at once, as it were, and towering over many established reputations. The prestige which he acquired was such that every obstacle was surmounted, and in one day he saw himself raised against his will, and without his having ever sought the honour, to the highest pinnacle of fashion and literary fame.

In a country where success is all, his enemies, and those who were jealous of his name, were obliged to fall back; but they did not give up their weapons nor their spite. One curious element was introduced in the national veneration for the poet. It was agreed that never had such an accumulation of various gifts been heaped upon the head of one man : he was to be revered and honoured, but on one condition. He was to be a mysterious being whose genius should not transgress the boundaries of the East; who was to allow himself to be identified with the imaginary beings of his own fancy, however disagreeable, nay, even criminal they might be in reality. True, his personal conduct (at twenty-four) was to be above all human weakness ; if not, he was to be treated, as certain superstitious votaries treat their idols if they do not obtain at once the miracles they ask for. His secret enemies perfidiously made use of these stupid demands of the public.

Insinuating and giving out at times one calumny after another, they always kept behind the scenes, resolved, however, to ruin him in the public esteem on the first opportunity, which they knew they would not have long to wait for from one so open, so passionate, so generous as Lord Byron. The greatest misfortune of his life—his marriage—gave them their opportunity. Then they came forth, threw down the mask which they had hitherto worn, to put on one more hideous still; overturned the statue from the pedestal upon which the public had raised it, and tried to mutilate its remains. But as the stuff of which it was made was a marble which could not be broken, they only defiled, insulted, and outlawed it.

Then it was that France made acquaintance with Lord Byron. She saw him first mysteriously enveloped in the romantic semblance of a Corsair, of a sceptical Harold, of a young lord who had despised and wounded his mother country, from which he had almost been obliged to exile himself, in consequence of a series of eccentricities, faults, and—who knows?—of crimes, perhaps. Thus caught in a perfidious net, Lord Byron left England for Switzerland.

He found Shelley, whom he only knew by name, at Geneva, where he stopped. Shelley was another victim of English fanatical and intolerant opinions; but he, it may be allowed at least, had given cause for this by some reprehensible writings, in which he had declared himself an atheist. No allowance had been made for his youth, for he was only seventeen when he wrote 'Queen Mab,' and he found himself expelled not only from the university but also from his home, which was to him a real cause of sorrow and misfortune.

Between these two great minds there existed a wide gulf—that which exists between pantheism and spiritualism; but they had one great point of resemblance, their mutual passionate love for justice and humanity, their hatred of cant and hypocrisy, in fact, all the elevated sentiments of the moral and social man. With Lord Byron these noble dispositions of the heart and mind were naturally the consequence of his tastes and opinions, which were essentially spiritualistic. With Shelley, though in contradiction with his metaphysics, they were notwithstanding in harmony with the beautiful sentiments of his soul, which, when he was only twenty-three years of age, had already experienced the unkindness of man. Their respective souls, wounded and hurt by the perfidiousness and injustice of the world, felt themselves attracted to each other. A real friendship sprang up between them. They saw one another often, and it was in the conversations which they held together at this time that the seed was sown which shortly was to produce the works of genius which were to see the day at the foot of the Alps and under the blue sky of Italy.

Although Lord Byron's heart was mortally wounded, still no feeling of hatred could find its way into it. The sorrow which he felt, the painful knowledge which he had of cruel and perfidious wrongs done to him, the pain of finding out the timidity of character of his friends, and the recollection of the many ungrateful people of whom he was the victim, all and each of these sentiments found their echo in the 'Prisoner of Chillon,' in the third canto of 'Childe Harold,' in 'Manfred,' in the pathetic stanzas addressed to his sister, in the admirable and sublime monody on the death of Sheridan, and in the 'Dream,' which, according to Moore, he must have written whilst shedding many bitter tears. According to the same authority, the latter poem is the most melancholy and pathetic history that ever came forth from human pen.

* ★ *

CHAPTER IV.

LORD BYRON'S RELIGIOUS OPINIONS.

" When the triumph of a cause of such importance to humanity is in question, there never can be too many advocates. . . . . But it is not enough to count up the votes; their value must, above all, be weighed."—SHERER.

THE struggles between heart and reason, in religious matters, began almost with Lord Byron's infancy. His desire of reconciling them was such, that, if unsuccessful, his mind was perplexed and restless. He was not, as it were, out of the cradle when, in the midst of his childish play, the great problems of life already filled his youthful thoughts; and his good nurse May, who was wont to sing psalms to him when rocking him to sleep, had also to answer questions which showed the dangerous curiosity of his mind.

"Among the traits," says Moore, "which should be recorded of his earlier years, I should mention, that, according to the character given of him by his first nurse's husband, he was, when a mere child, 'particularly inquisitive and puzzling about religion.'"

At ten years of age, he was sent to school, at Dulwich, under the care of the Rev. Dr. Glennie, who, in the account given by him to Moore, and after speaking of the amiable qualities of Byron, adds: that "At that age he already possessed an intimate acquaintance with the historical facts in the

Scriptures, and was particularly delighted when he could speak of them to him, especially on Sunday evenings after worship. He was wont then to reason upon all the facts contained in the Bible, with every appearance of faith in the doctrine which it teaches.

But while his heart was thus drawn towards its Creator, the power of his reason began imperiously to assert its rights. As long as he remained sheltered under his father's roof, under the eyes of his mother, and of young ecclesiastics who were his first teachers, and whose practice agreed with their teaching,—as long as his reason had not reached a certain degree of development,—he remained orthodox and pious. But when he went to college, and particularly when he was received at Cambridge, a vast field of contradictions opened before his observing and thinking mind. His reflections, together with the study of the great psychological questions, soon clouded his mind, and threw a shade over his orthodoxy. If Lord Byron, therefore, had really the misfortune to lose, at an earlier age than ordinary children, the simple faith of his childhood, the fact is not to be wondered at. By the universality of his genius he added to the faculties which form the poet, those of an eminently logical and practical mind; and being precocious in all things, he was likewise so in his powers of reflection and reasoning. "Never," says Moore, "did Lord Byron lose sight of reality and of common practical sense; his genius, however high it soared, ever preserved upon earth a support of some kind."

His intellectual inquisitiveness was likewise, with

him, a precocious passion, and circumstances stood so
well in the way to serve this craving, that when
fifteen years of age (incredible as it seems), he had
already perused two thousand volumes, amongst
which his powerful and vivid intellect had been
able to weigh the contradictions of all the principal modern and ancient systems of philosophy.
This thirst for knowledge (anomalous according to
the rules of both school and college) was the more
extraordinary that it existed in him together with
a passionate love for boyish play, and the indulgence
in all the bodily exercises, in which he excelled, and
on which he prided himself. But as he stored his
mind after the usual college hours, and apart from
the influences of that routine discipline, which, with
Milton, Pope, and almost all the great minds, he so
cordially hated, the real progress of his intellect
remained unobserved by his masters, and even by
his fellow-students. This mistake, on the part of
men little gifted with quickness of perception, was
not shared by Disraeli, who could so justly appreciate genius ; and of Byron he spoke as of a studious
boy, who loved to hide this quality from his comrades,
thinking it more amiable on his part to appear idle
in their eyes.

Whilst the young man thus strengthened his intellect by hard though irregular study, his meditative
and impassioned nature, feeling in the highest degree
the necessity of confirming its impressions, experienced more imperatively than a youth of fifteen
generally does, the want of examining the tradi-
tional teachings which had been transmitted to him.
Byron felt the necessity of inquiring on what irrevoc-

able proofs the dogmas which he was called upon to believe were based. Holy Writ, aided by the infallibility of the teachings of the Church, &c., were adduced as the proofs he required.

He was wont, therefore, to read with avidity a number of books treating on religious matters; and he perused them, both with artless ingenuity and in the hope of their strengthening his faith. But, could he truly find faith in their pages? Are not such books rather dangerous than otherwise for some minds?

"The truth is," says the author of the 'Essays,' "that a mind which has never entertained a doubt in revelation, may conceive some doubts by reading books written in its defence." And he adds elsewhere, in speaking of the writers of such controversial works, that "impatient of the least hesitation, they deny with anger the value of their adversary's arguments, and betray, in their way of getting over difficulties, a humour which injures the effects of their reasoning, and of the proofs they make use of to help their arguments." After reading several of these books, he must have found, as did the great Pitt, " that such readings provoke many more doubts than they dispel;" and, in fact, they rather disquieted and shook, than strengthened his faith. At the same time, he was alive to another striking contradiction. He noticed that the men who taught the doctrines, too often forgot to make these and their practice agree; and in losing his respect for his masters, he still further doubted the sincerity of their teaching. Thus, whilst remaining religiously inclined, he must have felt his faith becoming more and more shaken, and in the memorandum of his early days, after enumerating the books treating upon religious subjects which he had read, he says: "All very tedious. I hate books treating of religious subjects; although I adore and love God, freed from all absurd and blasphemous notions."

In this state of mind, of which one especially finds a proof in his earlier poems, the philosophy of Locke, which is that professed at Cambridge, and which he had already skimmed, as it were, together with other philosophical systems, became his study. It only added an enormous weight in the way of contradictions to the already heavy weight of doubt.

Could it be otherwise? Does not Locke teach that all ideas being the creation of the senses, the notion of God, unless aided by tradition, has no other basis but our senses and the sight of the external world? If this be not the doctrine professed by Locke, it is the reading which a logical mind may give to it.

He believes in God; yet the notion of God, as it appears from his philosophical teaching, is not that which is taught by Christian doctrine. According to him, God is not even proclaimed to be the Creator of the Universe. But even were He proclaimed such, what would be the result of this philosophical condescension, unless it be that God is distinct from the world? Would God possess then all those attributes which reason, independently of all philosophy, points to in the Divinity? Would power, goodness, infinite perfection, be God's? Certainly not: as we are unable to know Him except through a world of imperfections, where good and evil, order and confusion, are mixed together, and not by the conception of the infinite, which alone can give us a true and perfect idea of God, it follows that God would be much superior to the world, but would not be absolute perfection.

After this depreciation of the Omnipotent, what says this philosophy of our soul? It does away altogether with one of the essential proofs of its spiritual nature, and thereby compromises the soul itself, declaring as it does, that "it is not unlikely that matter is capable of thought." But then of what necessity would the soul be, if the body can think? How hope for immortality, if that which thinks is subject to dissolution and to death?

As for our liberty, it would be annihilated as a consequence of such doctrines; for it is not supposed to derive its essence from the interior activity of the soul, but would seem to be limited to our power of moving. Yet we are hourly experiencing what our weakness is in comparison with the power of the laws of nature, which rule us in every sense and way. In making, therefore, all things derivable from sensations, Locke, fell from one error into another, and nearly arrived at that point when duty and all principles of justice and morality might be altogether denied. Being himself, however, both good, honest, liberal, and Christian-minded, he could only save himself from the social wreck to which he exposed others, by stopping on the brink of the abyss which he had himself created, and by becoming in practice inconsistent with his speculative notions. His successors, such as Condillac and Cabanis, fell by following his system and by carrying it too far.

A doctrine which denies the right of discovering,

or of explaining the religious truths which are the grounds of all moral teaching, and which allows tradition the privilege only of bestowing faith; a system of metaphysics, which cannot avoid the dangers in which morality must perish, owing to its contradictions and its inconsistencies, must be perilous for all but those happily constituted minds for whom simple faith and submission are a part of their essence, who believe on hearsay and seek not to understand, but merely glance at the surface of the difficult and venturesome questions which are discussed before them, either because they feel their weakness, or because the light of revelation shines upon them so strongly as to make that of reason pale. For more logical minds, however, for such who are inquisitive, whose reason is both anxious and exacting, who want to understand before they believe, for whom the ties which linked them to tradition have been loosened, owing to their having reflected on a number of contradictions (the least of which, in the case of Lord Byron, was decidedly not that of seeing such a philosophy professed and adopted in a clerical university); for minds like these such doctrines must necessarily lead to atheism. Though Lord Byron's mind was one of these, he escaped the fearful results by a still greater effort of his reason, which made him reject the precepts of the sensualists, and comprehend their inconsistencies.

His protest against the doctrines of the sensualists is entered in his memorandum, where, after naming all the authors of the philosophical systems which he had read, and, coming to the head of that school, he exclaims from the bottom of his heart—

" Hobbes ! I detest him ! "

And notwithstanding the respect with which the good and great Locke must individually have inspired him, he evidently must have repudiated his precepts, inasmuch as they were not strong enough to uproot from his mind the religious truths which reason proclaims, nor prevent either his coming out of his philosophical struggle a firm believer in all the dogmas which are imperiously upheld to the human reason, or his proclaiming his belief in one God and Creator, in our free will, and in the immortality of the soul.

☆ ★ ☆

To sum up, we may declare, from what we have said, that as regards Lord Byron there has been a confusion of words, and that his scepticism has merely been a natural and inevitable situation in which certain minds who, as it were, are the victims of their own contradictory thoughts, are placed, notwithstanding their wish to believe. Faith, being a part of poetical feeling, could not but form a part likewise of Byron's nature, but there existed also in him a great tendency to weigh the merits of the opinions of others, and consequently the desire not to arrive too hastily at conclusions.

This combination of instinctive faith and a philosophical mind could not produce in him the belief in those things which did not appear to him to have been first submitted to the test of argument, and proved to be just by the convictions resulting from the test of reasoning to which they had been subjected. It produced, on the contrary, a species of expectant doubt, a state of mind awaiting some decisive explanation, to reject error and embrace the truth. His scepticism, therefore, may be said to have been the result of thought, not of passion.

In religion, however, it must be allowed that his scepticism never went so far as to cause him to deny its fundamental doctrines. These he proclaimed from heartfelt convictions, and his modest, humble, and manly scepticism may be said to have been that of great minds, and his failings, also, theirs. Is a day said to be stormy because a few clouds have obscured the rays of the sun?

Is it necessary to say anything about what he doubted? In showing what he believed, the exception will be found unnecessary. He believed in a Creator, in a spiritual and consequently immortal soul, but which God can reduce to nothing as He created it out of nothing. He believed in liberty of thought, in our responsibility, our privileges, our duties, and especially in the obligation of practising

the great precept which constitutes Christianity;
namely, that of charity and devotion towards our
neighbour, even to the sacrifice of our existence for his
sake. He believed in every virtue, but his experience forbade his according faith to appearances, and
trusting in fine phrases. He often found it wise and
prudent to scrutinize the idol he was called upon to
worship, but when once that idol had borne the
test of scrutiny no worship was so sincere.

"Was he orthodox?" will again be asked. To
such a question it may be justly answered, that
if he did not entertain for all the doctrines revealed
by the Scriptures that faith which he was called
upon to possess, it was not for want of desiring
so powerful an auxiliary to his reason. He felt
that, however strong reason might be, it always
retains a little wavering and anxious character;
and, though essentially religious at heart, he could
not master that blind faith required in matters which
baffle the efforts of reason to prove their truth
logically and definitively. This is to be accounted
for by the conflict of his conscience and his philosophical turn of mind. Conviction, for him, was a
difficult thing to attain. Hence for him the difficulty
of saying "I believe," and hence the accusation of
scepticism to which he became liable. He wanted
proofs of a decisive character, and his doubts belonged
to that school which made Bacon confess that a philosopher who can doubt, knows more than all the wise
men together. Byron would never have contested
absolutely the truth of any mystery, but have merely
stated that, as long as the testimonies of its truth were
hidden in obscurity, such a mystery must be liable

to be questioned. He was wont to add, however, that the mysteries of religion did not appear to him less comprehensible than those of science and of reason.

As for miracles, how could he think them absurd and impossible, since he admitted the omnipotence of God? His mind was far too just not to understand that miracles surround us, even from the first origin of our race. He often asked himself, whether the first man could ever have been created a child? "Reason," says a great Christian philosopher, "does not require the aid of the book of Genesis to believe in that miracle."

One evening at Pisa, in the drawing-room of the Countess G——, where Byron was wont to spend all his evenings, a great discussion arose respecting a certain miracle which was said to have taken place at Lucca.

The miracle had been accompanied by several rather ludicrous circumstances and of course laughter was not spared. Shelley, who never lost sight of his philosophy, treated miracles as deplorable superstitions. Lord Byron laughed at the absurdity of the history told, without any malice however. Madame G—— alone did not laugh. "Do you, then, believe in that miracle?" asked Byron. "I do not say I exactly believe in that miracle," she replied; "but I believe in miracles, since I believe in God and in His omnipotence; nor could I believe that God can be deprived of His liberty, when I feel that I have mine. Were I no longer to believe in miracles, it seems to me I should no longer believe in God, and that I should lose my faith."

Lord Byron stopped joking, and said—

" Well, after all, the philosophy of common sense is the truest and the best."

The conversation continued, in the jesting tone in which it had begun, and M. M——, an *esprit fort*, went so far as to condemn the supernatural in the name of the general and permanent laws which govern nature, and to look upon miracles as the legends of a by-gone age, and as errors which affect the ignorant. From what had gone before, he probably fancied that Byron was going to join issue with him. But there was often a wide gulf between the intimate thoughts of Byron and his expressions of them.

" We allow ourselves too often," he said, " to give way to a jocular mood, and to laugh at every thing, probably because God has granted us this faculty to compensate for the difficulty which we find in believing, in the same manner as playthings are given to children. But I really do not see why God should be obliged to preserve in the universe the same order which He once established. To whom did He promise that He would never change it, either wholly or in part ? Who knows whether some day He will not give the moon an oval or a square shape instead of a round one ? "

This he said smiling, but added immediately after, in a serious tone :—

" Those who believe in a God, Creator of the universe, cannot refuse their belief in the possibility of miracles, for they behold in God the first of all miracles."

Finally, Lord Byron determined himself the limits of what he deemed his necessary belief; and remained throughout life a stanch supporter of those opinions, but he never ceased to evince a tendency to steer clear of intolerance, which according to him only brought one back to total unbelief.

Let us not omit to add that, as he grew older, he saw better the arrogant weakness of those who screen themselves under the cover of science, and recognized more clearly each day the hand of the Creator in the works of nature.

" Did Lord Byron pray?" is another objection which will be made.

We have already seen what he thought of prayer ; we have shown that his poems often took the form of a prayer, and we have read with admiration various passages containing some most sublime lines which completely answer those who accused him of want of religion, while they exhibit the expansion of his soul towards God.

We also know with what feelings of respect he approached places devoted to a religious life, and what charms he found in the ceremonies of the Church. All this is proof enough, it would seem ; but, in any case, we must add that if his prayers were not those advised by Kennedy, they were at least the prayers of a great soul which soars upwards to bow before its Creator. " Outward ceremonies," says Fénélon, " are only tokens of that essential point, the religion of the soul, and Byron's prayer was rather a thanksgiving than a request." —" In the eyes of God," says some one, " a good action is worth more than a prayer."

Such was his mode of communing with God even in his early youth, but especially in his last moments, which were so sublime. Can one doubt, that at that

solemn moment his greatest desire was to be allowed
to live? He had still to reap all the fruits of his
sacrifices. His harvest was only just beginning to
ripen. By dint of heroism, he was at last becoming
known. He was young, scarcely thirty-six years
of age, handsome, rich. Rank and genius were
his. He was beloved by many, notwithstanding
a host of jealous rivals; and yet, on the point of
losing all these advantages, what was his prayer?
Was it egotistical or presumptuous? was it to solicit
a miracle in his favour? No, his last words were
those of noble resignation. "Let Thy holy will, my
God, be done, and not mine!" and then absorbed,
as it were, in the infinity of God's goodness, and,
confiding entirely in God's mercy, he begged that
he might be left alone to sleep quietly and peacefully
into eternity. On the very day which brought to us
the hope of our immortality, he would awake in the
bosom of God.

☆ ★ ☆

CHAPTER VIII.

QUALITIES OF LORD BYRON'S HEART.

GRATITUDE,—that honesty of the soul which is even greater than social honesty, since it is regulated by no express law, and that most uncommon virtue, since it proscribes selfishness, — was pre-eminently conspicuous in Lord Byron.

To forget a kindness done, a service rendered, or a good-natured proceeding, was for him an impossibility. The memories of his heart were even more astonishing than those of his mind.

His affection for his nurses, for his masters, for all those who had taken care of him when a boy, is well known ; and how great was his gratitude for all that Doctor Drury had done for him! His early poems are full of it. His grateful affection for Drury he felt until his last hour.

This quality was so strong in him, that it not only permitted him to forget all past offences, but even rendered him blind to any fresh wrongs. It sufficed to have been kind to him once, to claim his indulgence. The reader remembers that Jeffrey had been the most cruel of the persecutors of his early poems, but that later he had shown more impartiality. This act of justice appeared to Byron a generous act, and one sufficient for him in return to forget all the harm done to him in the past. We accordingly find in his memoranda of 1814 :—

" It does honour to the editor (Jeffrey), because he once abused me : many a man will retract praise; none but a high-spirited mind will revoke its censure, or *can* praise the man it has once attacked."

Yet Jeffrey, who was eminently a critic, gave fresh causes of displeasure to Byron at a later period, and then it was that he forgot the present on recalling the past.

In speaking of this Scotch critic, he considered himself quite disarmed. When at Venice, he heard that he had been attacked about Coleridge in the ' Edinburgh Review,' he wrote as follows to Murray :—

" The article in the ' Edinburgh Review' on Coleridge, I have not seen ; but whether I am attacked in it or not, or in any other of the same journal, I shall never think ill of Mr. Jeffrey on that account, nor forget that his conduct towards me has been certainly most handsome during the last four or more years." *

And instead of complaining of this attack, he laughed at it with Moore :—

" The ' Edinburgh Review ' had attacked me . . . Et tu, Jeffrey ! ' there is nothing but roguery in villanous man.' But I absolve him of all attacks, present and future ; for I think he had already pushed his clemency in my behoof to the utmost, and I shall always think well of him. I only wonder he did not begin before, as my domestic destruction was a fine opening for all who wished to avail themselves of the opportunity." †

His great sympathy for Walter Scott became quite enthusiastic, owing also to a feeling of gratitude for a

* Moore, Letter 261.   † Venice, 1817.

service rendered to him by Scott. Shortly after his arrival in Italy, and the publication of the third canto of 'Childe Harold,' public opinion in England went completely against him, and an article appeared in the 'Quarterly Review,' by an anonymous pen, in his defence. Byron was so touched by this, that he endeavoured to find out the name of its writer.

"I cannot," he said to Murray, "express myself better than in the words of my sister Augusta, who (speaking of it) says, 'that it is written in a spirit of the most feeling and kind nature.' It is, however, something more: it seems to me (as far as the subject of it may be permitted to judge) to be very well written as a composition, and I think will do the journal no discredit; because, even those who condemn its partiality, must praise its generosity. The temptations to take another and a less favourable view of the question have been so great and numerous, that what with public opinion, politics, &c., he must be a gallant as well as a good man, who has ventured in that place, and at this time, to write such an article even anonymously.

"Perhaps, some day or other, you will know or tell me the writer's name. Be assured, had the article been a harsh one, I should not have asked it."

He afterwards learnt that the article had been written by Walter Scott, and his sympathy was so increased by his gratitude for the service rendered, that he never after seemed happier than when he could extol Scott's talents and kindness.

Gratitude, which often weighs upon one as a duty, so captivated his soul, that the remembrance of the kindness done to him was wont to turn into an affectionate devotion, which time could not change.

Long after the appearance of the article, he wrote as
follows to Scott from Pisa :—

" I owe to you far more than the usual obligations
for the courtesies of literature and common friendship, for you went out of your way in 1817 to do
me a service, when it required, not merely kindness, but courage to do so ; to have been mentioned
by you, in such a manner, would have been a proud
memorial at any time, but at such a time, ' when
all the world and his wife,' as the proverb goes,
were trying to trample upon me, was something still
more complimentary to my self-esteem. Had it been a
common criticism, however eloquent or panegyrical,
I should have felt pleased, undoubtedly, and grateful,
but not to the extent which the extraordinary good-
heartedness of the whole proceeding must induce
in any mind capable of such sensations. The very
tardiness of this acknowledgment will, at least, show
that I have not forgotten the obligation; and I can
assure you, that my sense of it has been out at com-
pound interest during the delay."

Gratitude, with him, was oftentimes a magnifying-
glass which he used when he had to appreciate
certain merits. No doubt Gifford was a judicious,
clear-sighted, and impartial critic, but Byron. extolled him as an oracle of good taste, and submitted
like a child to his decisions.

Gratitude levelled every social condition in his
eyes, as we may see by his correspondence with
Murray, where the proud aristocrat considers his publisher on a par with himself. Moore marvelled at
this ; but Moore forgets that Murray was no ordinary
publisher, and that, generous by nature, he made to

Byron on one occasion, in 1815, when the noble poet was in great difficulties, the handsomest offers. Lord Byron refused them; but the act was so noble, that its impression was never effaced from Byron's mind, and modified the nature of their relations.

When he had recovered his fortune, he wrote to Murray from Ravenna:—"I only know of three men who would have raised a finger on my behalf; and one of those is yourself. It was in 1815, when I was not even sure of a five-pound note. I refused your offer, but have preserved the recollection of it, though you may have lost it."

To calculate the degree of gratitude due to a service rendered, would have seemed ingratitude in his eyes. He could create beings who were capable of doling it out in that way, but to apply it to himself was an impossibility.

His predilection for the inhabitants of Epirus, of Albania, and for the Suliotes, is known. This predilection originated in the gratitude which he felt for the care taken of him by two Albanian servants who doted on him, during an illness which he had at Patras at the time when he visited that place for the first time. It was also on the Albanian coast that he was wrecked on one occasion, and where he received that hospitality which he has immortalized in Don Juan.

Byron's predilection for this people even overcame the effects which their ingratitude might have produced, for it is matter of history, how badly the barbarous Suliotes behaved to him at Missolonghi a short time before his death; they who had been so benefited by his kindness to them!

The memory of services done to him was not susceptible of change, and neither time nor distance could in the least affect it. The moment he had contracted a debt of gratitude, he believed himself obliged to pay interest upon it all his life, even had he discharged his debt. One single anecdote will serve to illustrate the truth of these remarks. On the eve of his last departure from London in 1816, when the cruelty of his enemies, powerfully seconded by the spite of Lady Byron, had succeeded in so perverting facts as to give their calumnies the colour of truth, and to throw upon his conduct as a husband so false a light as to hold him up to universal execration, it required great courage to venture on his defence. Lady Jersey did it. She—who was then quite the mistress of fashion by her beauty, her youth, her rank, her fortune, and her irreproachable conduct—organised a fête in honour of Byron, and invited all that was most distinguished in London to come and wish Byron farewell.

Among those who responded to the noble courage of Lady Jersey was one equally deserving of praise, Miss Mercer, now Lady K——. This conduct of Miss Mercer was all the more creditable that there had been a question of her marriage with Lord Byron, and that Miss Milbank had been preferred to her.

This party gave Byron a great insight into the human heart, and showed him all its beauty and all its baseness. The reflections which it caused him to make, and the frank account he gave of it in his memoirs—(the loss of which can never be too much regretted)—would not have pleased his survivors. This was unquestionably a powerful reason why the memoirs were destroyed. But Byron cared not so much for the painful portion of this recollection, as he loved to remember the noble conduct of these two ladies.

"How often he spoke to me of Lady Jersey, of her beauty and her goodness," says Madame G——. "As to Miss M——," he said, "she was a woman of elevated ideas, who had shown him more friendship than he deserved."

One of the noblest tributes of gratitude and admiration which can be rendered to a woman was paid by Lord Byron to Miss Mercer. As he was embarking at Dover, Byron turned round to Mr. Scroope Davies, who was with him, and giving him a little parcel which he had forgotten to give her when in London, he added : "Tell her that had I been fortunate enough to marry a woman like her, I should not now be obliged to exile myself from my country."

"If," pursues Arthur Dudley (evidently a name adopted by a very distinguished woman biographer), "the rare instances of devotion which he met in life reconciled him to humanity, with what touching glory used he not to repay it. The last accents of the illustrious fugitive will not be forgotten, and history will preserve through centuries the name of her to whom Byron at such a time could send so flattering a message."

But, as if all this were not enough, he actually consecrated in verse, a short time before his death, the memory of his gratitude to the noble women who had done so much honour to their sex :—

> "I've also seen some female *friends* ('tis odd,
> But true—as, if expedient, I could prove),
> That faithful were through thick and thin, abroad,
> At home, far more than ever yet was Love —

Who did not quit me when Oppression trod
Upon me; whom no scandal could remove;
Who fought, and fight, in absence, too, my battles,
Despite the snake Society's loud rattles."

It was on that occasion that Hobhouse said to Lady
Jersey, "Who would not consent to be attacked in
this way, to boast such a defence?" To which Lady
Jersey might have replied, "But who would not be
sufficiently rewarded by such gratitude, preserved in
such a heart and immortalised in such verses?"

IMPULSES OF LORD BYRON.

All those who have studied human nature agree
that impulses show the natural qualities of the soul.
"Beware of your first impulses, they are always
true," said a diplomatist, the same who insisted that
speech was given us to conceal our thoughts. If such
be the case, Lord Byron's goodness of heart is palpa-
ble, for all who knew him agree in bearing testimony
to the extraordinary goodness of all his impulses.
"His lordship," says Parry, "was keenly sensitive at
the recital of any case of distress, in the first instance;
and advantage being taken of this feeling immediately, he would always relieve it when in his
power. If this passion, however, was allowed to cool,
he was no longer to be excited. This was a fault of
Lord Byron's, as he frequently offered, upon the
impulse of the moment, assistance which he would
not afterwards give, and thereby occasionally compromised his friends."

To multiply quotations would only be to repeat the
same proof. I shall therefore merely add that it was
often the necessity of modifying the nobility of his

first impulses which made him appear inconstant and changeable.

EFFECTS OF HAPPINESS AND MISFORTUNE UPON BYRON.

"The effect of a great success," writes some one, "is ever bad in bad natures, but does good only to such as are really good in themselves."

As the rays of the sun soften the honey and harden the mud, so the rays of happiness soften a good and tender heart, while they harden a base and egotistical nature. This proof has not been wanting in Byron. His wonderful successes, which laid at his feet the homage of nations, and which might easily have made him vain and proud, only rendered him better, more amiable, and brighter.

"I am happy," said Dallas, on the occasion of the great success which greeted the publication of the first canto of 'Childe Harold,' "to think that his triumph, and the attention which he has attracted, have already produced upon him the soothing effect I had hoped. He was very lively to day."

Moore says the same; and Galt is obliged to grant that, as Byron became the object of public curiosity, his desire to oblige others increased. After giving a personal proof of Byron's goodness to him, he ends by saying :—

"His conversation was then so lively, that gaiety seemed to have passed into habit with him." It was also at that time that he wrote in his memoranda :—
"I love Ward, I love A——, I love B——," and then, as if afraid of those numerous sympathies, he adds : "Oh! shall I begin to love the whole world?" This

universal love was only the expression of the want of his soul which had mollified under the rays of that mild sun which is called happiness.

EFFECTS OF MISFORTUNE AND INJUSTICE UPON BYRON.

If his natural goodness had so large a field to develop itself in happiness, it reached a degree of sublimity in misfortune.

That Byron's short life was full of real sorrows, I have shown in another chapter, when I had to prove their reality against those imputations of their being imaginary made by some of his biographers. He required a strength of mind equal to his genius and to his sensibility, to be able to resist the numerous ills with which he was assailed throughout his life :—

"Have I not had to wrestle with my lot?
Have I not suffered things to be forgiven?
Have I not had my brain sear'd, my heart riven,
Hopes sapp'd, name blighted, Life's life lied away?"

Such beautiful lines speak loudly enough of the intensity of his sufferings. Great as they were, they did not, however, produce in him any feeling of hatred. To forgive was his only revenge ; and not only did he forgive, but, the paroxysm of passion over, there was only room in his soul for those nobler feelings of patience, of toleration, of resignation, and of abnegation, of which no one in London can have formed a notion. The storms to which his soul was at times a prey only purified it, and discovered a host of qualities which are kept back often by the more powerful passions of youth. If he never attained that calmness of spirit which is the gift of those who cannot feel, or perhaps of the saints, he at any rate, at the age of thirty-two, began to feel a contempt of all worldly and frivolous matters, and came to the resolution of forgiving most generously all offences against him.

Shelley, who went to see him at Ravenna, wrote to his wife "that if he had mischievous passions he seemed to have subdued them; and that he was becoming, what he should be,—a *virtuous man.*"

Mme. de Bury, in her excellent essay upon Byron, expresses herself thus, "had his natural goodness not been great, the events which compelled him to leave his country, and which followed upon his departure, must have exercised over his mind the effect of drying it up; and, in lessening its power, would have forced him to give full vent to his passions." Instead of producing such a result, they on the contrary purified it, and developed in him the germs of a host of virtues. I shall not tarry any longer, however, on this subject, as in another chapter I intend to consider Byron's kindness of disposition from a far higher point of view. I shall only add his own words, which prove his goodness of character. "I cannot," said he, "bear malice to any one, nor can I go to sleep with an ill thought against anybody."

James Kennedy: *Conversations on Religion with Lord Byron* (London, 1830)

James Kennedy's *Conversations on Religion with Lord Byron* are one of the very few memoirs of Byron that appear to have been published without a view to making a profit from the poet's reputation. Instead the intention was to spread to a wider audience the Evangelical message of religious conversion which Kennedy had preached to Byron himself. The implication of this is that there is no obvious reason to posit the reliability of Kennedy's account any more than that of any other of Byron's memoirists. However they are of especial interest to the Byronist in that they are one of the few remaining first-hand accounts that remain of the meaning of Byronism for the Evangelicals – a still relatively little-understood but extremely important grouping in Regency England.

The very little that is known about the short life of James Kennedy can be summarised as follows. He was born around 1793, and graduated in medicine at Edinburgh University in 1813; in the following year he became a hospital assistant to the British Army, and in 1815 he was promoted to the rank of Assistant Staff Surgeon, spending most of his time in Malta and the Ionian Islands, which had been fought over in the French Wars. He quickly acquired a reputation for his good-natured and sincere desire to spread his own religious beliefs, and spent his spare time establishing schools and performing other acts of charity. In the early 1820s he was posted for a time in Greece; in 1824 he was ordered out to the West Indies, where, two years later, he died after contracting yellow fever.

The entirety of Kennedy's claim to fame rests on his meeting Byron while stationed at Cephalonia between 10 August and 29 December 1823 – Byron having paused there en route to Missolonghi. The best description of this encounter was that written by Galt, and is reproduced in this volume. Kennedy had agreed to give a series of lectures on popular evidences of Christianity, during which he would attempt to convert a rather sceptical local audience of officers and expatriates with his own brand of sincere if plodding evangelism. His friendship with Byron was probably the most remarkable of the poet's last years: his respect for Byron was returned, both men being agreeably surprised at their ability to communicate with each other. Byron, however, was clearly a little abashed at being seen to get on with a man of such overtly evangelical views, and recorded his impressions of Kennedy in typical fashion in a letter to his half-sister Augusta Leigh dated August the 12th 1823:

There is a clever but eccentric man here a Dr. Kennedy – who is very pious and tries in good earnest to make converts – but his Christianity is a queer one – for he says that the priesthood of the Church of England are no more Christians than 'Mahmoud or Termagant' are. – He has made some converts I suspect rather to the beauty of his wife (who is pretty as well as pious) than of his theology. – I like what I have seen of him – of *her* I know nothing – nor desire to know – having other things to think about. *He* says that the dozen shocks of an Earthquake we had the other day – are a sign of his doctrine – or a judgement on his audience – but this opinion has not acquired proselytes.

Kennedy clearly made an impression on Byron, not least for being one of the very few people he met in his life who thought him 'so nearly a tolerable Christian that he is trying to make me a whole one', as he wrote to tell Charles Barry on the 23rd of August 1823. It is nearly impossible to say at this distance whether this was because Kennedy had the penetration to discover in the poet the elements of a belief in Christianity that very few others would have thought possible, or whether his earnest and possibly rather dim sincerity laid him open to one of Byron's favourite pastimes – that of making a fool out of his listener by retailing absurd stories. Finally, it is worth noting that Kennedy's book was edited by his wife, and there is no way of telling the extent to which is has been altered in the editorial process. His book remains an original and highly unorthodox contribution to the Byronic corpus. It deserves attention on this account.

We then began to talk on other subjects, and at last poetry was talked of. I said, " A lady in Argostoli had expressed to me, how much it is to be regretted that your lordship has not chosen some other subjects for your works, especially for some of your tragedies. She thinks that the scene of a tragedy laid in Babylon during the Jews' captivity there, would give full and irreproachable scope for all your powers."

" I am tired of tragedies, having so completely failed in them, as they say ; but does the lady you allude to write poetry ?" I said, " She wrote a little for her own amusement, and as the subject I had just mentioned had struck her, she had amused herself by sketching out a few scenes, till it occurred to her that it would be an excellent subject for your lordship, and draw you from others which might afford room for objection."

" Bring it," said his lordship, " and shew me what the lady has written, and I shall consider the subject, and whether I engage in it or not, I shall feel obliged if you can allow me to look at it." I said, " I was not sure that I could succeed; but if it was in my power, I would bring it the next time I came."

Some days afterwards, I called upon the Resident, and found Lord B. there; a glass of brandy was on the table untouched, brought, I suppose, for his lordship, as he had come in from the country, and the day was rainy. A gentleman in a few moments after entered, he had come from the Castle (Fort St. George), another glass was brought for him, which he took. Lord B. begged me to observe, that he had not taken any brandy, as it was still untouched on the table. The conversation was desultory, but it soon turned on an officer, who was said to have been converted to the truth, and whose conduct, an individual present deemed to be inconsistent with his principles, and he mentioned some things which he had done. I begged them to consider dates, and stated, that I had access to know that these things were done before the gentleman alluded to had become religious ; that since that time, his conduct was irreproachable, except, perhaps, in too assiduous attention to, and courting of his superiors,—a fault, I said, which would also in time be removed.

" I am sorry," said Lord B., "to hear of this failure in one of your converts : it will throw me ten years back in mine." "A proof," I replied, " that your lordship's conversion is not yet begun ; for if it was, no real or alleged failure would ever affect your opinions, unless to excite a regret for those who could not adhere to the principles they profess."

About this time Lord B. was busy preparing all things for his departure ; having hired two small vessels, he sent his things to Argostoli, and left his house at Metaxata. I met him as I was walking, coming into town, attended by a Suliote, who was also on horseback. He took up his residence at an English gentleman's house. Next day Count Gamba called upon me, and after some conversation, requested a French Bible. While he was with me, a servant came to say that the vessel in which they were to embark was ready to sail, and only waited for him. He arose, and I accompanied him; and as he had already taken leave of Lord B., he embarked at once, with the Bible in one hand, and an eye-glass in the other. I then went to take leave of Lord B., who, with his physician, was to embark in a smaller vessel that same afternoon. I found him alone, reading

Quentin Durward. He was, as usual, in good spirits. I said, " I am sorry that your lordship is at last to leave us, though it is pleasing to reflect that you are going to engage in so good a cause. I hope that you may be blessed with good health, and that you may be the means of doing much good, and above all, that you will prosecute the study of the sacred Scriptures as you have pro-mised."

Lord B. thanked me, and said, " he would do his best in assisting the Greeks, and that his in-clination would lead him to continue the investiga-tion of the subjects about which we had conversed. I have taken," he said, "all your books with me, which I shall peruse carefully; I feel some re-luctance in depriving you of them." " Think nothing of that. So far from wishing them re-turned, I have a box of other books ready for you, which I would have sent now, but I thought you would be too much engaged, and would have so many things to carry with you; I have therefore deferred it for the present; I shall, however, send them by the first opportunity to Missolunghi." " Do so," said Lord B. " I shall dispose of them prudently ; and in everything in which you think me likely to be of any use in promoting education

and useful knowledge among the unfortunate and
ignorant Greeks, you may always rely on me."

Here the gentleman of the house entered, with
Dr. Bruno. "Is Gamba gone?" asked Lord B.
"He is," replied one of them. "He has carried
with him all my money. Where is Fletcher?"
One of them answered he did not know. "Send
some one after him, we must embark immediately ;
send down to the Mess-house, you will probably
find him there, taking a parting glass with some of
his cronies."

"If your lordship wants any money," said the
gentleman of the house, "I can supply you with
whatever sum you please." "I thank you," said
Lord B.; "I believe I shall have enough till I
reach Zante." He then went into the next room,
and soon returned with fifteen dollars, which he
presented to me. "Take them," said he, "as a
very small donation from me to the school for
Greek females which Mrs. K. is establishing, as
a mark of my approbation and sincere good
wishes for the success of so useful an institution.*"

* Many others had subscribed very liberally to this little establishment: Lord Guildford gave twenty dollars annually; the
Lord High Commissioner gave the same. The Resident, Colonel
N., has acted with great generosity, and under his patronage, it
is confidently hoped that this school, which after Mrs. K.'s depar-

I thanked him, and said, " that some of the ladies had requested me to ask his lordship's assistance, which I declined, knowing the many claims and applications which had been, and would yet be made upon his generosity."

"The ladies did right, and you did wrong," said Lord B.; " for I should at any time be ready to lend my aid, however small, to such useful institutions." I shook hands with him, and he said, " I shall write to you, and give you an account of my proceedings in assisting Stanhope in establishing schools, and in forwarding the moral and religious improvement of the Greeks."

I answered, " I shall always esteem it an honour to hear from your lordship. From what has occurred, I shall ever feel a warm interest and anxiety in whatever concerns you, especially till such time as I hear that you have arrived at that point of religious knowledge and improvement, towards which I have, in our conversations, been

ture sunk into a temporary abeyance, will again flourish. The ladies of Edinburgh have instituted a Society for the promotion of Female Education among the Greeks, and a governess has left England for Corfu. It is ardently hoped that the English ladies will not be backward in giving their aid to so benevolent an undertaking. The Lord High Commissioner has entered with great kindness into the plan, and has held out every prospect of encouragement.—1830.

desirous of leading you. You have complained that many, who professed themselves strict Christians, have inveighed against you. Be assured that there is one at least who will not do so, but who will, on the contrary, always pray for your welfare, particularly for that of your soul."

" I shall always feel myself indebted to you," said Lord B. We again shook hands, and departed, never to see each other more.

Lord B. embarked the same evening. Next day his vessels touched at Zante. After leaving this island they were separated, and during the night, that in which Lord B. sailed came close upon a Turkish vessel, but escaped to one of the Strophades; and after a few days, he arrived at Missolunghi, and was received by the Greeks with every demonstration of honour, and with universal enthusiasm *.

Count Gamba was not so fortunate. He was taken by a Turkish frigate, and the lives of the crew were in some danger, till the Captain of the Turkish vessel discovered in the person of Spiro Valsimachi (Count G.'s Captain), one who had preserved his life when shipwrecked in the Black Sea. They were detained a few days at Patras,

* See Appendix—Count G.'s letter.

and were hospitably treated by the Pasha, and were then liberated, and rejoined Lord Byron at Missolunghi *.

His lordship was now engaged in a new scene. His rank, his talents, his wealth, and influence, naturally made him an object of much importance to the Greeks, and his time was completely occupied in doing all the good he could among this turbulent and thoughtless people. His stedfast object was to promote an union among all parties; to organize a corps of artillery, fortify Missolunghi, and, at last, prepare for an attack on Lepanto; which, from circumstances, appeared likely to be taken by assault without much difficulty. He had occasion to send some of the English officers repeatedly to Cephalonia, both for warlike stores, and for part of his baggage, which he had left behind. From them we had opportunities of learning how matters were going on. All were unanimous in their praises of Lord B., and of his incessant efforts to do something

* Their papers or manifestoes were not taken out for Missolunghi, or they would have fallen inevitable victims to Turkish policy, for the Turks would not have tolerated any who were about to enter an hostile town. As it was, Jusuf Pasha felt some degree of difficulty in releasing them. This Count D. related, and the Captain also, to Dr. K.

among the Greeks, whose discord, selfishness, and supine thoughtlessness, they as uniformly censured.

Colonel Stanhope addressed two letters to me, which will be seen in the Appendix. This gentleman's constant attention to the promotion of education is well known, and deserves every commendation. I received, also, two letters from Count Gamba, written with a view of gaining the assistance of my friend, Professor Bambas, for the Greek Chronicle.

I told Bambas that the patriots of Missolunghi were desirous that he should furnish them with something from his pen, to promote the cause of liberty, and that he might have his own price.

"Tell his lordship," said this true patriot, " that the efforts of my pen will, as a matter of course, be at the service of my oppressed country. It would be base in me to take money for any of my labours for her good ; they are due from me to her ; or, indeed, to any country similarly situated, and struggling nobly for her freedom.*

* Bambas often came to our house in Cephalonia, and was particularly pleased with the literature and periodical works of England. We sometimes translated pieces from the Quarterly Review, which were remitted for insertion in the Missolunghi Gazette. One article, I particularly remember, was on the literature of the ancient Greeks,

The second letter was to request my consent to
take under my own charge and that of Mrs. K.,
a young Turkish girl whom his lordship, from
feelings of humanity, had resolved to educate as
a companion to his daughter, if it met with Lady
B.'s approbation; and in the mean time he was
to write to his sister, the Honourable Mrs. Leigh;
and at all events, he promised to provide for her
respectably.

To this we readily consented. In writing to
Count Gamba, I forwarded at the same time a box
of Bibles and tracts for Lord B., and I said to
Gamba, that as his lordship was much engaged,
I begged, after he had taken as many Bibles as

and on the present struggle for freedom. B. entered with all the
spirit of the writer, into that apostrophe—

> ὦ Παῖδες Ἑλλήνων, ὅτι
>
> Ἐλευθεροῦτε πατρίδ', ἐλευθεροῦτε δὲ
>
> Παῖδας, γυναῖκας, θεῶν τε πατρῴων ἕδη
>
> Θήκας τε προγόνων· νῦν ὑπὲρ πάντων ἀγών.

He stands next to Korai in the estimation of the Greeks, and is
highly respected and esteemed by all who have the pleasure of
knowing him. He was formerly one of the Professors in the College of Scio, and is now a Professor in the College at Corfu; but
when Dr. K. knew him, he had a classical academy in Cephalonia.
Although he does not speak English, he understands the language
well. I have by me some of his translations, into Greek, of some
of Lord Byron's and Sir Walter Scott's poems. Bambas was five
years in Paris, and he always regrets that he never went to England; but he was deterred by the expense of education and of
living in this country.

he pleased in order to disperse himself, that Lord
B. would give the remainder to some respectable
person to distribute. Lord B. entrusted them to
the care of Dr. Meyer, a Swiss physician, long
settled in Missolunghi, and the editor of the ' Missolunghi Chronicle.' After Dr. Meyer had received and distributed the books, he wrote me the
interesting letter, No. 7, of the Appendix.

About the 15th of February, Lord B. was
seized with an epileptic fit, which gave much concern to all his friends in Cephalonia. As his physician, though ingenious and well educated, was
young, and could not have had much experience,
three medical officers in Cephalonia consulted together, and we agreed that each of us should write
to Dr. Bruno, giving our opinion of the best mode
of treating his lordship, should a second attack
return, and begging for a particular account of
the first.

It was generally reported in Cephalonia, that
his lordship's case was said to have been nervous
spasms, and to have been treated with valerian
and bark, and hence it was that we were induced
to take the liberty of writing to Dr. Bruno, apolo-
gizing at the same time for our interference, and
ascribing it to the interest which we naturally felt

in our distinguished countryman. We all wrote
that in such a complaint, or indeed in any of an
acute nature, his lordship's case should be treated
with blood-letting, and purgatives should be freely
used, especially at the outset; and we pointed out
to Dr. Bruno, that from Lord B.'s habits such a
practice would be particularly necessary, for it was
probable that in any acute disease a determination to the brain would ensue.

Dr. Bruno received our letters with great politeness, corrected the false rumours which had been
circulated, and stated that he agreed with us in
opinion respecting his lordship's complaint and
mode of treatment.

As in my letter I had expressed my opinion
that it would be advisable for Lord B. to leave
Missolunghi, which, from its low and marshy situation, would be unhealthy in the summer months, I
advised him either to persuade Lord B. to return
to the islands, or make short and easy journies
through Greece; to go as far as the scat of government, but not to occupy himself with much political
care and business, till his health was completely
re-established. Dr. Bruno disagreed with me, as
will be seen in the Appendix, No. 8; he thought
that no reason for change of place existed, and

that, in fact, Missolunghi was more healthy than the islands.

Feeling, as I did, a considerable degree of interest in Lord B., I took the liberty of addressing a letter to himself, in which I advised the same things I had urged to Dr. Bruno. In answer to this, Lord Byron wrote me the letter No. I, in which he expresses his determination to remain at all hazards, as long as his presence was supposed likely to be of use. I again wrote to Lord Byron on the same subject, and on that of the Turkish girl *. About this time, his boat, or felucca, came to Argostoli, on board which was Mr. Hodges, who brought a prospectus of the Greek Telegraph. As from the motto and style of the prospectus there was an appearance of radicalism, and an air of irreligion, we all expressed our apprehension to Mr. Hodges, and our regret at such a proceed-

* Mr. Hobhouse has this letter and the papers and books which Dr. K. sent to Lord Byron. Lord B. had proposed, that should Lady B. not consent to receive Haidee, that she should be educated in Italy. To this Dr. K. remonstrated, for after we had received the child we should have considered ourselves her guardians, and could but feel an interest in her future welfare. A slight demur arose from the mother's wishing to accompany her daughter ; but as Lord B. had put us to the test, as Christians opposed to Mahometans ; although highly inconvenient, we consented to receive both.—Vide Lord B.'s letter, Appendix.

ing, not only because it was essentially wrong, but was likely to injure the cause in which they were engaged. Mr. Hodges said, if we thought so, I ought to write to Lord Byron on the subject, as he was sure he would receive my advice kindly. I complied with this suggestion, and addressed a letter to his lordship, stating our reasons for dis-approving of the motto, and the prospectus.

In answer to this, Lord B. wrote the letter No. 2, in the Appendix. As I kept no copies of my correspondence, I am unable to give their contents ; but they are still preserved by his lord-ship's executors *.

We continued to take an interest in all that was going on in Missolunghi, from whence we had arrivals at intervals. As we heard of Lord B.'s preparations for Lepanto, and of his in-creasing influence and popularity among the Greeks; and learned from Dr. Bruno's letters, that his lordship's health regularly continued to improve,—we had ceased any longer to have ap-prehension. The intelligence came suddenly and unexpectedly, that Lord B. was dead. The shock that this excited, both among the Greeks and English, was very strong. The singularly great

* I regret that I cannot give Dr. K.'s answer.

character, thus prematurely cut off in the midst of his years and fame, just as he was entering on the noblest cause in which he had ever been engaged, and appeared likely to redeem his former errors by the splendour and virtue of his future life ; made a deep impression on all, and which I hope may be salutary to many.

It appears from Count Gamba's Journal, that on the 1st of March, Lord B. complained of frequent vertigos, which made him feel as though he were intoxicated ; but it does not seem that bleeding, which would now have been useful, or indeed that any medical treatment, was judged necessary. From this time till the fatal attack, his mind must have been full of anxiety, from the numerous applications of the Greeks for money,—from the turbulence and refractory conduct of the Suliotes, —and from the failure of the projected expedition to Lepanto, of which he was to have been the leader. On the 9th of April, he was overtaken by the rain, yet went into the boat, and two hours afterwards was seized with rigors, fever, and rheumatic pains. On the 10th, he was affected with almost constant shivering ; on the 11th, he found himself so well that he rode out; on the 12th, he was confined to his bed with fever. He

rose on the 13th, with pain in the bones and head,
and had not slept; on the 14th, he rose at 12,
the fever was less, the debility greater, and he
complained of pain in the head ; on the 15th,
fever, but the pains were abated, and he trans-
acted business ; on the 16th, he wrote a letter,
but became worse in the evening ; on the 17th,
his countenance was suspicious,—in the morning
he was bled, and also in the afternoon, and two
pounds of blood were taken : that night he was
delirious, and raved about fighting ; on the 18th,
Dr. Bruno wished to bleed him. " No," said he,
" if my hour is come I shall die, whether I lose
my blood or keep it." At three in the afternoon,
Dr. Bruno and Mr. Millingen called in Dr.
Turber, a German, and Dr. Luca Veja, a Greek
physician. At four o'clock, his lordship seemed
to be aware of his approaching end ; he became
delirious for a short time, and when he revived he
was anxious to give orders. He muttered about
twenty minutes, but nothing was distinctly understood. He said, " Now, then, I have told you all."
Fletcher said, " I have not understood a word
you have been saying." Lord B. was distressed
at this. " Not understand me? what a pity!
then it is too late." " I hope not," said Fletcher ;

" but the Lord's will be done!" His lordship
continued, " Yes, not mine." He then tried to
utter a few words, of which none were intelligible,
except, " My sister! my child!" At six in the
evening, he said, " I want to go to sleep now,"
and turning round, he fell into a slumber, from
which he never awoke. Leeches were applied to
the temples, and bled freely all night. He continued lethargic twenty-four hours, and at a quarter
past six in the afternoon of the 19th, he opened
his eyes—shut them again—and expired. His
remains were carried to England.

Thus died Lord Byron, in the thirty-seventh
year of his age. It would appear from the
accounts of his physicians, who differed in opinion
(see Dr. Bruno's letter) with respect to the treatment, that his lordship was averse to be bled, and
said, that the lancet had killed more than the
lance.

It was industriously spread abroad, that I was
going to prove that I had converted his lordship.
After trying in vain to stop the idle rumour, I
allowed it to take its course. Several of the
gentlemen in Cephalonia furnished me with copies
of Lord Byron's letters to them, and gave me
some curious details of his conversation.

From the time that Lord Byron arrived at Argostoli, on the 6th of August, 1823, to the time of his death, on the 19th of April, 1824,—short as this period was,—it may be said with truth, that it was the happiest and brightest of his life. During the whole of that time, he was not engaged in writing any poem, nor was he in the practice of any open vice. The flattering reception which he met with from his countrymen in Cephalonia gave him no small pleasure, which was enhanced by the feeling which he had entertained that his reception would be very different.

He remained on board the Hercules for nearly a month, except a short tour which he made to Ithaca, before he went to reside at Metaxata. In returning from Ithaca, he was accompanied by a Scotch gentleman, who asked him his opinion of the epitaph on Sir John Moore, written by Mr. Wolfe. He said, it was the finest epitaph ever written *.

* Not a drum was heard, nor a funeral note
 As his corse to the rampart we hurried;
Not a soldier discharged his farewell shot
 O'er the grave where our hero we buried.

We buried him darkly at dead of night,
 The sods with our bayonets turning,
By the struggling moon-beam's misty light,
 And the lantern dimly burning.

" You must have been highly gratified by the classical remains, and the classical recollections of Ithaca during your visit there," said Colonel D. " You quite mistake me," said Lord B. " I have no poetical humbug about me; I am too old for that. Ideas of that sort are confined to rhyme.— The people at home have very absurd notions of the Greeks, as if they were the Greeks of

> No useless coffin enclosed his breast;
>   Nor in sheet nor shroud we bound him ;
> But he lay like a warrior taking his rest,
>   With his martial cloak around him.
>
> Few and short were the prayers we said,
>   And we spoke not a word in sorrow;
> But we steadfastly gazed on the face of the dead,
>   And we bitterly thought of the morrow.
>
> We thought, as we hollowed his narrow bed,
>   And smoothed down his lonely pillow,
> That the foe and the stranger would tread o'er his head,
>   And we far away on the billow.
>
> Lightly they'll talk of the spirit that's gone,
>   And o'er his cold ashes upbraid him ;
> But nothing he'll reck, if they let him sleep on
>   In the grave where a Briton has laid him.
>
> But half of our heavy task was done,
>   When the clock told the hour for retiring;
> And we heard, by the distant and random gun,
>   That the foe was suddenly firing.
>
> Slowly and sadly we laid him down,
>   From the field of his fame, fresh and gory ;
> We carved not a line, we raised not a stone,
>   But we left him alone with his glory.

Homer's time. I have travelled through the country and know the contrary. I have tried to remove these notions." He said he would do every thing for them, but would take no command. He added, " A Turk's word could always be depended on, but not a Greek's, if his interest were in question." Speaking of his intention to go to Constantinople to redeem some Greek captives which he promised to their families when he came from Genoa, Colonel D. dissuaded him from it on account of the danger. " Oh, the worst would be," he said, " they will put me in the seven towers, from which I do not think Strangford would release me ; besides he is a poet, and two of a trade you know——" Speaking of Moore, he said, " He is, like all the fraternity, at present employed in writing heroic and patriotic songs in favour of the Spaniards or Greeks ; the last work he has dedicated to myself." He said he would give his travels in the Morea to the world ; but laughing, added, it would depend on the reception he met with, whether they should be written in the Childe Harold or the Don Juan style. When any one spoke finely, he used to say, " That will do very well for rhyme." Whether Homer lived or not, he said he did not know ; " but we poets must swear by him."

One night he was out at a gentleman's house ; the weather was very hot, and he said when he went on board, that he would bathe ; some one expressed surprise that he should bathe at so late an hour ; " Oh," said T. (a gentleman who from too great vivacity of imagination and thoughtlessness exaggerated a little), " we were two hours in the water late last night." " Yes," said Lord B. emphatically, " by Shrewsbury clock."

Dr. —— when on board one evening, was narrating to his lordship some wonderful act of legerdemain which he witnessed at Paris ; Lord B. smiled : " You look incredulous, my lord," said the Doctor. " No, not at all," replied Lord B. ; " where is T.? I dare say, he saw the same thing."

When he went out to Metaxata he spent the day in an easy and tranquil manner. He seemed to have no fixed hour for his meals, and at the time lived very low, on account of his health. He sometimes forgot himself in the warmth of conversation, and often both ate and drank more than he intended, though I never saw him do either except in a moderate degree. He was fond of riding,—an exercise he daily took. He was a bold and graceful horseman, and appeared to great advantage on horseback. One day, when he was riding, he met Colonel D., who had taken out his regiment into the country for exercise. The Colonel took his lordship in front of the line of the whole regiment ; " After all," said he, " there are not finer looking soldiers in the whole world than the English."

Lord B.'s right foot was what is called club-footed, which he took care to conceal, by wearing his pantaloons as much over the foot as possible, and the weakness of feeling shame for this deformity was frequently apparent, in his care to place this leg behind the other when he was sitting so as to have himself exposed to view. I am persuaded that this deformity was a cause of frequent vexation and chagrin to him. At times, however, as might be expected, he was superior to this weakness, and would make allusions to it. " Take care," said a gentleman who was riding with him, when they came to a difficult pass of the road,— " take care, lest you fall and break your neck." " I should not like that," said his lordship, " but should this leg of mine be broken, of which I have not much use, I should not mind, and perhaps I might get a better."

He was an excellent marksman, and was accustomed to exercise himself with some of his friends very often in firing at a mark, and he invariably surpassed them all in dexterity. He was personally brave.

The woman who washed for him, a soldier's widow, had a smart, genteel-looking girl, her daughter, about fifteen, whom she occasionally sent to his lordship's house with the linen. Lord B. noticed this, and wrote to Mr. H., of the regiment to which she belonged, requesting him to tell the mother not to send her daughter any more. " You know," he said, " what a parcel of rascals my household is composed of, and I should not like the poor girl to get any injury ; and don't fail," he added, " to let Dr. K. know this good action of mine."

He displayed great humanity when some Greeks were buried beneath a part of the road, by the falling in of the sand ; some of them were killed, and some seriously injured. He rode instantly to the spot, and was incensed at the indifference which the Greeks collected shewed to the fate of their countrymen *. Alluding to this circumstance,

* A new and handsome road had been projected by Colonel N., leading from the town of Argostoli to the district of Levato, in which district his lordship's house was situated, and many Greeks were engaged in this work. Owing to the negligence or inexperience of the workmen, the earth fell in and covered several.

he said that he came out to the Islands prejudiced against Sir T. Maitland's tight government of the Greeks, " but I have now changed my opinion. They are such barbarians, that if I had the government of them, I would pave these very roads with them." He sent Dr. Bruno, his physician, to attend the sufferers and to supply them with medicines.

He was very glad to see any of the English gentlemen who visited him at Metaxata: they were, always hospitably entertained and welcomed, as were also the principal Greeks, who often went out to him. His conversation was invariably lively, polite, and pleasing. He was fond of saying smart and witty things, and never allowed an opportunity of punning to escape him. He generally showed high spirits and hilarity. His conversation and manners varied according to his company. With some of the young officers, whose chief pleasure consisted in excitement and

The news reached Metaxata immediately ; Lord B. rode up to the spot, and inquired whether there were any below the earth. The Greeks (about forty) said they did not know, but they believed there were. "Why," he asked, " do they not get them out ?" when he was told their laziness prevented them, he ordered his valet to get off his horse and thrash them soundly, if they did not immediately commence their work.

370 LIVES OF THE GREAT ROMANTICS: BYRON

amusement, he was among the first for wit and
repartee, and according to the accounts I have
heard, he was not on every occasion scrupulous in
refraining from indelicacy, and even infidelity.
This account, however, depends on the authority
of others. When he visited one of the officers
with whom he seemed pleased, he was accustomed
to jest, laugh, smoke, drink brandy and water, and
porter, with the best of them. I never saw him
guilty of any such actions. Although once or twice
his puns were not the most pure, yet they were
never gross ; and I never heard him utter any im-
proper expression against religion. I have heard
him say several witty things ; but as I was always
anxious to keep him grave, and present important
subjects for his consideration, after allowing the
laugh to pass, I again endeavoured to resume the
seriousness of the conversation, whilst his lordship
constantly did the same. Those sayings, to which
of course my attention was not directed, I have
forgotten, and it is the less material, since there
was nothing particular in them, and they were
exactly of such a nature as are heard every day.
My impression from them was, that they were
unworthy of a man of his accomplishments: I mean

the desire of jesting. A gentleman, who frequently visited him, told me, that his lordship mentioned that he had generally a sullen and ill-natured fit every evening at eight o'clock, and then vented his ill-humour on those around him, and often abused his servants, especially Fletcher, till this splenetic fit had passed. Another gentleman, who spent several evenings with him, affirmed that he never saw any of these ill humours, but that while he was there, his lordship ever retained his good humour and politeness. About this time there were frequent paragraphs in the papers respecting Lord B. When a paper arrived, or when one was sent from the mess, he retired to his bed-room for a few minutes, and then returned and talked, and jested at the reproaches which were cast upon him.

When he first arrived at Cephalonia, the Captain of his ship anchored just before the military hospital. When Lord B. saw it, he complained of it laughingly to Captain Scott, as a thing of bad omen. "But," said his lordship, when he told the story, "the Captain, in order to remedy the evil, made it still worse; for next morning when we awoke, we found he had moored us on the opposite

side, it is true, but it was just against the burying-
ground." He was accustomed to spend a good
deal of his time in joking with the Captain, who
was a sort of humourist himself. "Scott," said
Lord B., "when these fellows of yours take me
over to Greece, are you not afraid that they will
be inspired with a love of liberty, desert you, and
join the glorious cause of the Greeks?" "I am
not at all afraid of that," said the Captain; "I
have taken care that they shall not do that."
"Why, what have you done?" "I have done
to them as your lordship does to me." "What
is that?" "I have kept them three months in
arrears." Lord Byron laughed heartily at the
Captain's joke.

At Metaxata his lordship was visited by many
poor refugee Greeks from the Continent and the
Isles of the Archipelago. He not only relieved
their present distresses, but allotted a certain sum
monthly to the most destitute, and this was paid
till his death. A list of these poor pensioners was
given me by the nephew of Professor Bambas,
which I have not at present by me.

When Lord B. was in the harbour, on board
the ship, although I had not called on him myself,
I persuaded my friend Professor Bambas to pay

his respects to his lordship, as due to one who came to befriend his country, and I had no doubt that his lordship would receive a patriot so distinguished as Bambas, with pleasure. Bambas called, but it appeared that Lord B. was quite unacquainted with his reputation and character, and as he was reposing himself, he sent his compliments, and said, that he could not then see him. He, however, soon heard of Bambas after his arrival at Argostoli, and one day when I mentioned the subject, and expressed my surprise that he had not received him, he said he did not know that he was anything but a common priest, and was at the time tired, and did not wish to be disturbed. Some one had told him, he said, that Bambas was a wild democrat. This I mentioned to Bambas. He replied, " No ; I would prefer democracy, or rather republicanism, were all my countrymen Phocions, but not till then." When we again spoke of Bambas, Lord B. said he would go and pay him a visit. This, however, mere circumstances prevented ; but he sent Count Gamba to make his apologies.

It was from Metaxata he wrote those fine letters to the Greek government, in which he warned them of the consequences of dissensions, and

exhorted them to true patriotism and peace.
Here he waited intelligence from Greece of the
state of parties, from the gentleman whom he sent
over to report to him the situation of affairs, and
in whose fidelity he could confide.

Count Delladecima assured me, and he had
ample opportunities of ascertaining the fact, that
in conversing with him on the affairs of Greece,
Lord Byron shewed a profound, cool, and deliberate judgment; a patience in examining, and
a soundness of political views, which did honour
both to the strength of his understanding, and to
the goodness of his heart, which was the more
surprising to him, he said, as he had formed an idea
from Lord Byron's poetical genius, that he would
find him full of imaginary and fanciful schemes, or
fickle and changeable in his judgment; but, he
added, of all the men whom I have had an opportunity of conversing with, on the means of establishing the independence of Greece, and rege-
nerating the character of the natives, Lord B.
appears to entertain the most enlightened and
correct views.

How well Lord B. spent his time in Missolunghi
—the utility which his presence and his councils
produced to the Greeks—the advances of money

that he made to the government, which enabled
the Greek fleet to move to Hydra—and above all,
the fortification of Missolunghi erected by Parry,
chiefly at his expense, without which the town
could never have made so memorable a resistance, are well known, and those who wish for a
detail of them, may find their curiosity gratified
by perusing Count Gamba's narrative. A friend
of mine, who was in Greece, and was intimate with
Lord Byron, amused me with the following
account of affairs, which is too curious to be
omitted.

" There was little comfort, or even appearance
of comfort, in his mode of living in Missolunghi;
his house was small and incommodious, though
one of the best in the town ; and it was in a low
and damp situation. It was frequently necessary
to use boats to get at it. Count Gamba lived in
lodgings, and often took his meals by himself.
Parry and some others lived on the ground-floor,
or in houses near his lordship. Bruno was seldom
in his company. When my friend arrived at
Missolunghi, Lord B. was under a strict regimen ;
this was probably after his first attack, and hence
there was no regular meal prepared for him : his
scanty meals he generally took by himself, at

whatever hour suited him. P. was officious, pompous, and jealous of any having access to, or influence with Lord B. The household appeared in confusion : all the servants had uniforms, each according to his fancy, and some of them were of the most grotesque kind : they seemed to have exchanged duties ; the cook, for example, became groom, and the groom became something else, and *vice versâ ;* each appeared to be doing something else than that which lay within his province."

As most of the officers were dependent on Lord B., either on account of his influence, or for their actual pay, they did not disturb him often. My friend, who thought that Lord B. would not be displeased with company, visited him every night, and took F. with him. Lord B. always received them kindly : there was, however, often as little ceremony in the house, as if it had been an inn ; and G. F. was often accustomed to take up a book, and lounge over it till Lord B. had time, or was in the humour for conversing with them. Sometimes he was animated and gay, telling them many amusing anecdotes and stories. He told them that, once when Mr. Murray was complaining of the high price which he gave for his book,

he answered him in rhyme, the short line always
terminating in " My Murray." One of the lines
which he remembers was,

> " But you have the printing of the Navy List,
> My Murray."

He said that when he and Hobhouse were
together in Albania, Hobhouse laid hold of a great
quantity of manuscript paper, which had fallen
out of his portmanteau, and asked what it was—
on being told that it was an account of Lord B.'s
early life and opinions, he persuaded him to burn
it ; " for," said he, "if any sudden accident occur,
they will print it, and thus injure your memory."
" The loss is *irreparable,*" said Lord B. One
evening they were talking of the separation between him and Lady B. ; he desired them to mention all the causes which they had heard assigned
for it, and seemed amused at the absurdity and
falsehood of them. When he had heard all, he
said, " The causes were too simple to be soon
found out."

He often professed his admiration of Sir Walter
Scott. He was much engaged about uniforms,
and appeared very particular about his dress.
Some of the agents of the committees of Switzerland and Germany published something in the

Missolunghi Chronicle against Baron Freidel, as
having authority to act for the English Committee.   Lord B. insisted that they should retract
their assertion of having authority from England.
He disliked Dr. Meyer, and some of the Ger-
mans ; one in particular who was suspected of
having assumed a title, and Meyer, because he
was so fond of displaying his new ones, such as
President of the Missolunghi School, Redacteur,
&c.   In one of his notes, in order to be as bitter
as possible, he wrote, " Be assured that Dr. M.
and Baron —— cannot have a greater contempt
for borrowed titles than your humble servant,
N. Byron." The German came to him, and made
many apologies with tears, and became on so
good a footing with Lord B., that he consented
to buy his rich and gaudy uniforms.   One day,
Lord B. shewed all these to G. F., who said, " I
thought the German was your enemy ?"   " Oh,"
said Lord B., " I have pardoned him, for I can
never resist a man's tears." He sent the uniforms
all back, because he thought them too dear.

One of his household, G., sent to Corfu for a
great many articles of dress, all exceedingly fine,
and among them was a pair of jack-boots and
spurs.   Lord B. was very angry when they

arrived, either because they were ordered without his knowledge, or because they were too expensive; to G. F. he exclaimed, " See what my buffoon has done ; he has ordered such and such things, but I shall send them all back except the elegant jack-boots, which he *shall* wear." And he did wear them to the no small amusement of some of his friends.

The Turkish girl and her mother were captives, and inhabited the house allotted to Millingen for an hospital. M., from pity, allowed them to remain. Lord B. took a fancy to the girl, and had her dressed in fine gaudy clothes, but she became pert and forward. G. F. told this to Lord B., and said if he were M. he would drive them from the house. Lord B. sent for the girl and scolded her.

At this time he gave no dinner parties to the Greeks, and G. F. thinks that this produced no bad effects, as distance increases respect, especially with such people as the Greeks. Mavrocordato came often to Lord Byron, and sat, and smoked, and conversed. One evening when he came, Lord Byron was out of humour, and said to G. F. and F., " Do not go away, for this fellow comes teasing me to give him money ; I have already lent him one thousand dollars, and he *shall not have more."* One of them whispered, Mavrocordato understands English; "So much the better," said he; "he will go away the sooner if he understood me." Mavrocordato sat awhile quietly smoking, and then went away *.

Lord B. was often suspicious, and seemed to think that those who approached him had some interested views, and in general he had too much reason for these conclusions. He at first thought that G. F. came to be admitted into his corps and get some of his money, till his acquaintance with him removed the error. Such of the Greeks as were in office were accustomed to dress in state,

* It has been suggested to me, that the above paragraph may give an unjust impression of Mavrocordato's character, whose disinterested conduct in pecuniary matters has never been doubted. It may here be observed, though perhaps scarcely necessary, that the loan spoken of was not made to Mavrocordato, as an individual, but as governor of Missolunghi, for the good of the public service. The character of no one of the Greek leaders stands so high as that of Mavrocordato for disinterested zeal for his country's cause; and after filling, for some years, the highest office in the Greek government, he has left it in honourable poverty. Lord Byron, whose little sally was made when out of humour, held Mavrocordato in high esteem, as may be seen from the following passage in a letter to Mr. Murray, dated February 25, 1824.

" Prince Mavrocordato is an excellent person, and does all in his power; but his situation is perplexing in the extreme; still we have great hopes of the success of the contest."

and visit him in ceremony : on such occasions
Lord B. hurried to his room to throw on his uniform, and the Greeks were evidently under great
awe while before him.

His presence in Missolunghi at times appeared
to increase the confusion which prevailed, and
Lord B. seemed sometimes to enjoy it, especially the burlesque manner in which P. vapoured
about and displayed his power, as Adjutant to
the Commander-in-chief. He used to say, " His
lordship, as commander-in-chief, never gives
orders directly, but only through ME. *We*," he
said one day, " *we* will subscribe twenty dollars
to your Infirmary." Lord B. gave fifty. G. F.
sold a pair of tight leather breeches one day to
G., who strutted about the dirty streets of Missolunghi in them, to the perfect amazement of the
Greeks. " Do not laugh at him," said G. F. to
his lordship, " or you will cause him to give me
them back, and break my bargain." He seemed
sometimes to wish that T. would return, merely
to drive away the people that pestered him,
and put his house in order ; for though he
took an obstinate fit occasionally, and would not
budge, merely to shew that he was not led by any
one, yet in general from indolence, or some other

cause, he was facile on many points, and allowed himself to be led and influenced.

During his illness, he said to M., who differed in opinion from B., "You differ, that you may have the credit of curing me." At another time he said, " I see that neither of you know anything about the matter." He returned T.'s gun which he had with him, either because he was reluctant to part with so much money, as it was dear, or, as was probable, he thought if T. was scarce of money, he would the sooner rejoin him.

He differed on many points with Colonel Stanhope. G. F. is inclined to think, that had he gone to Salona, he might have prevented the civil war by his influence ; but he was careful not to write a letter to Ulysses, who had sent him a letter of compliment. One day he desire Count G. to write a letter, which he did. Lord B. took it up, read it, and then coolly tore it to pieces.

A letter was afterwards written to Ulysses, and when Lord B. was told that it had been lost in the river Phidari, with some valuables, he uttered an exclamation of joy, and said, " they should not again prevail on him to write."

S. had been acquainted with T., and attended the funeral of Williams and Shelley. When it

was finished, he went away, and Lord B. asked
T. who that gentleman was. T. replied, "that
he was an English officer, who would not intrude, because he had heard that his lordship
wished to live retired." "Then I shall be acquainted with him," said Lord B. ; spurring his
horse, he soon overtook S. ; introduced himself,
and invited S. to breakfast. After this, he had frequent opportunities of seeing Lord B., who used
to say, T. was an excellent fellow till his Lara
and Corsair spoiled him, by his attempting to
imitate them.

G. F. told me, that Lord B. liked and seemed
pleased with F., who admired him excessively,
and with the greatest simplicity and singleness of
heart: but he did not like H., who was stiff and
formal. When they were disputing about the
motto for the Greek Telegraph, (the first having
given offence to many,) Lord B. insisted that the
old one should not be retained. Count G. entered one day, and said, "Pray, my lord, what
motto shall we have?" Lord B. pettishly replied, " Foolishness to the Greeks."

We all seemed at this time, said G. F., to have
lost our high sense of honour, and were occupied
in selling and buying, from one another, guns,

horses, breeches, uniforms,—each endeavouring to make the best bargain he could, influenced, probably, added G. F. by the contagious example of the Greeks around us. G. F. did not think that Lord B. was fitted for the place; it required one of stern demeanour, and of iron nerve. T. was of the same opinion. Lord Murray, he thought, was much better qualified for it : he was a great favourite with the Greeks, from speaking their language so well; and, from the undeviating gentleness of his manner, he would have attached to himself all the English around him.

Lord B. was rather above the middle size ; his countenance was fine, and indicated intelligence, but especially benevolence. His forehead was large and ample, his eyes were of a grey colour, his nose well-proportioned, his mouth wide, and his chin projecting; his hair was light brown, inclining to grey, particularly about the temples: his appearance was full and robust*. He had high shirt collars, sometimes embroidered, but without frills ; he wore often nankeen jacket

---

* Colonel D. told him that many persons had supposed he was quite *en-bon-point*. He said, "two years ago I was much stouter, and as fat as the captain of my brig."

and trowers, sometimes a plaid jacket; he generally wore a gold chain about his neck, on which
a locket was suspended, and the end of the chain
was placed in his waistcoat pocket, and a cameo,
with the head of Napoleon.

His countenance generally exhibited a smile, or
a look of softness, and thoughtfulness; and when
animated in conversation, there was a keen and
perçant expression of eye, with a slight colour
in his face, which was usually pale and clear.

He spoke with energy, vivacity, and freedom;
his utterance was rapid, and varied in its in-
tonations; his language was select, forcible, and
pure; and his ideas were expressed with unusual
ease and propriety. His voice was soft and melodious, to a degree which at first appeared to be
the result of affectation. His manners were dignified and well-bred; he was invariably polite.

The impression which he left on me, judging of
his manner merely, was that of a perfectly polished
man, with much affability, cheerfulness, vivacity,
and benevolence. In the conversations which I
had with him, he appeared to shew an acute and
cultivated mind, rather than a profound understanding. There was no appearance of extensive
science or erudition, nor that coolness and so-

briety of judgment, which a learned philosopher
might be expected to exhibit: but his manner
was lively, witty, and penetrating, shewing that
he had a mind of strong powers, and capable of
accomplishing great things, rather than affording a constant proof that he had already accomplished them. He was so easy, affable, and kind
that you required at times to recall to mind his
rank and fame, lest his manner should unconsciously betray you into undue familiarity,—an
error into which one gentleman fell,—and was
punished by Lord B.'s avoiding him as much as
politeness permitted. Although he must have
looked into a variety of books, and was acquainted
with a little on every subject, yet I was not
impressed with an idea of the profoundness of his
knowledge, nor should I have been disposed to rely
on the solidity of his judgment. He often spoke
for effect, and appeared to say fine and brilliant
things, without having any other end in view; a
practice which might display quickness of discern-
ment, eloquence and wit, but which, of course,
could not excite the decided admiration which the
display of a richly-furnished mind, or a superior
and solid understanding, would have elicited.
Though not insensible to renown and distinction,

and though raised to the highest pitch of poetical
eminence, he had no poetical enthusiasm, or fantastic frenzy in his manner and conversation. He
felt that these were useful, and to be studied
and valued only as they lead to something more
substantial ; and as he had a quick perception of
the ridiculous, he seemed to have a feeling, that
frequently crossed his mind, as if fame and poetry,
and every thing else, which men so eagerly court,
was, in reality, hollow and vain ; and contempt
for the whole human race—including himself—
was often predominant.

His varied fortunes in life, his unhappiness
amidst such means of happiness, his splendid fame,
his personal defects, and his domestic calamities,
his mortified pride, and vanity, might naturally
lead him often to such a conclusion. It is true,
that all I say is but my own opinion, and what I
cannot affirm as certan, yet, as far as one can
judge of another by looks, hints, or the train of
associations, such seem often to have been the predominant feelings of his mind. I have been asked
by some, if his appearance and manner did not
convey the idea of a fiend incarnate. On the
contrary, his appearance and manner gave the idea
of a kind-hearted, benevolent, and feeling man,

with an amiable and pleasing countenance, but a man who was led by passions, by prejudice, and not by coolness of judgment, nor the steady self-denial, and heroical feelings of Christian principles. That his was a mind often agitated in private by gloomy meditations and melancholy feelings appeared at times, when he gave for a moment repose to the mind, from the exertion of acting his part in company, and allowed his countenance to assume those features which were habitual, for then the expression which I saw once or twice was that of melancholy and woeful forlornness ; but it was surprising to see the quick and striking change, passing immediately from this, to a sprightly, animated, and amiable expression, whenever he saw that it was expected of him to resume his part ; which was always the principal in conversation. Sometimes it struck me, that in reality, in his solitary hours, he was melancholy and unhappy, and that the very great hilarity and vivacity which he shewed in company was a proof of it, as if he were glad to escape, for the sake of variety, from his habitual frame of mind. I often looked at Lord Byron with admiration, sympathy, and compassion : admiration for his great abilities, sympathy with his unfor-

tunate life, and compassion for one who, with all
the wealth, rank, and fame which fell to the lot of
few, and which, when founded on a proper basis,
are calculated so much to promote happiness,
appeared unhappy ; not merely because he was
not virtuous, but because he was not religious.
Many talents he possessed, calculated to excite
wonder and envy ; yet the highest of all blessings,
piety, he possessed not.

The vanity of all earthly things, if the favour of
God attends them not, was strongly impressed on
the mind in listening to him, and considering his
character. He possessed many virtues, such as
friendship and benevolence, yet he was not
happy ; and what could these avail, without that
peace and tranquillity of mind here, under every
situation and circumstance, and that strong and
certain hope of a blessed immortality in heaven,
which can alone be obtained through faith in the
merits of our Redeemer ? Yet Lord B. excited
intense interest and sympathy in my mind.

☆ ★ ☆

He vaguely hoped, no doubt, that if the Scriptures were true, he should ascertain the truth of
them some time or other ; and hence, surrounded
as he was with such companions and so many
public and private duties, it was a matter of ap-
prehension, that even this desire might be suspended, or even extinguished. His patience,
however, in listening to me, his candour in never
putting captious objections, his acknowledgment
of his own sinfulness, gave hope that the bless-
ing of religious truth might be opened to his
understanding ; and though these were damped by
an occasional levity, at least by the want of that
seriousness which the subject required, yet, on
the whole, the general result was favourable.

It may be useful to consider Lord B.'s character in the following points of view—as a man, as
a poet, and, lastly, in reference to Christianity.
Of the minute details of his early life I am ignorant, as no full and authentic account of it has
yet been given*. He first appeared as a poet
before he reached the age of majority, and his
work was received with an overwhelming ridi-

---

* Mr. Moore's work contains a full and interesting narration of
Lord B.'s early years, and most strikingly exemplifies that paradox,
" The Child is father of the Man."

cule and scorn by a critic in the Edinburgh Review. There was no excuse for defects or failings—no candid indulgence—no kind encourage
ment to try again, and endeavour to do better,
but a cruel and inhuman taunting and mockery.
That Lord B.'s vanity was mortified by the blow,
is certain. It struck to his very heart, and roused
his bitterest feelings; and in every variety of
scene, when wandering in the regions of Greece
or on the smiling shores of Turkey, the effects
were severely felt and powerly expressed. This
disappointment, joined to his personal deformity,
and his scantiness of fortune when compared
with others of his rank, affected him deeply, and
he felt as if nature and man had treated him
unkindly; instead of yielding to circumstances
or to the dictates of reason, he only exerted
his faculties to fight the battle into which he had
been so unexpectedly dragged. Had he been
educated in strictness of moral virtue, or in resignation to religion; and had those habits been
strengthened by example, his fate and his feelings
might have been different; but, left an orphan,
placed in society where ambition and wealth were
the only objects—where the passions had no particular restraint, he unfortunately chose not to

restrain his. He determined to engage in the fight with the Reviewers, and exhibited the same spirit of malevolent and angry feeling, unworthy of a virtuous and noble mind, but justifiable, or at least excusable in his case, as he was ungently attacked without having even given provocation. His opponents had no excuse, and his critic is not to be envied, if his judgment be now sobered, when he looks back on his wanton attack, and reflects how much his cruel criticism may have contributed to the chequered, unfortunate life of his victim. Lord B., in the execution of his vengeance against his critic, unfortunately attacked many others in terms of contempt and derision, and thus was guilty of the same fault which had been committed against himself. He assailed the most distinguished critics, poets, and writers; and the satirical powers of a young and noble author, who was thus daring and impetuous, were not likely to conciliate the forbearing hand and the kindly praise of others *. In the mean

* Colonel D. took up a book, which was "the English Bards and Scotch Reviewers." "You need not look at this," said D.; "it is your own." "This book did me a great deal of harm," replied his lordship; "I lost a great number of friends who have never forgiven me." "It is the best you ever wrote." "Why," said Lord B., "I published a few silly songs, written when I was young; and

time he went on rapidly, adding poem to poem; the subjects were strange and unusual, and his lordship seemed to care little about the sympathy of his readers or the rules of poetry. His progress was watched—his fame rose bright amidst all distrust and opposition: many, however, grudged his reputation, and praised him with reluctance. It was his lot to be constantly before the public eye. His marriage, his sudden separation, to which he imprudently gave publicity;—his departure for Italy, his mode of living there; his poems, which became more and more descriptive, as it was deemed, of his character, and were equally deserving of censure and praise,—all were calculated to excite a host of enemies who

when the Reviewers treated me so severely, I wished to show them that I would not put up with their insolence so tamely as they expected. But one thing I regret very much in this book, is what I wrote of Lord Carlisle. I am sorry for it." Colonel D. mentioned the Quarterly Review on his Cain. " Oh, you should read the Edinburgh Quarterly—this gives it much sharper; for though on my own side, it is always hardest against me."

One day, when talking of one of his aunts whom the colonel knew, he said, " We have been an unfortunate family; none of us have come to any good." The colonel said, " He hoped to see him a Methodist yet, though he regretted that in the interval much time was lost, as his lordship should now be writing some beautiful hymns." " When I do become one," he replied, " I shall not be a lukewarm Christian."

had hitherto lain quiet. As censure and criticism reached him, and he was always sensible to them, instead of endeavouring to remove the cause, he seems to have been still further roused, by his passions, and by a consciousness that he was censured far more than he deserved,—by many whose conduct was worse than his own,—to continue the battle with unabating vigour. As religion had never much engaged his thoughts, and as unfortunately many religious people, from a preposterous fear of the injury he would do, inveighed against him from the pulpit, and spoke or wrote against him, his anger seems to have been excited towards them also, and he resolved to write in defiance of them all; and as he did so on the spur of the moment and under malignant passions, and not from an ambition of the praise of the present or future good men, his poems became increasingly defective in purity, and were even tainted with the appearance of infidelity.

There are circumstances which induce me to believe that Lord Byron never doubted the divine authenticity of the Scriptures, arising probably from the influence of early education, if no higher principle was in operation, and that those hints of

infidelity were thrown out by way of desperate or
contemptuous bravado. His conduct, however,
was not to be excused. Writing, as he did, under
the influence of impetuous feelings, and stung by
what he considered unnecessarily cruel and un-
merited reproach and censure, he fell into greater
mistakes than he did at first. He libelled and
ridiculed his native country, from which he was
a voluntary exile; he satirized his king; he satirized his political enemies, and his vengeance
followed them even after they were laid in the
grave. These things were highly culpable; but
who does not perceive that his public life was a
warfare, a combat excited by his critic, and continued by a host of others? and who could expect
that a man so vain, so disappointed, so mortified,
and who fought with such feelings,—with the
added spirit of vengeance, would do so with
soberness and moderation?

His character as a man, if separated from that
of a poet, has no unusual feature, and is, indeed,
a common one. Deprived early of his parents, he
grew up without correction or control, and he
displayed some of those extravagances and eccentricities which distinguish too many of our young
noblemen. He married early; soon separated

from his wife ; lived in Italy for some years, in
comparative seclusion : then engaged in the
cause of Greece, and died at an early age. His
private life, like that of many others, was a mixture of virtues and vices ; and his vices, there is
reason to believe, were those which are most in-
dulgently looked upon by the world, nor were
they more numerous than most of those of his own
rank ; while his charities and benevolence were,
perhaps, more than can usually be found.

His writings, however, have given a tinge of
his private character; and hence it is impossible
to form an estimate of the latter, without taking
into view the former. Had he not written, it is
obvious that there was nothing unusual in his character, nothing that is not paralleled in the lives
of many private gentlemen. From the choice of
his subjects, he has had the peculiar fate of its
having been supposed that his imaginary characters were, in almost all instances, the representation of his own ; and hence many have judged of
his private character by those which he has drawn
in his writings. That there is some foundation
for this cannot be denied ; but that the conclusion
has been carried too far, a slight consideration will
readily convince any one. His first work against

the Edinburgh Reviewers exhibited a fearless
and undaunted mind, equally prepared for attack
and defence, and not very scrupulous in the
means. That it had the misfortune to keep his
mind in this state, ready for warfare with all his
passions awakened, has already been hinted at ;
and this consideration seems to account, sometimes, for the choice of subjects in his future
poems, and for those hints and remarks which
he incidentally scatters through them. As his
life was one of change and bustle—as his feelings and passions were never subjected to any
steady control—as he wrote often under the
sting and writhing of mortified pride and disappointment—as he also wrote with a feeling that
his sins were too severely punished by many
whose conduct did not justify them in doing so,
it may be supposed that he was not always happy
in his subjects and delineation, nor prudent and
guarded in his remarks. Though some of these
circumstances led him into errors, they contributed, there is room to conjecture, to that free,
unshackled style of writing, which, leaving his
genius uncramped by rules or criticisms, which he
both feared and despised, enabled him to reach
some of those excellencies which place him on a

level with the very first poets of this or any country.
The subject of Childe Harold, the finest, and,
upon the whole, the most unexceptionable of his
poems, was that of a man sated with all the sins
of his youth, and experiencing, like Solomon, the
vanity of all human things,—wandering from his
native country, and giving vent to his feelings and
sentiments, as the places he wandered over, and
the persons he met with, excited. As there
were some points of resemblance between this
imaginary character and his own, the mind naturally connects them together, and dwells with
some sort of mysterious curiosity on the innumerable vices which the young wanderer must
have committed, when, tired with all and stung
with remorse, he leaves his country to seek ease
in variety, to his troubled conscience. The impression that such must have been Lord Byron's
character in his youth is made by this poem;
though sober reflection might teach us, that it
could have been conceived and written by one
whose youth was spent in the exercise of every
virtue, and whose conduct was unstained by vice
or crime. The character of the Giaour, Lara,
the Corsair, Manfred, and, finally, that of Don
Juan, confirm these impressions. The poet

seemed to delight in imagining and delineating
all that was bad in human nature. Impetuous,
stormy, and violent passions ; insatiable revenge,
unconquered pride, ferocity, and the ungovern-
able and unlawful omnipotence of love, seem
subjects which engaged his thoughts and his
pen : in them were mixed expressions of discontent with all earthly enjoyments; with the
established order of things ; with feelings of contempt for all that man takes pride in ; the vanity
of ambition, of rank, of warlike or scientific
glory. He pourtrays the misery which man
brings on man, from the exercise of unruly passions ; the evils of tyranny and war ; the disorders
in the physical, as well as in the moral world : he
tries in vain to penetrate the inscrutable mysteries
of Providence ; and, failing in his attempt to account for what he sees, he throws out doubts
against the Divinity of the Scriptures. He is
not the poet of virtue. No character ennobled by
virtue, or by piety, is sung by him. Beauty is a
plaything, an object of desire ; and though his
descriptions of female beauty of face and figure
are in the highest degree poetical, yet they are
drawn without any other virtue than that which
education, or the opinion of society, gives them ;

and they are drawn in order to display that devotedness of love,—whether lawful or unlawful, it matters not with the poet,—that sacrifice of every worldly interest, that encountering of every misery and woe, and death itself, in pursuit of its gratification, or in its devotedness to the object beloved. With him, love must reign paramount to all laws and principles, moral and divine ; and death and damnation must be encountered, rather than restrain its impetuous and uncontrollable force. In short, it is a species of insanity, that takes possession of the mind, which absorbs every other feeling and interest.

Such is the general character of his poetry. I speak not of his style, of his invention, of his versification, of the grandeur of his delineations, of his frequent sublime descriptions, both of moral and physical portraits, and the various excellencies and defects of his compositions. These I leave to others, as my object is simply to endeavour to ascertain his character as a man. On these points I shall only remark that, considering Lord B. merely in the light of a poet, he has not only surpassed all his contemporaries, but, passing over a long list of great names, he places himself on a level with Shakspeare and Milton.

The question however recurs, how far his poetry
illustrates his moral and intellectual character, and
how far it is a faithful impression of it.

It can be conceived, that a moral man might
form conceptions such as he has done, and publish
them, merely as best suiting his genius, and as
being more likely to produce effect than others
which have presented themselves to his imagination. The mind of man is delighted at that which
is wonderful, astonishing, and striking, whether
the impressions are favourable to virtue or not;
and a poet, conversant with human naure, will
find that such pictures of new, splendid, grand,
and horrid views of human nature will produce
a greater impression than those that are soft,
pleasing, and virtuous. But though these subjects may be permitted to a poet, as within the
province of his art, yet he is amenable to censure and condemnation if his descriptions are
calculated to destroy or diminish virtue, piety,
loyalty, and all those feelings which contribute to
private or social happiness. Every man is under
obligations to maintain these; and whoever violates
them, whatever may be the object, whether to display the power of his talents, or to efface those
principles, the existence of which he disbelieves or

hates, is justly condemned. Lord B., therefore, is amenable to the same tribunal, in as far as he has violated those obligations which are due to the peace and welfare of society. That he has violated them to a great extent, few will venture to deny; but what were his motives for doing so, it is more difficult to ascertain. The events of his life encourage the idea, that he drew such portraits as were most congenial to his own mind, and that the sentiments he ascribes to others are entirely his own; but, to carry this belief to the length which some have carried it, would violate every principle of candour and charity, and would award to him a more severe and uncharitable judgment than has been pronounced on any other poet. The poet having a choice of characters, can draw them as he considers most likely to produce effect, and for that purpose he has a wide range allowed him; but it does not therefore follow, that these are characters which he himself loves, and admires, and wishes to be held up for imitation, or that the sentiments which he ascribes to them are his own. —It is true that such conceptions of character have passed through his mind, but they are no more to be considered his fixed and habitual sentiments, than are the evil thoughts and ima-

ginations which often pass through the minds
of men, to their great regret. With respect,
therefore, to Lord B., no positive judgment can be
drawn, but that the same charity and candour
should be exercised towards him, which has been
exercised towards every other poet. From what
I saw of him, I am induced to conclude, that most
of his characters were drawn, because he considered
them to have a more striking poetical effect than
others of a different kind, and that the sentiments
they utter are for the purpose of filling up his conception of the consistency and individuality of the
character; that he had no specific object either to
recommend vice or promote virtue, and that he
neither considered the moral nor immoral effect of
his writings. This remark I would not, however,
apply to his writings without exception, because
there are many expressions in his works, and
especially in that of Don Juan, the effects of which
he must have known were likely to be positively
prejudicial, and in writing which, he violated all
that indulgence which is properly allowed to a
poet. I am inclined to believe that occasionally
the sentiments which he ascribes to his characters
were, at the time he wrote them, really his own:
thus his discontent with the state of society, his

hatred of tyranny and oppression, might be judged in general to be the habitual sentiments of his own mind, arising from that melancholy view of human nature which his early misfortunes and disappointments might impress upon him. His abuse of individuals, his forgetfulness of what was due to loyalty, and his ridicule of the king, were the result of the prejudice and passion of the moment, and the subjects of after regret. His abuse of Lord Castlereagh I conceive to have been the effect of his really believing him to have been an enemy to the true interests of his country; and this feeling being carried to excess, he considered it was just to hold him up to the execration of posterity. His doubts of the inspiration of the Scriptures were not the actual convictions of his mind, but transient,—uttered in the feeling of the moment, and springing from a mixture of doubt and of bravado, that people might stare and wonder at his boldness.

I would acquit him, therefore, of a preference to vice, instead of virtue, merely because he has painted vicious characters; most of the sentiments which he has attributed to them are, it appears to me, imaginings of the brain, and not the convictions of the heart; and many others, which are more directly applicable to himself, were the result of passing impressions, and not expressive of his fixed and habitual belief. I would also acquit him of any determinate view of destroying virtue, encouraging vice, and promoting infidelity ; and candour requires that we should believe that his characters and subjects were chosen for their poetical and striking effect, and not with any other other secret and insidious view.

But, acquitting him of all this, we are still to ascertain that degree of praise and blame which the nature of his writings lead us to bestow upon him. In the first place he is not entitled to the praise of noble, enlightened, virtuous, and pious sentiments and descriptions. In the second place he is not entitled to praise for his writings having left any favourable and pleasing impressions of human nature, or of pure and unmixed delight in the contemplation of his characters. In the third place he is blamable for the unfavourable impressions which are produced by strong, exalted delineations of vicious, though great passions, of unlawful loves, of wild ambition, discontent, and turbulence; by doubts of virtue and of piety, and in his descriptions of moral profligacy, particularly in Don Juan. Every good man must

regret that his extraordinary talents were not
better applied. His poems produce a mixed
feeling of wonder and astonishment, of horror
and regret. It is not more unpleasing to see the
horrid sublime of vice, than to contemplate that
of nature; and had the mind something, however
little, in his poems, in the praise of virtue and
piety, on which it might rest, giving a hint as it
were of the misery and woe which ever attends
violent passions, describing the remorse for crime
and the agony of guilt, he would have saved his
character from reproach, and would have left an
impression that his descriptions were selected and
drawn for practical effect. Had this been done,
and had Don Juan never been written, his poems
would have been read with pleasure and instruc-
tion, as adding new views, finely drawn, of the
vanities of human character. It is perhaps well,
however, that they have been written, though
many might wish that Byron had not been the
man. They are such as none but a genius of the
highest order could have written : they shew
a desperate disregard of virtuous fame, which
marks strongly the impetuous, energetic, and
daring character of the man, and the singular circumstances of life which drew it forth, and in

which no other man has been, or will perhaps be placed. As they were written under irritation and agitation of feeling, when judgment and reflection were asleep, they were the wild throes of passion, rather than the result of long and studied deliberation. As he wrote not for fame, nor for posterity, but from the impulse of the moment, so we need not be surprised that we find so much to censure and regret. But this very consideration will form his excuse with posterity, when time has mellowed the asperities of his character, when his failings are excued in consideration of the temptations to which he was exposed ; and it will acquit him of all attempts and settled plans of undermining virtue and promoting the cause of infidelity and vice,—an idea which never would have been entertained, had not circumstances prevented a cool reflection and a calm decision.

In short, the name of Byron will go down to posterity with those of the first poets of the country. His grossness will find an example in some of those whom England most admires. His slight tincture of infidelity will be attributed to the circumstances of his life, and he will be reckoned of a peculiar order, as having given the best paintings of vice and crime ; a class which, though not edifying in a moral way, may not be uninstructive in an intellectual point of view, as exhibiting examples of the strength and conceptions of the mind. Though Byron, therefore, cannot enter into the class of the good, the moral, and the virtuous poets,—the number of which is unfortunately too small,—he will rank among the highest in that of poets in general : nor will he have much to suffer in point of mere morality if compared with Shakspear, the first of that class, as there is far more grossness and indelicacy in the works of Shakspear than in those of Byron ; the manners of the age, it is true, present some excuse for the former. They are both the poets of nature, that is, of nature exhibiting, as it really does, a mixture of goodness and vice,—of crime, and guilt, and passion,—of virtue and iniquity. They are equally powerful in delineating the varied features of individual character; though, as Shakspear has represented it under a greater variety of forms, he may be thought to have excelled Byron in richness of invention, and in eloquence of poetry ; yet, while this is admitted, it may be contended that many of the delineations of Byron shew the same strength and vigour of intellect so strikingly peculiar to Shakspear. Of

neither of them can it be said, that they never
wrote a line, which, dying, they would wish to blot:
though both of them excel Cowper in strength of
poetical genius, they are far his inferiors in virtue
and moral poetry. His fame will extend as widely
as theirs; and while they excite the admiration,
he will preserve the love and gratitude of every
good man, who can recur to his pages with the
assurance that his feelings of reverence for virtue
and religion will not only receive no shock, but
be improved and invigorated by the charms of his
poetry and the truth and justness of his remarks.

It appears, therefore, from a review of Byron's
private character, that it was a common one,
being mixed with many virtues and stained with
some fashionable vices. We meet nothing in it
to command our veneration: we find many things
to pity and excuse, from the peculiarity of his
situation; but we are not entitled to call him a
virtuous, pious man. In his poetical character,
we find much reason to admire his wonderful
talents. We may regret that his poems were
not finished with a greater end in view than he
seems to have had; that is, that he did not propose to himself more distinctly the promotion of
virtue. We may blame him for his indelicacy

and licentiousness of description in some of his
works, and also for many of his sentiments, and
especially for the levity, and appearance of infidelity, with which he sometimes alludes to sacred
subjects. We observe in them, however, no
proof of fixed opinions, or reason to believe that
in general he pourtrayed the features of his own
character; and we may readily believe, without any
breach of candour, that his most reprehensible
descriptions and sentiments, written under the
influence of passion and prejudice, or the result of
ignorance, would have been an object of regret
to himself had he lived, and perhaps often were
so. With respect to religion, we find nothing
like a bitter enmity to it, or a settled conviction
that it was an imposture. Some passages display
a levity and an appearance of incredulity, but
nothing like a deliberate denial, or a rejection of
its truth. We find, in fact, that he was like all
those nominal Christians who are unregenerate :
—he knew not its spirit. His conduct was not
regulated by it, and he differed simply from many
of those who hold in the world a very respectable
character, in his having treated it with seeming
ridicule in his writings, while they, perhaps, have
done the same in conversation.

He was, in fact, what he represented himself to be when I saw him,—unsettled in his religious opinions. He rejected the appellation of infidel ; he said it was a cold and chilling word. He confessed he was not happy ; he said, he wished to be convinced of the truth of religion.—We have now to consider if his conduct confirmed this statement.

NOTE

p. 366, l. 5: 'T' appears to be Trelawny, Byron's Cornish friend. See the headnote to Trelawny, *Recollections* in this volume.

Edward Trelawny, *Recollections of the Last Days of Shelley and Byron* (London, 1858)

Edward Trelawny's *Recollections* are the key source for one of the most enduring legends of British Romanticism, that of the dissolution of the 'Pisan circle' following the deaths of Shelley and Byron. His lurid and intensely personal account, at times poetic and at times merely bitter, peoples the Italian coast with heroes in their own day – amongst whom he himself figures as strongly as any bar Shelley. It has been as influential in the construction of the story of this highpoint and last chapter of British Romanticism as anything the poets themselves wrote, and for that reason merits serious attention.

Trelawny was born in 1792, the younger son of an ancient Cornish family. His father, who was from a military background, appears to have treated him harshly when young, for at the tender age of thirteen Trelawny ran away to join the Navy. Having the good (or, as he wrote, bad) fortune to miss out on most of the major naval engagements of the Napoleonic wars, he sailed with his ship as far as Bombay, where he was wounded in action and invalided back to England. By 1813 he was unhappily married; the next few years (of which few details survive) were to be taken up in public and embarrassing divorce procedings. In 1820, however, he reappeared in Geneva, where he met and befriended Edward Williams and Thomas Medwin, who later invited him to join them in Italy. Here (in January 1822) he encountered Byron and Shelley. He struck up a friendship with each, and was eventually to be of great service to both men. He assisted Byron in the planning and construction of the *Bolivar*, and was made captain of the ship. For Shelley his employment was less happy; it was Trelawny who arranged for the cremation of the remains of Shelley and Williams following the capsizing of their boat. He was even supposed to have snatched the heart of Shelley from the flames when it became apparent that it was not going to burn. Oddly enough, biographers tend to stress how much respect he gained from Byron for arranging the details of this famous but messy episode in British poetical history. But then Byron always prided himself on his eye for detail, and no doubt respected the same in others. It is likely that Shelley the idealist would have seen things differently.

Byron and Trelawny soon parted company following their voyage in July 1823 to join the Greek War of Independence – Trelawny claiming to be impatient at Byron's sluggardliness in joining the military campaign in person. Although he claimed to have hurried to Byron's bedside on hearing news of the poet's illness, he was too late to witness his death. He continued, however, to work with the Greeks and was seriously wounded in an assassination attempt which ended his active career. In later life Trelawny seems to have settled down remarkably well. He became what would today be called a successful property developer, and, absurdly enough, acquired a reputation for growing figs. In 1831 he unsuccessfully proposed marriage to Mary Shelley. With the marked improbability that characterized most of Trelawny's colourful existence, death came 'from mere natural decay', in 1881.

Without doubt one of the most colourful of Byron's friends, Trelawny unfortunately suffered from an insuperable aversion to telling the truth. His greatest problem was his tendency to view his acquaintances as challenges to his self-image. Thus a figure like Shelley, who was in many ways the opposite of Trelawny, escapes with little more than faint ridicule, while Byron, posing much more of a threat, sends Trelawny into fits of smears and sneers. It was not that Trelawny was entirely incapable of generosity; in Colonel Stanhope's *Greece* (1824) he recorded of Byron 'With all his faults, I loved him truly; if it gave me pain in witnessing his frailties, he only wanted a little excitement to awaken and put forth virtues that redeemed them all'. But the mood could not hold him for long. In later life he wrote what must have been the most absurd letter Mary Shelley had ever received (and she had many) to tell her 'I now feel my face burn with shame that so weak and ignoble a soul [Byron's] could so long have influenced me. It is a degrading reflection, and ever will be. I wish he had lived a little longer, that he might have witnessed how I would have soared above him here [in Greece], how I would have triumphed over his mean spirit.'

The problem in Trelawny's relationship with Byron was the curious similarity of the two men. In many ways Trelawny's mission in life was to out-Byron Byron (he is said to have slept with a copy of *The Corsair* under his pillow) and it is this that (as far as we can tell) has resulted in his leaving a more distorted picture of the poet than any other of his acquaintances bar Leigh Hunt. Like Byron, Trelawney habitually constructed a mythical persona for himself based on extensive reference to the heroes and (more often) the villains of Shakespeare and Milton. Both men were intensely proud of their lineage, and both tended to see themselves as rebels against a hypocritical conservative establishment. But unlike Trelawny, Byron possessed a keen sense of humour, and never quite let his habit of fantasizing about his own life and achievements gain the upper hand over the truth. He simply didn't take himself seriously enough for the grandiloquent and faintly ridiculous Cornishman. Even worse was that he was the only member of the Pisan circle who was not for a moment taken in by Trelawny's mythologizing of his own past: Byron once commented that he could make a gentleman out of Trelawny if only he could be persuaded to wash his hands and stop telling lies (quoted in Raphael, p. 179). This of course made Byron an opponent to be brought tumbling to the ground in the *Recollections* – hence the recurring note of peevish irritation on most occasions that the character of Byron is raised:

'If Byron's reckless frankness and apparent cordiality warmed your feelings, his sensitiveness, irritability, and the perverseness of his temper, cooled them. I was not then thirty, and the exigences of my now full-blown vanities were unsated, and my credulity unexhausted. I believed in many things then, and believe in some now; I could not sympathise with Byron, who believed in nothing.'

Byron is 'a dangerous mischief-maker'; however often Trelawny applies the epithet 'great' to him, he nevertheless claims to have experienced rapture on departing from him: 'When I left his gloomy hall, and the echoes of the heavy iron-plated door died away, I could hardly refrain from shouting with joy' (see Trelawny, pp. 24–49). The exaggeration is strongly suggestive of Trelawny's insecurity. Of course the result of the persistent carping is that Trelawny risks turning himself, as Leigh Hunt was to manage after him, into the clown he attempts to make of Byron. His account is yet more testimony to Byron's ability to inspire intense envy at some stage in almost all of those who knew him well.

For all this, the *Recollections* rank amongst the most valuable memorials we have of the poet. Trelawny was perhaps the only acquintance of Byron's last years who fully understood the bragging, bullying side of the poet's nature, and it can safely be assumed that the two men's many conversations on the less poetical aspects of existence would have made Trelawny privy to a part of Byron's character that Moore or Medwin would simply not have understood. Even without this, the *Recollections* are valuable for the light they shed on the character of a superb eccentric – a man who was considerably more than Joseph Severn's description of him as 'Lord Byron's jackal'.

CHAPTER IV.

---- ◆ ----

This should have been a noble creature—he
Hath all the energy which would have made
A goodly frame of glorious elements
Had they been wisely mingled.

MANFRED.

AT two o'clock on the following day, in company
with Shelley, I crossed the Ponte Vecchio, and went
on the Lung 'Arno to the Palazzo Lanfranchi, the
residence of Lord Byron. We entered a large
marble hall, ascended a giant staircase, passed
through an equally large room over the hall, and
were shown into a smaller apartment which had
books and a billiard-table in it. A surly-looking
bull-dog (Moretto) announced us, by growling,
and the Pilgrim instantly advanced from an inner
chamber, and stood before us. His halting gait was
apparent, but he moved with quickness; and although pale, he looked as fresh, vigorous, and ani-

mated, as any man I ever saw. His pride, added to his having lived for many years alone, was the cause I suppose that he was embarrassed at first meeting with strangers ; this he tried to conceal by an affectation of ease. After the interchange of commonplace question and answer, he regained his self-possession, and turning to Shelley, said,

" As you are addicted to poesy, go and read the versicles I was delivered of last night, or rather this morning—that is, if you can. I am posed. I am getting scurrilous. There is a letter from Tom Moore ; read, you are blarneyed in it ironically."

He then took a cue, and asked me to play billiards ; he struck the balls and moved about the table briskly, but neither played the game nor cared a rush about it, and chatted after this idle fashion:

" The purser of the frigate I went to Constantinople in called an officer *scurrilous* for alluding to his wig. Now, the day before I mount a wig—and I shall soon want one—I'll ride about with it on the pummel of my saddle, or stick it on my cane.

" In that same frigate, near the Dardanelles, we nearly ran down an American trader with his cargo

of notions. Our captain, old Bathurst, hailed, and
with the dignity of a Lord, asked him where
he came from, and the name of his ship. The
Yankee captain bellowed,—

"'You copper-bottomed sarpent, I guess you'll
know when I 've reported you to Congress.'"

The surprise I expressed by my looks was not
at what he said, but that he could register such
trifles in his memory. Of course with other such
small anecdotes, his great triumph at having swum
from Sestos to Abydos was not forgotten. I had
come prepared to see a solemn mystery, and so
far as I could judge from the first act it seemed
to me very like a solemn farce. I forgot that
great actors when off the stage are dull dogs; and
that even the mighty Prospero, without his book
and magic mantle, was but an ordinary mortal.
At this juncture Shelley joined us; he never laid
aside his book and magic mantle; he waved his
wand, and Byron, after a faint show of defiance,
stood mute; his quick perception of the truth of
Shelley's comments on his poem transfixed him,
and Shelley's earnestness and just criticism held
him captive.

I was however struck with Byron's mental vivacity and wonderful memory; he defended himself with a variety of illustrations, precedents, and apt quotations from modern authorities, disputing Shelley's propositions, not by denying their truth as a whole, but in parts, and the subtle questions he put would have puzzled a less acute reasoner than the one he had to contend with. During this discussion I scanned the Pilgrim closely.

In external appearance Byron realised that ideal standard with which imagination adorns genius. He was in the prime of life, thirty-five; of middle height, five feet eight and a half inches; regular features, without a stain or furrow on his pallid skin, his shoulders broad, chest open, body and limbs finely proportioned. His small, highly-finished head and curly hair, had an airy and graceful appearance from the massiveness and length of his throat : you saw his genius in his eyes and lips. In short, Nature could do little more than she had done for him, both in outward form and in the inward spirit she had given to animate it. But all these rare gifts to his jaundiced imagination only served to make his one personal defect (lameness) the more apparent, as

a flaw is magnified in a diamond when polished; and
he brooded over that blemish as sensitive minds will
brood until they magnify a wart into a wen.
His lameness certainly helped to make him sceptical, cynical, and savage. There was no peculiarity
in his dress, it was adapted to the climate; a tartan
jacket braided,—he said it was the Gordon pattern,
and that his mother was of that ilk. A blue velvet
cap with a gold band, and very loose nankeen
trousers, strapped down so as to cover his feet:
his throat was not bare, as represented in drawings.
At three o'clock, one of his servants announced
that his horses were at the door, which broke off his
discussion with Shelley, and we all followed him to
the hall. At the outer door, we found three or four
very ordinary-looking horses; they had holsters on
the saddles, and many other superfluous trappings,
such as the Italians delight in, and Englishmen eschew. Shelley, and an Irish visitor just
announced, mounted two of these sorry jades. I
luckily had my own cattle. Byron got into a
calêche, and did not mount his horse until we had
cleared the gates of the town, to avoid, as he said,
being stared at by the " d—d Englishers," who gene-

rally congregated before his house on the Arno.
After an hour or two of slow riding and lively talk,—
for he was generally in good spirits when on horseback,—we stopped at a small *podere* on the road-
side, and dismounting went into the house, in which
we found a table with wine and cakes. From thence
we proceeded into the vineyard at the back; the
servant brought two brace of pistols, a cane was
stuck in the ground and a five paul-piece, the size
of half-a-crown, placed in a slit at the top of the
cane. Byron, Shelley, and I, fired at fifteen paces,
and one of us generally hit the cane or the coin:
our firing was pretty equal; after five or six shots
each, Byron pocketed the battered money and
sauntered about the grounds. We then remounted.
On our return homewards, Shelley urged Byron to
complete something he had begun. Byron smiled
and replied,

"John Murray, my patron and paymaster, says
my plays won't act. I don't mind that, for I told
him they were not written for the stage—but he
adds, my poesy won't sell: that I do mind, for I
have an 'itching palm.' He urges me to resume
my old ' Corsair style, to please the ladies.'"

Shelley indignantly answered,

" That is very good logic for a bookseller, but not for an author: the shop interest is to supply the ephemeral demand of the day. It is not for him but you ' to put a ring in the monster's nose' to keep him from mischief."

Byron smiling at Shelley's warmth, said,

" John Murray is right, if not righteous: all I have yet written has been for women-kind; you must wait until I am forty, their influence will then die a natural death, and I will show the men what I can do."

Shelley replied,

" Do it now—write nothing but what your conviction of its truth inspires you to write; you should give counsel to the wise, and not take it from the foolish. Time will reverse the judgment of the vulgar. Cotemporary criticism only represents the amount of ignorance genius has to contend with."

I was then and afterwards pleased and surprised at Byron's passiveness and docility in listening to Shelley — but all who heard him felt the charm of his simple, earnest manner; while Byron knew him to be exempt from the egotism, pedantry, cox-combry, and, more than all, the rivalry of authorship, and that he was the truest and most discriminating of his admirers.

Byron looking at the western sky, exclaimed, "Where is the green your friend the Laker talks such fustian about," meaning Coleridge—

> "'Gazing on the western sky,
> And its peculiar tint of yellow green.'
> *Dejection : an Ode.*

"Who ever," asked Byron, "saw a green sky?"

Shelley was silent, knowing that if he replied, Byron would give vent to his spleen. So I said, "The sky in England is oftener green than blue."

"Black, you mean," rejoined Byron; and this discussion brought us to his door.

As he was dismounting he mentioned two odd words that would rhyme. I observed on the felicity he had shown in this art, repeating a couplet out of Don Juan ; he was both pacified and pleased at this, and putting his hand on my horse's crest, observed,

"If you are curious in these matters, look in Swift. I will send you a volume ; he beats us all hollow, his rhymes are wonderful."

And then we parted for that day, which I have
been thus particular in recording, not only as it
was the first of our acquaintance, but as containing
as fair a sample as I can give of his appearance,
ordinary habits, and conversation.

CHAPTER V.

— ◆ —

His house, his home, his heritage, his lands,
The laughing dames in whom he did delight.

*   *   *   *   *

Without a sigh he left, to cross the brine
And traverse Paynim shores and pass Earth's central line.

CHILDE HAROLD.

MEN of books, particularly Poets, are rarely men
of action, their mental energy exhausts their bodily
powers. Byron has been generally considered an
exception to this rule, he certainly so considered
himself: let us look at the facts.

In 1809, he first left England, rode on horseback through Spain and Portugal, 400 miles,
crossed the Mediterranean on board a frigate, and
landed in Greece; where he passed two years in
sauntering through a portion of that small country :
this, with a trip to Smyrna, Constantinople, Malta,
and Gibraltar, generally on board our men-of-war,
where you have all the ease, comfort, and most

of the luxuries of your own homes;—this is the extent of the voyages and travels he was so proud of. Anything more luxurious than sailing on those seas, and riding through those lands, and in such a blessed climate, I know from experience, is not to be found in this world. Taking into account the result of these travels as shown in his works, he might well boast; he often said, if he had ever written a line worth preserving, it was Greece that inspired it. After this trip he returned to England, and remained there some years, four or five; then abandoned it for ever, passed through the Netherlands, went up the Rhine, paused for some months in Switzerland, crossed the Alps into Italy, and never left that peninsula until the last year of his life. He was never in France, for when he left England, Paris was in the hands of the Allies, and he said he could not endure to witness a country associated in his mind with so many glorious deeds of arts and arms, bullied by " certain rascal officers, slaves in authority, the knaves of justice!"

To return, however, to his travels. If you look at a map you will see what a narrow circle comprises his wanderings. Any man might go, and many have gone without the aid of steam, over the same ground in a few months—even if he had to walk with a knapsack, where Byron rode. The Pilgrim moved about like a Pasha, with a host of attendants, and all that he and they required on the journey. So far as I could learn from Fletcher, his yeoman bold—and he had been with him from the time of his first leaving England,—Byron where-ever he was, so far as it was practicable, pursued the same lazy, dawdling habits he continued during the time I knew him. He was seldom out of his bed before noon, when he drank a cup of very strong green tea, without sugar or milk. At two he ate a biscuit and drank soda-water. At three he mounted his horse and sauntered along the road —and generally the same road,—if alone, racking his brains for fitting matter and rhymes for the coming poem, he dined at seven, as frugally as an-chorites are said in story-books to have done, at nine he visited the family of Count Gamba, on his return home he sat reading or composing until two or three o'clock in the morning, and then to bed, often feverish, restless and exhausted—to dream, as he said, more than to sleep.

Something very urgent, backed by the impor-
tunity of those who had influence over him, could
alone induce him to break through the routine I
have described, for a day, and it was certain to be
resumed on the next,—he was constant in this alone.
His conversation was anything but literary, except
when Shelley was near him. The character he
most commonly appeared in was of the free and
easy sort, such as had been in vogue when he was
in London, and George IV. was Regent; and his
talk was seasoned with anecdotes of the great actors
on and off the stage, boxers, gamblers, duellists,
drunkards, &c., &c., appropriately garnished with
the slang and scandal of that day. Such things
had all been in fashion, and were at that time considered accomplishments by gentlemen; and of this
tribe of Mohawks the Prince Regent was the chief,
and allowed to be the most perfect specimen. Byron,
not knowing the tribe was extinct, still prided himself on having belonged to it; of nothing was he
more indignant, than of being treated as a man of
letters, instead of as a Lord and a man of fashion:
this prevented foreigners and literary people from
getting on with him, for they invariably so offended.

His long absence had not effaced the mark John Bull brands his children with; the instant he loomed above the horizon, on foot or horseback, you saw at a glance he was a Britisher. He did not understand foreigners, nor they him; and, during the time I knew him, he associated with no Italians except the family of Count Gamba. He seemed to take an especial pleasure in making a clean breast to every new comer, as if to mock their previous conceptions of him, and to give the lie to the portraits published of him. He said to me, as we were riding together alone, shortly after I knew him,

"Now, confess, you expected to find me a 'Timon of Athens,' or a 'Timur the Tartar;' or did you think I was a mere sing-song driveller of poesy, full of what I heard Braham at a rehearsal call '*Entusamusy*;' and are you not mystified at finding me what I am,—a man of the world—never in earnest—laughing at all things mundane."

Then he muttered, as to himself,—

"The world is a bundle of hay,
Mankind are the asses who pull."

Any man who cultivates his intellectual faculty so highly as to seem at times inspired, would be too much above us, if, on closer inspection, we should not find it alloyed with weaknesses akin to our own. Byron soon put you at your ease on this point. Godwin, in his ' Thoughts on Man,' says, " Shakespeare, amongst all his varied characters, has not attempted to draw a perfect man;" and Pope says,—

" A perfect man's a thing the world ne'er saw."

At any rate I should not seek for a model amongst men of the pen; they are too thin-skinned and egotistical. In his perverse and moody humours, Byron would give vent to his Satanic vein. After a long silence, one day on horseback, he began :

" I have a conscience, although the world gives me no credit for it; I am now repenting, not of the few sins I have committed, but of the many I have not committed. There are things, too, we should not do, if they were not forbidden. My Don Juan was cast aside and almost forgotten, until I heard that the pharisaic synod in John Murray's back parlour had pronounced it as highly immoral, and unfit for publication. ' Because thou art virtuous thinkest thou there shall be no more cakes and ale?' Now my brain is throb-

bing and must have vent. I opined gin was inspiration, but cant is stronger. To-day I had
another letter warning me against the Snake
(Shelley). He, alone, in this age of humbug, dares
stem the current, as he did to-day the flooded
Arno in his skiff, although I could not observe he
made any progress. The attempt is better than
being swept along as all the rest are, with the filthy
garbage scoured from its banks."

Taking advantage of this panegyric on Shelley,
I observed, he might do him a great service at
little cost, by a friendly word or two in his next work,
such as he had bestowed on authors of less merit.

Assuming a knowing look, he continued,

" All trades have their mysteries; if we crack up
a popular author, he repays us in the same coin,
principal and interest. A friend may have repaid
money lent,—can't say any of mine have; but who
ever heard of the interest being added thereto ? "

I rejoined,

" By your own showing you are indebted to
Shelley; some of his best verses are to express
his admiration of your genius."

" Ay," he said, with a significant look, " who

reads them? If we puffed the Snake, it might not
turn out a profitable investment. If he cast off
the slough of his mystifying metaphysics, he would
want no puffing."

Seeing I was not satisfied, he added,

" If we introduced Shelley to our readers, they
might draw comparisons, and they are ' *odorous.*' "

After Shelley's death, Byron, in a letter to Moore,
of the 2nd of August, 1822, says,

" There is another man gone, about whom the
world was ill-naturedly, and ignorantly, and brutally
mistaken. It will, perhaps, do him justice *now*,
when he can be no better for it."

In a letter to Murray of an earlier date, he
says,

" You were all mistaken about Shelley, who was
without exception, the best and least selfish man
I ever knew."

And, again, he says, " You are all mistaken about
Shelley; you do not know how mild, how tolerant,
how good he was."

What Byron says of the world, that it will,
perhaps, do Shelley justice when he can be no
better for it, is far more applicable to himself.

If the world erred, they did so in ignorance; Shelley was a myth to them. Byron had no such plea to offer, but he was neither just nor generous, and never drew his weapon to redress any wrongs but his own.

CHAPTER VI.

Few things surpass old wine ; and they may preach
Who please, the more because they preach in vain.
Let us have wine and women, mirth and laughter,
Sermons and soda-water the day after.

DON JUAN.

BYRON has been accused of drinking deeply. Our universities, certainly, did turn out more famous drinkers than scholars. In the good old times, to drink lustily was the characteristic of all Englishmen, just as tuft-hunting is now. Eternal swilling, and the rank habits and braggadocio manners which it engendered, came to a climax in George IV.'s reign. Since then, excessive drinking has gone out of fashion, but an elaborate style of gastronomy has come in to fill up the void; so there is not much gained. Byron used to boast of the quantity of wine he had drunk. He said, "We young Whigs imbibed claret, and so saved our constitutions : the

Tories stuck to port, and destroyed theirs and their country's."

He bragged, too, of his prowess in riding, boxing, fencing, and even walking; but to excel in these things feet are as necessary as hands. It was difficult to avoid smiling at his boasting and self-glorification. In the water a fin is better than a foot, and in that element he did well; he was built for floating,—with a flexible body, open chest, broad beam, and round limbs. If the sea was smooth and warm, he would stay in it for hours; but as he seldom indulged in this sport, and when he did, over-exerted himself, he suffered severely; which observing, and knowing how deeply he would be mortified at being beaten, I had the magnanimity when contending with him to give in.

He had a misgiving in his mind that I was trifling with him; and one day as we were on the shore, and the Bolivar at anchor, about three miles off, he insisted on our trying conclusions; we were to swim to the yacht, dine in the sea alongside of her, treading water the while, and then to return to the shore. It was calm and hot, and seeing he would not be fobbed off, we started. I reached the boat a long time before he did; ordered the edibles to be ready, and floated until he arrived. We ate our fare leisurely, from off a grating that floated alongside, drank a bottle of ale, and I smoked a cigar, which he tried to extinguish, — as he never smoked. We then put about, and struck off towards the shore. We had not got a hundred yards on our passage, when he retched violently, and, as that is often followed by cramp, I urged him to put his hand on my shoulder that I might tow him back to the schooner.

"Keep off, you villain, don't touch me. I'll drown ere I give in."

I answered as Iago did to Roderigo,

" 'A fig for drowning! drown cats and blind puppies.' I shall go on board and try the effects of a glass of grog to stay my stomach."

"Come on," he shouted, "I am always better after vomiting."

With difficulty I deluded him back; I went on board, and he sat on the steps of the accommodation-ladder, with his feet in the water. I handed him a wine-glass of brandy, and screened him from the burning sun. He was in a sullen mood, but after a time resumed his usual tone. Nothing could induce him to be landed in the schooner's boat, though I protested I had had enough of the water.

"You may do as you like," he called out, and plumped in, and we swam on shore.

He never afterwards alluded to this event, nor to his prowess in swimming, to me, except in the past tense. He was ill, and kept his bed for two days afterwards.

To return to his drinking propensities, after this digression about his gymnastic prowess : I must say, that of all his vauntings, it was, luckily for him, the emptiest—that is, after he left England and his boon companions, as I know nothing of what he did there. From all that I heard or witnessed of his habits abroad, he was and had been exceedingly abstemious in eating and drinking. When alone, he drank a glass or two of small claret or hock, and when utterly exhausted at night a single glass of grog ; which when I mixed it for him I lowered to what sailors call " water bewitched," and he never made any remark. I once, to try him, omitted the alcohol; he then said, " Tre, have you not forgotten the creature comfort?" I then put in two spoonfuls, and he was satisfied. This does not look like an habitual toper. His English acquaintances in Italy were, he said in derision, all milksops. On the rare occasions of any of his former friends visiting him, he would urge them to have a carouse with him, but they had grown wiser. He used to say that little Tommy Moore was the only man he then knew who stuck to the bottle and put him on his mettle, adding, "But he is a native of the damp isle, where men subsist by suction."

Byron had not damaged his body by strong drinks, but his terror of getting fat was so great that he reduced his diet to the point of absolute starvation. He was of that soft, lymphatic temperament which it is almost impossible to keep within a moderate compass, particularly as in his case his lameness prevented his taking exercise. When he added to his weight, even standing was painful, so he resolved to keep down to eleven stone, or shoot himself. He said everything he swallowed was instantly converted into tallow and deposited on his ribs.

He was the only human being I ever met with

who had sufficient self-restraint and resolution
to resist this proneness to fatten : he did so; and
at Genoa, where he was last weighed, he was
ten stone and nine pounds, and looked much
less. This was not from vanity about his personal appearance, but from a better motive; and
as, like Justice Greedy, he was always hungry, his
merit was the greater. Occasionally he relaxed
his vigilance, when he swelled apace.

I remember one of his old friends saying,
" Byron, how well you are looking!" If he had
stopped there it had been well, but when he
added, " You are getting fat," Byron's brow
reddened, and his eyes flashed—" Do you call
getting fat looking well, as if I were a hog ?"
and, turning to me, he muttered, " The beast, I
can hardly keep my hands off him." The man who
thus offended him was the husband of the lady
addressed as ' Genevra,' and the original of his
' Zuleika,' in the ' Bride of Abydos.' I don't think
he had much appetite for his dinner that day, or
for many days, and never forgave the man who, so
far from wishing to offend, intended to pay him a
compliment.

Byron said he had tried all sorts of experiments to stay his hunger, without adding to his bulk. "I swelled," he said, "at one time to fourteen stone, so I clapped the muzzle on my jaws, and, like the hybernating animals, consumed my own fat."

He would exist on biscuits and soda-water for days together, then, to allay the eternal hunger gnawing at his vitals, he would make up a horrid mess of cold potatoes, rice, fish, or greens, deluged in vinegar, and gobble it up like a famished dog. On either of these unsavoury dishes, with a biscuit and a glass or two of Rhine wine, he cared not how sour, he called feasting sumptuously. Upon my observing he might as well have fresh fish and vegetables, instead of stale, he laughed and answered,

"I have an advantage over you, I have no palate; one thing is as good as another to me."

"Nothing," I said, "disagrees with the natural man, he fasts and gorges, his nerves and brains don't bother him; but if you wish to live?"——

"Who wants to live?" he replied, "not I. The Byrons are a short-lived race on both sides, father and mother : longevity is hereditary : I am nearly at the end of my tether. I don't care for death a d—n : it is her sting ! I can't bear pain."

His habits and want of exercise damaged him, not drink. It must be borne in mind, moreover, that his brain was always working at high pressure. The consequences resulting from his way of life were low or intermittent fevers; these last had fastened on him in his early travels in the Levant; and there is this peculiarity in malaria fevers, that if you have once had them, you are ever after peculiarly susceptible to a renewal of their attacks if within their reach, and Byron was hardly ever out of it. Venice and Ravenna are belted in with swamps, and fevers are rife in the autumn. By starving his body Byron kept his brains clear; no man had brighter eyes or a clearer voice; and his resolute bearing and prompt replies, when excited, gave to his body an appearance of muscular power that imposed on strangers. I never doubted, for he was indifferent to life, and prouder than Lucifer, that if he had drawn his sword in Greece, or elsewhere, he would have thrown away the scabbard.

☆ ★ ☆

CHAPTER XII.

All things that we love and cherish,
Like ourselves, must fade and perish ;
Such is our rude mortal lot,
Love itself would, did they not.
SHELLEY.

I GOT a furnace made at Leghorn, of iron-bars and strong sheet-iron, supported on a stand, and laid in a stock of fuel, and such things as were said to be used by Shelley's much loved Hellenes on their funeral pyres.

On the 13th of August, 1822, I went on board the 'Bolivar,' with an English acquaintance, having written to Byron and Hunt to say I would send them word when everything was ready, as they wished to be present. I had previously engaged two large feluccas, with drags and tackling, to go before, and endeavour to find the place where Shelley's boat had foundered ; the captain of one of the feluccas having asserted that he was out in the fatal squall, and had seen Shelley's boat go

down off Via Reggio, with all sail set. With light
and fitful breezes we were eleven hours reaching our
destination—the tower of Migliarino, at the Bocca
Lericcio, in the Tuscan States. There was a
village there, and about two miles from that place
Williams was buried. So I anchored, landed,
called on the officer in command, a major, and
told him my object in coming, of which he was
already apprised by his own government. He
assured me I should have every aid from him. As
it was too late in the day to commence operations,
we went to the only inn in the place, and I wrote
to Byron to be with us next day at noon. The
major sent my letter to Pisa by a dragoon, and made
arrangements for the next day. In the morning he
was with us early, and gave me a note from Byron,
to say he would join us as near noon as he could.
At ten we went on board the commandant's boat,
with a squad of soldiers in working dresses, armed
with mattocks and spades, an officer of the quarantine service, and some of his crew. They had their
peculiar tools, so fashioned as to do their work without coming into personal contact with things that
might be infectious—long handled tongs, nippers,

poles with iron hooks and spikes, and divers others
that gave one a lively idea of the implements of
torture devised by the holy inquisitors. Thus
freighted, we started, my own boat following with
the furnace, and the things I had brought from
Leghorn. We pulled along the shore for some
distance, and landed at a line of strong posts and
railings which projected into the sea—forming the
boundary dividing the Tuscan and Lucchese States.
We walked along the shore to the grave, where Byron
and Hunt soon joined us : they, too, had an officer
and soldiers from the tower of Migliarino, an officer
of the Health Office, and some dismounted dragoons,
so we were surrounded by soldiers, but they kept
the ground clear, and readily lent their aid. There
was a considerable gathering of spectators from the
neighbourhood, and many ladies richly dressed
were amongst them. The spot where the body lay
was marked by the gnarled root of a pine tree.

A rude hut, built of young pine-tree stems, and
wattled with their branches, to keep the sun and
rain out, and thatched with reeds, stood on the
beach to shelter the look-out man on duty. A few
yards from this was the grave, which we commenced

opening—the Gulf of Spezzia and Leghorn at equal
distances of twenty-two miles from us. As to fuel
I might have saved myself the trouble of bringing
any, for there was an ample supply of broken spars
and planks cast on the shore from wrecks, besides
the fallen and decaying timber in a stunted pine
forest close at hand. The soldiers collected fuel
whilst I erected the furnace, and then the men of
the Health Office set to work, shovelling away the
sand which covered the body, while we gathered
round, watching anxiously. The first indication of
their having found the body, was the appearance of
the end of a black silk handkerchief—I grubbed this
out with a stick, for we were not allowed to touch
anything with our hands—then some shreds of
linen were met with, and a boot with the bone of the
leg and the foot in it.   On the removal of a layer of
brushwood, all that now remained of my lost friend
was exposed—a shapeless mass of bones and flesh.
The limbs separated from the trunk on being touched.

   " Is that a human body ? " exclaimed Byron ;
" why it 's more like the carcase of a sheep, or any
other animal, than a man : this is a satire on our
pride and folly."

I pointed to the letters E. E. W. on the black silk handkerchief.

Byron looking on, muttered, " The entrails of a worm hold together longer than the potter's clay, of which man is made. Hold! let me see the jaw," he added, as they were removing the skull, " I can recognise any one by the teeth, with whom I have talked. I always watch the lips and mouth : they tell what the tongue and eyes try to conceal."

I had a boot of Williams's with me ; it exactly corresponded with the one found in the grave. The remains were removed piecemeal into the furnace.

" Don't repeat this with me," said Byron; " let my carcase rot where it falls."

The funereal pyre was now ready ; I applied the fire, and the materials being dry and resinous the pine-wood burnt furiously, and drove us back. It was hot enough before, there was no breath of air, and the loose sand scorched our feet. As soon as the flames became clear, and allowed us to approach, we threw frankincense and salt into the furnace, and poured a flask of wine and oil over the body. The Greek oration was omitted, for we had lost our Hellenic bard. It was now so insufferably hot that the officers and soldiers were all seeking shade.

"Let us try the strength of these waters that drowned our friends," said Byron, with his usual audacity. "How far out do you think they were when their boat sank?"

"If you don't wish to be put into the furnace, you had better not try; you are not in condition."

He stripped, and went into the water, and so did I and my companion. Before we got a mile out, Byron was sick, and persuaded to return to the shore. My companion, too, was seized with cramp, and reached the land by my aid. At four o'clock the funereal pyre burnt low, and when we uncovered the furnace, nothing remained in it but dark-coloured ashes, with fragments of the larger bones. Poles were now put under the red-hot furnace, and it was gradually cooled in the sea. I gathered together the human ashes, and placed them in a small oak-box, bearing an inscription on a brass plate, screwed it down, and placed it in Byron's carriage. He returned with Hunt to Pisa, promising to be with us on the following day at Via Reggio. I returned with my party in the same

way we came, and supped and slept at the inn.
On the following morning we went on board the
same boats, with the same things and party, and
rowed down the little river near Via Reggio to the
sea, pulled along the coast towards Massa, then
landed, and began our preparations as before.

Three white wands had been stuck in the sand to
mark the Poet's grave, but as they were at some
distance from each other, we had to cut a trench
thirty yards in length, in the line of the sticks, to
ascertain the exact spot, and it was nearly an hour
before we came upon the grave.

In the mean time Byron and Leigh Hunt arrived
in the carriage, attended by soldiers, and the
Health Officer, as before. The lonely and grand
scenery that surrounded us so exactly harmonised
with Shelley's genius, that I could imagine his
spirit soaring over us. The sea, with the islands
of Gorgona, Capraji, and Elba, was before us;
old battlemented watch-towers stretched along the
coast, backed by the marble-crested Apennines
glistening in the sun, picturesque from their diver-
sified outlines, and not a human dwelling was in
sight. As I thought of the delight Shelley felt

in such scenes of loneliness and grandeur whilst living, I felt we were no better than a herd of wolves or a pack of wild dogs, in tearing out his battered and naked body from the pure yellow sand that lay so lightly over it, to drag him back to the light of day; but the dead have no voice, nor had I power to check the sacrilege—the work went on silently in the deep and unresisting sand, not a word was spoken, for the Italians have a touch of sentiment, and their feelings are easily excited into sympathy. Even Byron was silent and thoughtful. We were startled and drawn together by a dull hollow sound that followed the blow of a mattock; the iron had struck a skull, and the body was soon uncovered. Lime had been strewn on it; this, or decomposition, had the effect of staining it of a dark and ghastly indigo colour. Byron asked me to preserve the skull for him; but remembering that he had formerly used one as a drinking-cup, I was determined Shelley's should not be so profaned. The limbs did not separate from the trunk, as in the case of Williams's body, so that the corpse was removed entire into the furnace. I had taken the precaution of having more and larger pieces of timber, in consequence of my experience of the day before of the difficulty of consuming a corpse in the open air with our apparatus. After the fire was well kindled we repeated the ceremony of the previous day; and more wine was poured over Shelley's dead body than he had consumed during his life. This with the oil and salt made the yellow flames glisten and quiver. The heat from the sun and fire was so intense that the atmosphere was tremulous and wavy. The corpse fell open and the heart was laid bare. The frontal bone of the skull, where it had been struck with the mattock, fell off; and, as the back of the head rested on the red-hot bottom bars of the furnace, the brains literally seethed, bubbled, and boiled as in a cauldron, for a very long time.

Byron could not face this scene, he withdrew to the beach and swam off to the 'Bolivar.' Leigh Hunt remained in the carriage. The fire was so fierce as to produce a white heat on the iron, and to reduce its contents to grey ashes. The only portions that were not consumed were some fragments of bones, the jaw, and the skull, but what surprised us all, was that the heart remained entire.

In snatching this relic from the fiery furnace, my hand was severely burnt; and had any one seen me do the act I should have been put into quarantine.

After cooling the iron machine in the sea, I collected the human ashes and placed them in a box, which I took on board the ' Bolivar.' Byron and Hunt retraced their steps to their home, and the officers and soldiers returned to their quarters. I liberally rewarded the men for the admirable manner in which they behaved during the two days they had been with us.

As I undertook and executed this novel ceremony, I have been thus tediously minute in describing it.

Byron's idle talk during the exhumation of Williams's remains, did not proceed from want of feeling, but from his anxiety to conceal what he felt from others. When confined to his bed and racked by spasms, which threatened his life, I have heard him talk in a much more un-orthodox fashion, the instant he could muster breath to banter. He had been taught during his town-life, that any exhibition of sympathy or feeling was maudlin and unmanly, and that the appearance of daring and indifference, denoted blood and high breeding.

✫ ★ ✩

CHAPTER XXI.

———◆———

Arnold !—Do you—dare you—
Taunt me with my born deformity.
                        Deformed Transformed.

WITH desponding thoughts I entered Missolonghi on the third day from my leaving Salona.
Any spot on the surface of the earth, or in its
bowels, that holds out a prospect of gain, you will
find inhabited ; a morass that will produce rice,
the crust of a volcano in which the vine will grow ;
lagunes, in which fish abound, are temptations which
overcome the terror of pestilence or death. So I was
not surprised at seeing Missolonghi, situated as it
is on the verge of the most dismal swamp I had ever
seen. The marvel was that Byron, prone to fevers,
should have been induced to land on this mud-
bank, and stick there for three months shut in by a
circle of stagnant pools which might be called the
belt of death. Although it was now the early spring,

I found most of the strangers suffering from gastric fevers. It was the 24th or 25th of April when I arrived; Byron had died on the 19th. I waded through the streets, between wind and water, to the house he had lived in; it was detached, and on the margin of the shallow slimy sea-waters. For three months this house had been besieged, day and night, like a bank that has a run upon it. Now that death had closed the door, it was as silent as a cemetery. No one was within the house but Fletcher, of which I was glad. As if he knew my wishes, he led me up a narrow stair into a small room, with nothing in it but a coffin standing on trestles. No word was spoken by either of us; he withdrew the black pall and the white shroud, and there lay the embalmed body of the Pilgrim—more beautiful in death than in life. The contraction of the muscles and skin had effaced every line that time or passion had ever traced on it; few marble busts could have matched its stainless white, the harmony of its proportions, and perfect finish; yet he had been dissatisfied with that body, and longed to cast its slough. How often I had heard him curse it! He was jealous of the genius of

Shakspeare—that might well be—but where had he
seen the face or form worthy to excite his envy ?   I
asked Fletcher to bring me a glass of water.   On
his leaving the room, to confirm or remove my
doubts as to the cause of his lameness, I uncovered
the Pilgrim's feet, and was answered—the great
mystery was solved.   Both his feet were clubbed,
and his legs withered to the knee—the form and
features of an Apollo, with the feet and legs of a
sylvan satyr.   This was a curse, chaining a proud
and soaring spirit like his to the dull earth.   In
the drama of 'The Deformed Transformed,' I knew
that he had expressed all he could express of what
a man of highly-wrought mind might feel when
brooding over a deformity of body : but when he said

" I have done the best which spirit may to make
   Its way with all deformity, dull deadly,
   Discouraging weight upon me,"

I thought it exaggerated as applied to himself;
now I saw it was not so.   His deformity was always
uppermost in his thoughts, and influenced every
act of his life, spurred him on to poetry, as that was
one of the few paths to fame open to him,—and as

if to be revenged on Nature for sending him into
the world "scarce half made up," he scoffed at her
works and traditions with the pride of Lucifer; this
morbid feeling ultimately goaded him on to his last
Quixotic crusade in Greece.

No other man, afflicted as he was, could have
been better justified than Byron in saying,

> " I ask not
> For valour, since deformity is daring;
> It is its essence to o'ertake mankind
> By heart and soul, and make itself the equal—
> Ay, the superior of the rest. There is
> A spur in its halt movements, to become
> All that the others cannot, in such things
> As still are free to both, to compensate
> For step-dame Nature's niggardness at first ;
> They war with fearless deeds, the smiles of fortune,
> And oft, like Timour the lame Tartar, win them."

Knowing and sympathising with Byron's sensitiveness, his associates avoided prying into the cause of
his lameness ; so did strangers, from good breeding
or common humanity. It was generally thought his
halting gait originated in some defect of the right foot
or ankle—the right foot was the most distorted, and
it had been made worse in his boyhood by vain efforts
to set it right. He told me that for several years he

wore steel splints, which so wrenched the sinews and tendons of his leg, that they increased his lameness; the foot was twisted inwards, only the edge touched the ground, and that leg was shorter than the other. His shoes were peculiar—very high heeled, with the soles uncommonly thick on the inside and pared thin on the outside—the toes were stuffed with cotton-wool, and his trousers were very large below the knee and strapped down so as to cover his feet. The peculiarity of his gait was now accounted for; he entered a room with a sort of run, as if he could not stop, then planted his best leg well forward, throwing back his body to keep his balance. In early life whilst his frame was light and elastic, with the aid of a stick he might have tottered along for a mile or two; but after he had waxed heavier, he seldom attempted to walk more than a few hundred yards, without squatting down or leaning against the first wall, bank, rock, or tree at hand, never sitting on the ground, as it would have been difficult for him to get up again. In the company of strangers, occasionally, he would make desperate efforts to conceal his infirmity, but the hectic flush on his face, his swelling veins, and quivering nerves betrayed him, and he suffered for many days after such exertions. Disposed to fatten, incapable of taking exercise to check the tendency, what could he do? If he added to his weight, his feet would not have supported him; in this dilemma he was compelled to exist in a state of semi-starvation; he was less than eleven stone when at Genoa, and said he had been fourteen at Venice. The pangs of hunger which travellers and shipwrecked mariners have described were nothing to what he suffered; their privations were temporary, his were for life, and more unendurable, as he was in the midst of abundance. I was exclaiming, "Poor fellow, if your errors were greater than those of ordinary men, so were your temptations and provocations," when Fletcher returned with a bottle and glass, saying, "There is nothing but slimy salt water in this horrid place, so I have been half over the town to beg this bottle of porter," and, answering my ejaculation of "Poor fellow?" he said—

"You may well say so, sir, these savages are worse than any highwaymen; they have robbed my Lord of all his money and his life too."

Whilst saying this, Fletcher, without making any

remark, drew the shroud and pall carefully over the feet of his master's corpse—he was very nervous and trembled as he did it ; so strongly had his weak and superstitious nature been acted upon by the injunctions and threats of his master, that, alive or dead, no one was to see his feet, for if they did, he would haunt him, &c., &c.

NOTES

p. 415, l. 10: 'the Pilgrim': Byron was usually identified with the pilgrim hero of *Childe Harold's Pilgrimage*.

p. 427, l. 17: The Mohawks appear in Byron's day to have been a group of riotous young rich men about town. The use of the word here, however, is slightly anachronistic, as the Mohawks are more usually associated with the London of the eighteenth century.